Losing a Parent to Suicide

The suicide of a parent has lifelong consequences; few more traumatic scenarios exist, and counselors often struggle for ways to help clients deal with its impacts. Few understand the pain and life-altering impacts of these tragedies better than children who have experienced them. Despite this, there are few texts that incorporate and evaluate the first-person accounts of grief following the suicide of a parent while advancing a method for helping. *Losing a Parent to Suicide* analyzes stories of parent suicides and explores the grief and coping processes that follow, revealing the strategies and approaches that have empowered such individuals and helped them rebuild their lives.

Marty Loy, PhD, is professor of health promotion and dean of the College of Professional Studies at the University of Wisconsin–Stevens Point. He is the author of *Children and Stress: A Handbook for Parents, Teachers and Therapists*. He and his wife, Becky, are cofounders of Camp HOPE, a camp for grieving children that has served as a model for similar camps around the USA.

Amy Boelk, MSSW, PhD, is associate professor and social work field coordinator in the Department of Sociology and Social Work at the University of Wisconsin–Stevens Point. She is a former hospice social worker whose research and writing have spanned a variety of topics related to grieving and end-of-life care.

Losing a Parent to Suicide

Using Lived Experiences to Inform Bereavement Counseling

MARTY LOY AND AMY BOELK

Routledge
Taylor & Francis Group
NEW YORK AND LONDON

First published 2014
by Routledge
711 Third Avenue, New York, NY 10017

Simultaneously published in the UK
by Routledge
27 Church Road, Hove, East Sussex BN3 2FA

Routledge is an imprint of the Taylor & Francis Group, an informa business

Library of Congress Cataloging in Publication Data

Loy, Marty.
Losing a parent to suicide: using lived experiences to inform bereavement counseling / Marty Loy and Amy Boelk.
pages cm
Includes bibliographical references and index.
1. Grief in children. 2. Children of suicide victims—Psychology. 3. Parents—Death. 4. Suicide. 5. Grief therapy. I. Boelk, Amy. II. Title.
BF723.G75L69 2013
155.9'370854—dc23 2013009299

ISBN: 978-0-415-81617-5 (hbk)
ISBN: 978-0-415-81618-2 (pbk)
ISBN: 978-0-203-59347-9 (ebk)

Typeset in Minion
by Apex CoVantage, LLC

Contents

Foreword by Amanda Maule vii

Acknowledgments ix

CHAPTER 1—Introduction 1

CHAPTER 2—Challenges 21
Amber's Story: Renounced 47
Fred's Story: Dad's Right-Hand Man 53
Dirk's Story: The Man of the House Now 56
Brooke's Story: On My Way Out 61

CHAPTER 3—Support 65
Lisa's Story: It Is So Powerful 86
Shane's Story: My Family, My Support 90
Kevin's Story: Every Time I Look Above 93
Guy's Story: Finding My Way Back 95

CHAPTER 4—Coping 100
Rachel's Story: Reevaluating 116
Melissa's Story: A Journey of Self-Discovery 120
Zach's Story: My Life-Defining Moment 124
Jenna's Story: Relief 128

CHAPTER 5—Posttraumatic Growth **130**
Jake's Story: A Positive Outlook on Life 139
Trevor's Story: Taking His Letter to Heart 142
Jerome's Story: Tomorrow Is a New Day 146
Suzanne's Story: It Hits You in Ways That You Don't Expect 148

CHAPTER 6—Professional Implications and Best Practices **153**
Camp HOPE 175

Epilogue **185**

References **187**

Index **201**

Foreword

I am a daughter without a mother, a daughter who's been asked hundreds of times how her mother died. I never get to plainly say, "She tied a blue extension cord around her neck and hung herself from a pipe in our basement." Besides being too long, this explanation is too shocking. In the short answer to the "how" question, I say, "suicide," and it's still shocking. People usually aren't sure how to respond, and almost everyone offers an apology. After "suicide" come the silent questions: why, was she depressed, and "what if" As honest and needed as it is in these conversations, I've never been asked, "So, what does that make you?"

Your hands and mind on this book give our 16 stories range and, at least for me, relief. Rather than standardizing and simplifying grief, you are about to help prove the importance of individual stories, and it's my hope that the examples and patterns gleaned from our stories lead to more productive help because—I'll say this my way—in the short and long term, suicide sucks.

Suicide is a summary like "heart attack" and "cancer" are summaries, but folks are more surprised to hear suicide, especially when children say it was their mother or father. In our culture, younger people are presumed to have parents; we mass-market Mother's Day and Father's Day. When people are shocked and that shock is emotionally weighted, they often avoid talking about it or offer an automated response, which, in the case of suicide, can do the disservice of making us feel more ignored, more isolated, more infected, more troubled, more at fault, more "at risk," more sad, and less able to think of ourselves as more than the aftermath of our parents' suicides.

I'm Amber in this book, Amanda to most, and "the Mauler" to many. The more I've matured in my awareness of how Mom's hanging impacted my identity, the more I consider the question of what I deserve, what people deserve. I think everyone impacted by suicide, personally or professionally, deserves the precision, honesty, and advice in this book. We deserve to tell complete stories to authentic people and have those stories contextualized by others' stories and the cannon of academic theory and suicide study. Others who've lived the same circumstances deserve to know they're not alone and there are people they can relate to, scholarship they can consider. Professionals deserve data to continue to serve the bereaved. This form of suicide study deserves thoughtful attention from all of us.

Cheers,
Amanda Maule

Acknowledgments

Understandably, much effort and many long hours were spent by a number of people who contributed to the research and writing making up this book. Out of respect for the individuals whose stories provided the book's foundation, each person involved approached their work with great care and understanding. They can all share in the satisfaction of knowing that they contributed to something truly meaningful.

First and foremost, we would like to thank the individuals who participated in our study and helped us understand their unique experiences. They agreed to share personal aspects of their lives for the sole purpose of helping other children who, like themselves, have had a parent die by suicide. You will appreciate how honestly they convey their lived experiences.

We also express gratitude to the university students who served as research assistants, transcribers, and fact-checkers: Wendy Peterson, Amy Irwin, Cathey Hankison, Susie Lewis, Jennifer Smith, Torrie Kolbeck, Song Xiong, Jenna Barbian, Arielle Hardre, Sarah Siegel, and Kris Poncek. We offer a special thank you to graduate students Wendy Peterson and Amy Irwin, both of whom contributed greatly to this project. Wendy came to us with the original idea. Her initial questions, thoughts, and graduate project inspired our research. Amy was involved in the research from start to finish, and we relied heavily on her skills as an interviewer. Data collected on how the study participants coped with their parent's suicide became the topic of her master's thesis, and as such she provided a great foundation for the chapter entitled "Coping."

Finally, we offer much thanks to Becky Loy and Camp HOPE, who graciously put us in touch with many of the individuals featured in this book. Becky Loy's camp program, featured in the segment entitled "Camp HOPE," pages 175–184, has helped thousands of grieving children, many of whom have experienced parental suicide.

All sorrows can be borne, if you put them in a story.

—Isak Dinesen

one
Introduction

Suicide impacts thousands of parents every year; secondarily affected are between 10,000 and 20,000 bereaved children and thousands of children exposed to a parent's suicide attempt (Pfeffer, Karus, Siegel, & Jiang, 2000). For every person who dies by suicide, there are at least six people significantly touched by that death (Pompili, M., Innamorati, M., Raja, M., Falcone, I., Ducci, G., Angeletti, G., Lester, D., Girardi, P., Tatarelli, R., De Pisa, E. 2008). Among adults ages 25–44, the group most likely to have children at home, suicide is the fourth leading cause of death (Heron, 2012).

Children bereaved by the suicide of a parent are known to be particularly vulnerable, and according to Webb (1991) such children are left "profoundly and traumatically" bereft. In fact, one in five children bereaved by suicide will have emotional and behavioral difficulties at a level to justify referral to a specialist (Mitchell, A. M., Wesner, S., Brownson, L., Dysart-Gale, D. D., Garand, L., & Havill, A. 2006). Even so, the impact of parental suicide on children has been given little attention by the mental health field; though there are many studies related to suicide, few address the impact of parental suicide on surviving children (Cain, 2002). It is certain that the suicide of a parent has lifelong consequences, yet little is known about the long-term impacts of early responses, and no studies exist that allow adults to describe their experience with childhood parental suicide.

Overview of This Book

The information, insights, and stories shared in this book will help counselors better understand the experience of children who have had a parent die of suicide, allowing them to more effectively assist in the recovery process. In this first chapter we provide background on the underlying study used to inform the book, introduce the survivors whose stories will unfold, and through a brief review of the child and adolescent bereavement literature, place the book in context among other books written about suicide and its effects on survivors. Chapters 2 through 5 reveal the challenges, supports, coping mechanisms, and growth perceived by the survivors of parental suicide interviewed for our study. Within each chapter you will find a brief discussion of relevant literature, an elucidation of themes generated through our analysis of interview transcripts, and quotes from survivors in support of each theme. Implications for professionals are discussed in Chapter 6, giving credence to the experiences of survivors as valuable to our understanding of "best practices." Between chapters are interspersed the stories of 16 of the 22 parental suicide survivors that we interviewed. Each survivor reflects on his or her own particular experience and shares the story behind his or her grief.

This book confirms and strengthens much of what is already expressed in the literature. We identify unique challenges faced by children after losing a parent to suicide and describe support efforts that were helpful and not helpful. We highlight individual coping strategies and convey how survivors grew as a result of their trauma. While these topics have been discussed in other sources, this work gives voice to survivor perspectives, as they reflect on their lives immediately following the suicide and in subsequent years. Few have written of people's experiences beyond the suicide (Maple, 2005), or have captured the survivor's perspective. This is especially true in the case of child survivors, in which research is needed to reveal their particular experiences and identify longer-term needs and concerns (Cerel, Jordan, & Duberstein, 2008).

We also present new insights about suicide bereavement in children and teens. One participant used the term "*do nothing support*" to describe the importance of "*just being with someone.*" The importance of journaling and other forms of writing also emerged. We gained a better understanding of the roles of mental illness and family functioning in cases of parental suicide and the associated implications for recovery. We gained insight into the experience of a child having to participate in the notification of other family members of the death, and of the challenge of healing alongside a "*checked out mom.*" We were surprised by participants' reflections on the insensitivities of law enforcement, clergy, and teachers and how such interactions left lasting impressions. These and other important aspects of parental suicide are revealed as you read on and bear witness to the experiences of a courageous group of people.

Suicide of a Parent in Childhood: The Study

The study informing this book examined factors that helped and hindered recovery following the suicide of a parent during childhood. We asked 22 adult participants to tell us about their experiences as children following the suicide of their parent, and to describe how the experience shaped them. We aimed to discover what was helpful and what was not, learn participants' impressions of various interventions, gain insights to build on existing knowledge, and use information gained to inform professional practice.

We recruited participants using a convenience sample from a list of 92 adults who as children attended Camp HOPE, a camp for grieving children, or who asked to participate after learning of the study. In-depth interviews took place in person, utilizing a qualitative, semistructured interview process. This approach was chosen because it is more interactional and substantive when trying to understand the meaning of participants' experiences (Warren, 2002).

Open-ended questions helped guide conversation and seek information and understanding with the intent of gaining a deep level of understanding from the participants' perspectives (Johnson, 2002). In addition to asking participants to describe the circumstances surrounding their parent's death, we asked the following questions: What support did you have immediately following the death? What support did you have throughout your childhood and teen years? What challenges did you face throughout your childhood and teen years because of your parent's suicide? What have you done to cope with the suicide and its related challenges? How are you doing now? In what ways, if any, did your parent's death have a positive influence on your life? Probing questions were used gently as follow-ups to generate more detail and description when answers were brief.

Many safeguards were put into place. Pseudonyms were used to protect participant identities and data was stored securely. It was also important to keep in mind that children with a family history of suicide are two and a half times more likely to take their own lives (American Association of Suicidology, 2005). Interviewers were trained using the QPR (Question, Persuade, Refer) method of recognizing suicidal dispositions, assessing the immediacy of the threat, and knowing how to report it. In addition, participants were provided with contact information for local support services available to them.

While we were naturally concerned about the psychological strain involved with recounting a traumatic life experience, existing literature suggests that the retelling of traumatic events can be helpful in understanding, gaining control of, and making meaning of those events (Neimeyer & Sands, 2011). We found this to be true during our investigation. When asked later about the effect of our study on their healing, participants were clear that it was both difficult and healing at the same time. Amber, for example, commented that the interview was "*cathartic and allowed me to better understand my own journey.*"

The 40 hours of audiotaped interviews were transcribed word-for-word into nearly 600 pages for analysis. Obtaining a verbatim record of each interview is considered an ideal method to ensure that subsequent analyses are valid and meaningful (Johnson, 2002). We first used the transcriptions to construct autobiographical stories by rewriting each interview in a first-person story format. The participants then edited their stories for accuracy. Care was taken to preserve the voice of each participant, remove redundancies, improve readability, and logically organize each story chronologically or by theme. Several participants used the term "*committed suicide*" when telling their stories. This term can be viewed as insensitive, and because of its stigma and connotation of fault it is rarely used by professionals. However, in order to retain the participant voice, we kept the term within the story when it was used by the participant.

We further used the transcribed interviews for analysis of common themes across participant experiences. Transcripts were reviewed line by line, and code names, or labels, were given to chunks of data. We then organized this coded data into higher-order themes representing participants' experiences. Several techniques were used to enhance analytic rigor and trustworthiness of our findings, including (1) peer debriefing, a co-coding process involving ongoing comparative analysis and discussion of intersubjective agreement among the primary researchers at each step of the analysis; (2) auditing that involved careful documentation of the process followed in the development of codes, memos, and analytic decisions; (3) member checking whereby participants reviewed and validated the analysis; and (4) searching for disconfirming evidence, which involved combing the data to disconfirm various assertions made as a result of the analysis (Creswell, 1998; Lincoln & Guba, 1985; Padgett, 1998).

The Participants

As you read further, you will meet 22 courageous people and hear about their journeys. Several talk about what was gained and how they grew as a result of their experiences. You will be impressed with their resilience, strength, and insight. You will be inspired by what they have overcome, what they aspire to, and who they have become. As our way of introducing them to you, we now share their brief profiles.

Participant 1 is **Amber**, who was 22 years old at the time of the interview. Amber's mother died by suicide when she was 16, and she discovered the body. Amber is an aspiring poet. Participant 2 is **Fred**, age 28. His father died by suicide when he was 16 years old. Fred served in the Iraq war. He has six siblings. Participant 3 is **Dirk**, age 27. Dirk's father died when he was 16 years old, and he witnessed the suicide. As a child, Dirk had trouble with his temper. A parent himself, Dirk comes across as a hard worker, family man, and nice guy. Participant 4 is **Brooke**, age 28. Brooke's father died of suicide when she was 12. Brooke's grief was complicated because her father sexually abused her. She served time in prison as a result of her involvement in a homicide. Brooke feels good about telling her story "*so that others can learn from my mistakes.*" Participant 5 is **Lisa**, age 30. Her mother died when Lisa was 9, and her father died when she was 15, both by suicide. Attending Camp HOPE was a life-changing experience for her. She noted that "*Everyone was so focused on what they were going through that they kind of forgot about us . . . two little kids who just lost a mother.*" Lisa is now a caring mother for her own three children.

Participant 6 is **Shane**, age 18. His father died of suicide when he was 12. At one point he was expelled from school. He made a promise to himself that he "*will never ever commit suicide*" and "*abandon*" his family the way his father did. Participant 7 is **Kevin**, age 35. Kevin's father died of suicide when Kevin was 7 after being diagnosed with Parkinson's disease. Recently married, Kevin lives in a country home, which likely resembles the farm he lived on before his father's death.

Participant 8 is **Guy**, age 19. Guy's father was abusive to the entire family. Diagnosed with schizophrenia, he died of suicide when Guy was 3. "*Disturbed*" by finding his father's body, he still has nightmares. He used drugs to cope, and on several occasions he attempted suicide. His family was torn apart, but, according to Guy, slowly they are "*finding the way back to each other and to themselves.*"

Participant 9 is **Rachel**, age 21. Her father died of suicide when she was 7. She describes her memories as "*snapshots of traumatic events.*" Rachel expresses being more sensitive to loss and depression now, and has begun to reevaluate the effects of the suicide on her. She is an introspective college student.

Participant 10 is **Melissa**, age 20. Her father died of suicide when she was 14, and she discovered the body. With a family history of depression and suicide, Melissa learned all that she could about the factors that led to her father's death. Melissa's boyfriend has helped "*heal*" her and is her calming force.

Participant 11 is **Zach**, age 19. Zach's father was diagnosed with bipolar disorder and died of suicide when Zach was 8 years old. Initial support from teachers and friends was very helpful in his recovery. Zach is a soft-spoken, gentle young man. He was vice president of his high school's National Honor Society and was heavily involved in volunteer work.

Participant 12 is **Jenna**, age 20. Jenna's father died of suicide when she was 11 years old. She is very close to her nine siblings, is a college student, and wants to become a librarian upon completion of her social sciences degree.

Participant 13 is **Jake**, age 24. Jake's father was also diagnosed with bipolar disorder. He died of suicide when Jake was 4 years old, while in jail for the kidnapping of Jake's older brother. Jake is in college now to become a special education teacher, though his real dream is to become a firefighter.

Participant 14 is **Trevor**, age 22. Trevor's father died of suicide when he was 8. He took the advice in his father's note seriously. Trevor is currently a volunteer firefighter and fire prevention student.

Participant 15 is **Jerome**, age 23. Jerome's father died of suicide when he was only 3. He is an example of how a suicide can become part of one's life story even when the death happens at a very young age.

Participant 16 is **Suzanne**, age 50. Suzanne's father died of suicide when she was 8. She describes that day "*as if it were yesterday.*" She made suicide prevention part of her life's work. Suzanne wanted to see her story published, but was never able to because she died of cancer soon after her interview.

Participant 17 is **Kevin**, age 35. Kevin was 7 years old when his father died by suicide. To cope, he became involved in wrestling and football, and he relied on his "*buddies*" for support, especially one who also lost his dad to suicide.

Participant 18 is **Jeffery**, age 21. Jeffery's father died of suicide when he was 10 years old. Following the suicide, he was described as sad, depressed, and suicidal, as well as aggressive toward teachers and peers. As a result,

Jeffery was placed into foster care. He doesn't talk much about his dad's death anymore because, as he stated in his interview, "*what's in the past is in the past.*"

Participant 19 is **Julie**, age 25. Julie, the oldest of three siblings, is Jeffery's big sister; she was 15 when their father died. Julie felt responsible, and she vividly remembers seeing her dad cleaning his gun and "*going to bed just thinking . . . I wonder if anything bad is going to happen.*" Julie coped by smoking, drinking, and stealing. Julie is now a stay-at-home mom, and at the time of her interview she was 7 months pregnant. Her advice to other teens is to simply "*tell your feelings.*" Participant 20 is **Jared**, age 26.

Jared's father died of suicide when he was 12 years old; it was his father's fourth attempt. Jared's family couldn't afford to have his dad's body flown to the burial so he and his uncle drove their family car across the Midwest with the casket in the back. Jared talked about how the death made him emotionally stronger, self-sufficient, and more accountable to himself. Participant

21 is **Charlotte**, age 22. Charlotte's father died of suicide when she was 15. He left a short note to say that he was sorry. Charlotte says that the unanswered questions are the hardest part, and she still struggles with the question "*why, why would he do that?*" To cope, Charlotte writes in her journal daily. Participant 22 is **Louise**. Louise was 9 years

old when her father died of suicide. She described herself as "*daddy's girl*" and shared several memories of spending time with him, receiving help from him with her homework, and receiving his hugs. Her biggest challenge came from classmates who bullied and teased her, telling her that her dad wouldn't go to heaven because of the suicide. Louise has a 2-year-old son and wants to help other children who have gone through a similar loss.

A Brief Review of the Bereavement Literature

Bereavement Theory: Early Roots

Several theorists have had a major influence on bereavement work, and their resulting models have influenced counselors who work with bereaved children and adolescents. Freud (1917) was a pioneer of the psychoanalytic perspective on mourning and "melancholia." Psychoanalytic theories describe grief in individual, process-oriented ways, and their focus is on the emotional aspects of grief, with an emphasis on describing the progression of grief reactions. Psychoanalytic theorists generally believe that physical and cognitive reactions will dissipate once the emotional grief work is accomplished. Freud's initial works outline the need for detachment from the deceased, and the willingness to let go. He notes similarities between mourning (normal grief) and "melancholia" (pathological grief) by focusing on their distinguishing features. He defines mourning as the expression of grief emotions in response to the loss of a love object or person. Pain, loss of interest in the outside world, loss of capacity to adopt a new object of love, and a turning away from all thoughts of the dead are considered characteristic grief reactions. Freud proposes that grief work occurred in order for the libido to be withdrawn from its attachments to the object and that this work is accomplished "bit by bit, under great expense of time and cathartic energy" (Freud, 1917, p. 245).

Lindemann (1944) focuses on the somatic reactions of acute grief, and, like Freud, characterizes "grief work" as a psychological process. Lindemann, a psychoanalyst, devoted much of his work to the area of pathologic grief. He defines nine distorted grief reactions, ranging from psychosomatic illness, progressive social isolation, and furious hostility to agitated depression and self-punitive behavior. He held a fairly narrow view of "normal grief" (Middleton, Raphael, Martinek, & Misso, 1993), believing that pathologic grief reactions are common and can be easily managed by a psychiatrist. Lindemann asserts that early identification of the problem and proper psychiatric attention to facilitate grief work help the bereaved regain a normal course of grief. For this grief work to occur, Lindemann proposes several conditions to be met, including disconnection from the deceased, readjustment to the new environment (one without the deceased), and the formation of new relationships. He believed that if these conditions could be met, morbid grief could be shaped into normality in 8–10 counseling sessions.

Revolutionary at the time, Kubler-Ross (1969) challenges existing conservative theories and practices that suggest that death be swept under the carpet and not discussed. She proposes a model that suggests five stages of grief (denial, anger, bargaining, depression, and acceptance) that people move through. Though misconstrued by some as a rigid series of steps, Kubler-Ross intended her framework as a guide, believing that people do not always experience all five of the stages, some stages may be revisited over time, stages are not necessarily linear, and transitions between stages are more of an ebb and flow rather than a progression.

Parkes (1985) applies an attachment model to his observations on the course of grief. His model describes typical grief as consisting of denial and numbing, followed by searching for the lost object, anger and guilt, and finally mitigation and defense. Each of these periods was thought to include bouts of insomnia, anorexia, restlessness, irritability, outbursts of anger, and preoccupation with thoughts of the deceased. Early on, Parkes identifies three forms of pathological grief: chronic grief (prolonged grief with exaggerated symptoms), inhibited grief (normal grief responses are absent), and delayed grief (avoidance of painful emotions). Later, he relates grief outcome to attachment styles in relationships and advocates a wide range of bereavement services from use of professionals to self-help groups (Parkes, 1980).

Bowlby (1980), like Parkes, also proposes an attachment viewpoint. He emphasizes the ecological nature of yearning for the deceased and suggested that mourning lasts longer than had been previously thought. He found that several responses generally regarded as pathological were, in fact, common in healthy mourning. These include anger directed at self, the deceased, or others; disbelief that the loss has occurred; and the tendency to search for the lost person. Bowlby's attachment theory also makes a link between pathological grief, the subject's childhood experiences, and parental attachment behavior, indicating that individuals who experience "pathogenic parenting" are especially vulnerable following a major

TABLE 1.1 Select Historical Writings That Have Influenced the Understanding of Bereavement

Bowlby, J. (1980). *Attachment and loss: Vol. 3. Loss: Sadness and depression.* London: Harper Collins.
Freud, S. (1917). *The standard edition of the complete psychological works of Sigmund Freud: Vol. 14. Mourning and melancholia (1914–1916).* London: Hogarth Press.
Kubler-Ross, E. (1969). *On death and dying.* New York: Springer.
Lindemann, E. (1944). Symptomatology and management of acute grief. *American Journal of Psychiatry,* 101, 141–148.
Piaget, J. (1966). *The child's conception of physical causality.* London: Routledge.
Stroebe, W., & Stroebe, M. (1987). *Bereavement and health.* New York: Cambridge University Press.

loss. Like other theorists, Bowlby recommends the need to actively work through the pain associated with the loss, describing grief work as a process of redefining the self and situation, accomplished through the realization of the permanence of the loss and restructuring of the internal models to align them with any changes.

The influence of psychoanalytic and attachment theory have endured over time, not only on contemporary classifications of pathological forms of grief but also as the conceptual basis of counseling and therapy programs. Until recently, grief was viewed as a time-limited process where individuals, over time, detach from the deceased and reinvest in other love relationships, and those who fail to do so are considered pathologic in their grief (Bowlby, 1980; Freud, 1917; Parkes, 1980). As of late, this perspective has been replaced with grief work being viewed as an ongoing process, revisited indefinitely, one that may never be fully resolved (Horacek, 1991; Munholland, 1997; Palombo, 1981; Parkes, 1980; Worden, 1996). This perspective, that bereavement is a dynamic and fluid process requiring accommodation across time, has resulted in reform in professional practice. (For historical writings on bereaved theory, see Table 1.1)

Bereavement as an Adaptive Process: A Contemporary Viewpoint

Whereas traditional theories view healthy bereavement as a series of stages to progress through, tasks to complete, or a condition to resolve, modern research suggests that healthy bereavement is a lifelong process, where the bereaved seeks ways to hold on to emotional relationships rather than letting them go (Davies, 2004). Walter and McCoyd (2009), for example, describe bereavement as a normal, albeit destabilizing experience and process, where the instability promotes self-reflection and growth, particularly when the loss experience is supported. Certainly, the notion of grief as a time-limited process is too simplistic. Although most grief subsides over time, and grievers typically let go of emotional ties to the deceased over time, it is generally advised that they should not sever their ties with the deceased. In fact, most grievers retain emotional attachments to the deceased and are able to continue to involve them in everyday lives. Healthy grieving, then, involves the achievement of adapting to the loss, where the bereaved person adjusts to his or her new reality of life without the physical presence of the person who died (Howarth, 2011).

Present-day theorists see bereavement as a dynamic, ever-changing process, where the adaptation to loss has no timetable, and full "resolution" may never occur. Silverman, Nickman, and Worden (1992) advance the argument that one does not recover from bereavement but rather continually adjusts to the permanent changes. Therefore, the emphasis of grief work must be placed on the bereaved person's ability to transform his or her connections to the deceased, and to renegotiate the meaning of the loss over time (Neimeyer, Burke, Mackay, & Stringer, 2010; Worden, 1996). Many of the reactions and behaviors that were previously construed as defensive or pathologic are instead normal and adaptive ways to cope with and protect against the overwhelming nature of loss (Neimeyer, 2009; Silverman & Worden, 1992). Grief behaviors are viewed as self-protective responses allowing time for the bereaved to better deal with the emotional trauma of the loss. Stroebe and Schut (1999) describe this adaptive process as a "Dual Process Model" of coping with bereavement (see Figure 1.1). This model

FIGURE 1.1 The dual process model of coping with bereavement. Reprinted from "The Dual Process Model of Coping with Bereavement: Rationale and Description," by M. Stroebe & H. Schut, 1999, *Death Studies*, *23*, p. 276. Copyright 1999 by Maggie Stroebe and Henk Schut. Reprinted with permission.

recognizes the dynamic nature of grief in which coping is a regulatory process that fluctuates between confronting and avoiding the different tasks of grieving, and it acknowledges the normative need to both confront and take a break from the stress of the loss.

Theorists like Neimeyer (2011) advocate a narrative approach where the creation of meaning is central to the grief process. Neimeyer, a social constructivist, views loss as an event that upsets one's sense of security and worldview, and that after a loss it is important to reestablish meaning using psychological, social, cultural, emotional, and cognitive resources. Grief is a normal human experience that, although difficult, will produce personal insight and growth. The ability to assign meaning to the deceased person's life, death, and relationships is critical to the grief process (Neimeyer & Sands, 2011).

Bereavement theory has made a major paradigm shift, from a model where grief is considered a malady to recover from by accomplishing a predictable series of tasks or stages, to one where grief is a normal, dynamic, and sometimes cyclical process that is unique to the individual and leads to self-reflection and growth. Where the goals of successful bereavement were at one time to detach from the deceased loved one and achieve resolution, they are now to maintain a psychological relationship with the deceased and gain meaning from the loss.

Bereavement in Children and Adolescents

A Developmental Perspective

Our understanding of grief from a developmental perspective began in earnest when Nagy's (1948) study defined three broad developmental stages of child concepts of death. Building on these ideas, Piaget (1973) posited a theory that helped professionals to frame childhood bereavement and understanding of death as a developmental process that moves through preoperational, concrete operational, and formal operational stages according to age and maturity. Later, Kane (1979) performed a study to confirm previously derived developmental levels of death concepts, and to determine if experiences with death accelerated the development. She found a sequential flow in development, and determined that experience with death accelerated development only in children under age 6. Since then, researchers have focused on different age levels (Matter & Matter, 1982) and concepts (Speece & Brent, 1992), and contemporary frameworks such as the one presented in Table 1.2 have been developed for practical use.

Children grieve differently than adults. They often grieve in spurts and can regrieve at new developmental stages as their understanding of death and perceptions of the world change (Himebauch, Arnold, & May, 2008).

Many factors will affect a child's understanding of death—for example, cognitive age, past experience with death, personality, relationship with the deceased, and level of family communication and support. An understanding of age-appropriate grief is important when assessing a child's response to a death.

TABLE 1.2 Death Concepts in Children: Considerations of Age and Development Level

Age	Concepts of Death	The Child's Needs
0–2 (Infant)	Children at this age have no cognitive understanding of death. They will sense confusion or that something is wrong.	• Separation anxiety is a concern. • Provide warmth, security, and consistency. • Use transitional objects such as a favorite toy.
2–5 (Preschool)	For young children death is seen as reversible; thus their response is primarily a reaction to separation and confusion. Death is viewed as temporary, like being asleep, and they think "magically"—for example, death can be caused by wishing for it.	• Provide clear, precise language, correct misperceptions and avoid euphemisms—for example, death rather than "gone," "passed on," or "lost." • Regression is normal—for example, bed wetting, thumb sucking. • Be aware of secondary losses. • Encourage expression through play—for example, physical activity, doll play, stuffed animals.
6–9 (School age)	School age children understand that death is irreversible, but they may have difficulty accepting the finality of a death. They often lack the ability to verbalize feelings. Death is personified and children at this age can become fearful—for example, the dark, ghosts, or the "bogyman." Children at this age typically cannot verbalize thoughts and feelings. Anger can be an especially difficult emotion to appropriately express.	• Be honest and open, provide facts, concrete details, and death physiology. • Provide a variety of nonverbal ways of expression—for example, art, music, photography, physical activity. • Be aware of feelings of guilt and fears of abandonment. Provide reassurance—for example, "it wasn't your fault," and "I will always be here to love and support you." • Encourage memories and rituals. • Use stories and books to normalize the death. • Provide opportunities for fun and laughter.

(Continued overleaf)

TABLE 1.2 (*continued*). Death Concepts in Children: Considerations of Age and Development Level

Age	Concepts of Death	The Child's Needs
9–12 (Preadolescent)	Children at this age are developing a realistic understanding of death but often have not learned to identify and deal with feelings. They may become curious about the physical details of the death process and about religious and cultural death traditions. Preadolescent children have the ability to identify causal relationships, which can lead to feelings of guilt.	• Children at this age become more verbal. Ask them questions about what they are thinking and feeling. • Provide access to peers who have experienced similar loss. • Allow participation in decision making. • Create a safe environment to share personal thoughts. • Be aware of other losses. • Be aware of feelings of hopelessness.
13–18 (Adolescent)	Teenage children have the ability to reflect on themselves and the death experience. They have an extra tough time dealing with death because of the many conflicting emotions of adolescence. They are expected to "handle it like an adult," but they often lack coping skills to do so. Teens may be drawn toward unhealthy coping, leading to high-risk and often dangerous activities.	• Be truthful and straight-forward. • Role model positive coping strategies. • Expect strong feelings and allow for their expression. • Reading books helps normalize the experience. • Journal, essay, poetry, and letter writing encourages reflection, adaptation, and growth. • Encourage supportive relationships with friends and teachers, and through support groups. • It is important to reinforce self-esteem. • Allow for privacy and independence. • Watch for overcompliance—for example, "big man/big woman syndrome."

Child Reactions to Death

It is generally agreed that children are particularly vulnerable, and that the full impact of bereavement on them may not be realized until many years later (Currier, Holland, & Neimeyer, 2007; Moore & Herlihy, 1993). Most bereavement studies describe the death of a loved one during childhood as a trauma that carries the risk of a variety of short- and long-term issues. In the short term, children can struggle with issues such as depression, anxiety, conduct problems, poor school performance, withdrawal, insecurity, and lower internal control (Luecken, 2008). The lesser-known long-term consequences include a vulnerability to depression (Bowlby, 1980; Zisook, 1985), panic disorder and phobia (Kendler, Neale, Kessler, Heath, & Eaves, 1992), poor physical health (Luecken, 2008), and risk of suicide. It is evident that the experience of bereavement during childhood constitutes a risk for concurrent and sometimes chronic distress (Currier et al., 2007).

Silverman and Worden (1993) describe children's reactions to death in the early months of bereavement using three conceptual domains—specifically, the child's affective responses, efforts at maintaining a connection to the deceased, and impact of social networks and support systems. Affective responses reflect inner feelings about death and include crying, inability to sleep, inability to concentrate in school, and early health problems related to the somatization of feelings. Based on observations of children who participated in the Harvard Child Bereavement Study, Silverman and Worden (1993) report that reactions immediately upon hearing of the loss were more contained than one might have expected. Most children talked of feeling sad or confused upon hearing the news and of not being sure how to respond. Many felt dazed or shocked, some turned to family members for comfort, and others withdrew. Children often experience increased anxiety, focus on concerns about further loss and the safety of other family members, and have fears around separation. Mild depression is typical and can persist for a year or more (Akerman & Statham, 2011).

Children are considered at high risk for complicated grief reactions because of their developmental immaturity and dependency on others (Barbato & Irwin, 1992). Perhaps that is why, for a child, the loss of a parent is particularly hard to bear (Bowlby, 1980). Although the death of a loved one is stressful and disruptive for any child, there are certain factors that are more likely to cause heightened reactions and severe adjustment problems than others. How intensely a child will grieve and for how long are highly individual matters, influenced by dynamics such as personality, attachment style, genetic makeup and unique vulnerabilities, age, gender, health and mental health, spiritual and cultural identity, support and resources, additional stressors, previous loss experience, quality of the relationship, relation (e.g., parent, sibling, friend), and manner in which the death occurred (Bowlby, 1980; Parkes, 1993; Rando, 1992; Sanders, 1993; Stroebe, Stroebe, & Domittner, 1988; Vachon & Stylianos, 1988; Weller, Weller, Fristad, & Bowes, 1991; Wolfelt, 1996; Worden & Silverman, 1996; Zisook & Shear, 2009).

Adolescent Reactions to Death

Adolescent children face a unique set of difficulties during bereavement because they concurrently struggle through the developmental tasks of adolescence at the same time as they are navigating the complex emotions associated with their grief (Fulmer, 1983; Glass, 1991; Grollman, 1977; Kandt, 1994; Oaks & Bibeau, 1987; Rosen, 1991). Although researchers suggest that adolescents can develop strengths as they cope with grief, extensive evidence also exists that emphasizes its many adverse effects (Antonovsky, 1979; Bowlby, 1979; Furman, 1974; Garmezy, 1987; Stroebe & Stroebe, 1993).

After a significant death, adolescents often feel helpless and frightened (Glass, 1991), and may retreat to child-like behaviors, or, compelled by social expectations, act more like an adult. They may be unable or unwilling to share feelings, or they may put on a facade of independence and appear to be coping quite well (Rando, 1988). Anger is also a common adolescent expression of grief (McCown & Davies, 1995) as are denial, sadness, loneliness, and guilt. Although grief reactions in adolescents are similar to those of adults, the way they are expressed can be quite different, often through behavioral rather than cognitive or emotional means (Kandt, 1994). Fulmer (1983) describes hostility and acting out as typical responses to adolescent grief while Grollman (1977) suggests longing is a normal response in adolescence. Rosen (1991) indicates that adolescents often feel the need to take the place of the deceased by becoming a stand-in for a sibling or a replacement for a parent. Bereavement in adolescence can slow the mastery of developmental tasks necessary for emotional entry into adulthood and lead to depression in later life (Bowlby, 1980; Freud, 1917; Moore & Herlihy, 1993; Zisook, 1985).

Variables affecting an adolescent's progression through grief include emotional closeness to the deceased, reaction of others to the death, prior grief experiences, and the adolescent's own concept of the death, which is affected by the adolescent's personality (Kandt, 1994). Outside stressors such as moving, attending a new school, or having relationship difficulties can also play a role in grief outcome (Kalish, 1985). In short, the more stress, the more challenging it will be to successfully cope. A strong support system can positively impact the grief process in adolescents. Wolfelt (1996) found peer support especially important for this age group, but often lacking because of peers' anxieties about death.

Complicated Grief

Until recently, Complicated Grief was not recognized within the Diagnostic and Statistical Manual of Mental Disorders (DSM); however, that has begun to change with the recent publication of DSM-5. Although not included as a diagnosable disorder, this newest edition refers to Persistent Complex Bereavement Disorder under the "Disorders for Further Study" section of the manual. This inclusion suggests compelling evidence that grief, under some circumstances, is a definable condition that can impact individual functioning. Inclusion of Persistent Complex Bereavement Disorder will encourage further study of complicated grief so that it can be accurately described and reliably diagnosed. In defining Persistent Complex Bereavement Disorder, DSM-5 has added to our general understanding of grief and has helped identify the characteristics that differentiate normal from complicated grief (see DSM-5 criteria in sidebar).

TABLE 1.3 Criteria for Persistent Complex Bereavement Disorder, DSM-5 Section 3: Disorders for Further Study.

Persistent Complex Bereavement Disorder

Proposed Criteria

A. The individual experienced the death of someone with whom he or she had a close relationship.

B. Since the death, at least one of the following symptoms is experienced on more days that not and to a clinically significant degree and has persisted for at least 12 months after the death in the case of bereaved adults and 6 months for bereaved children:

1. Persistent yearning/longing for the deceased. In young children, yearning may be expressed in play and behavior, including behaviors that reflect being separated from, and also reuniting with, a caregiver or other attachment figure.
2. Intense sorrow and emotional pain in response to the death.
3. Preoccupation with the deceased.
4. Preoccupation with the circumstances of the death. In children, this preoccupation with the deceased may be expressed through the themes of play and behavior and may extend to preoccupation with possible death of others close to them.

C. Since the death, at least six of the following symptoms are experienced on more days than not and to a clinically significant degree, and have persisted for at least 12 months after the death in the case of bereaved adults and 6 months for bereaved children:

Reactive distress to the death

1. Marked difficulty accepting the death. In children, this is dependent on the child's capacity to comprehend the meaning and permanence of death.
2. Experiencing disbelief or emotional numbness over the loss.
3. Difficulty with positive reminiscing about the deceased.
4. Bitterness or anger related to the loss.
5. Maladaptive appraisals about oneself in relation to the deceased or the death (e.g., self-blame).
6. Excessive avoidance of reminders of the loss (e.g., avoidance of individuals, places, or situations associated with the deceased; in children, this may include avoidance of thoughts and feelings regarding the deceased).

Social/identity disruption

7. A desire to die in order to be with the deceased.
8. Difficulty trusting other individuals since the death.
9. Feeling alone or detached from other individuals since the death
10. Feeling that life is meaningless or empty without the deceased, or the belief that one cannot function without the deceased.

(*Continued overleaf*)

TABLE 1.3 (*continued*). Criteria for Persistent Complex Bereavement Disorder, DSM-5 Section 3: Disorders for Further Study.

Persistent Complex Bereavement Disorder
Proposed Criteria
Social/identity disruption
11. Confusion about one's role in life, or a diminished sense of one's identity (e.g., feeling that a part of oneself died with the deceased).
12. Difficulty or reluctance to pursue interests since the loss or to plan for the future (e.g., friendships, activities).
D. The disturbance causes clinically significant distress or impairment in social, occupational, or other important areas of functioning.
E. The bereavement reaction is out of proportion to or inconsistent with cultural, religious, or age-appropriate norms.
Specify if:
With traumatic bereavement: Bereavement due to homicide or suicide with persistent distressing preoccupations regarding the traumatic nature of the death (often in response to loss reminders), including the deceased's last moments, degree of suffering and mutilating injury, or the malicious or intentional nature of the death.

Is Suicide Bereavement Different?

While the intuitive answer to this question is "yes," study results are complex and contradictory (Jordan, 2001). Studies conducted over the past decade both support and negate the notion that those bereaved by suicide grieve or recover differently from those bereaved by other types of death (Brown, Sandler, Tein, Liu, & Haine, 2007; Cerel, Fristad, Weller, & Weller, 1999, 2000; Grossman, Clark, Gross, Halstead, & Pennington, 1995; McMenamy, Jordan, & Mitchell, 2008; Melhem, Moritz, Walker, Shear, & Brent, 2007; Nikulainen-Levine, 1997; Pfeffer et al., 2000; Sveen & Walby, 2008). One explanation could be that there are many similarities between suicide bereavement and bereavement by other types of death, and that differences are more subtle. This was, in fact, the conclusion made by McIntosh (1993), who, after reviewing 14 separate studies, made the following conclusions: (a) bereavement following a suicide is generally nonpathological; (b) there are more similarities than differences between suicide survivors and those of other modes of death; (c) there are a small number of grief reactions or aspects of grieving that may be unique or different in survivors of suicide; and (d) survivorship may be different between suicide loss and that of other types of loss over time. In their book *Grief After Suicide*, Jordan and McIntosh (2011) also posit that differences do exist, but that there is just not enough research-based evidence yet to identify clear, consistent differences or unique features of suicide bereavement.

Suspected Distinct Features of Suicide Bereavement

Ness and Pfeffer (1990) conducted one of the first examinations of the literature looking at the differences between suicide and other types of bereavement. They suggest that suicide bereavement is unique in that (a) it is characterized by shock and the need to make sense of the death; (b) it increases the risk of suicide in the survivors; and (c) social attitudes toward suicide survivors are more negative than after other types of losses. Jordan (2001) identifies similar aspects of suicide bereavement that he believed differentiate it, including (a) a greater struggle to find meaning in the loss of the loved one; (b) greater feelings of guilt, responsibility, and blame; and (c) greater feelings of rejection, abandonment, and anger toward the deceased. These characteristics have been supported by other authors, as discussed ahead. Similar notions are expressed by Calhoun, Selby, and Selby (1982), who indicate that people bereaved by suicide have a greater need to understand the death and experience more intense feelings of guilt, and Clark and Goldney (2000), who found that a need to make sense of the death was profound, as were feelings of shock and disbelief, horror, guilt, blame, and rejection. Perhaps the need to find meaning is why, as Calhoun et al. (1982) mention, a preoccupation with suicide and involvement in prevention efforts is common among suicide survivors.

Further, the violent death of a loved one appears to increase the risk for psychiatric issues such as depression, PTSD, prolonged grief disorder, and complicated grief (Armour, 2006; Currier, Holland, & Neimeyer, 2006; Green et al., 2001; Harwood, Hawton, Hope, & Jacoby, 2002; McMenamy et al., 2008; Melhem et al., 2004; Murphy et al., 1999; Murphy, Johnson, & Lohan, 2003; Rynearson, 2006). A number of characteristics related to violent death may account for this, including "the horror associated with the physical aspect of dying in a violent manner and the resulting mutilation of the body; an empathic anguish in the mourner when contemplating the physical and psychological suffering of the loved one just prior to that person's death; and the hazard created by direct exposure to the death scene, which is likely to contribute to the development of PTSD" (Jordan & McIntosh, 2011, pp. 34–35). Individuals who discover the body of an individual following suicide might be considered a special case of such exposure (Andress & Corey, 1978).

In terms of social attitudes, the stigma of suicide loss results in feelings of being misunderstood or blamed for the death, a need to conceal the cause of death from others, and a search for meaning (Calhoun et al., 1982; Range, 1998). Clark and Goldney (2000) also report unique feelings of stigmatization and social isolation, anger, and regret at the wasted life of the deceased.

In their attempt to answer the "*is suicide bereavement different*" question, Jordan and McIntosh (2011) separate past research on the differences into two categories: those findings supported by "convincing evidence" and those supported only anecdotally by clinicians and survivor accounts (see Table 1.4).

TABLE 1.4 Factors that Differentiate Suicide Behavior

Differences in suicide bereavement supported by convincing evidence

1. Feelings of abandonment and rejection by a loved one who chose to leave them
2. Feelings of shame and stigma because of the traumatic nature of the death
3. Attempt to conceal the cause of death as suicide, most likely related to shame or stigma, or to protect the image of the deceased
4. Blaming of others either out of anger or as a way of "scapegoating" to cast the focus away from oneself

Differences in suicide bereavement supported anecdotally by clinicians and survivor accounts but not currently supported sufficiently by the literature

1. Feelings of guilt and concern with what one did, did not do, or could have done
2. Feelings of intense or complicated anger directed at the deceased, oneself, or others
3. Searching for explanation or a desire to understand why, which is somewhat less distinctive because it is seen in other types of traumatic or sudden loss; a sense of relief, especially in cases where the deceased person's mental state was disruptive and difficult
4. Feelings of shock and disbelief as with any sudden or unexpected death
5. Effects on family systems (breaking up or becoming closer), social support (ambiguity about norms of interacting or discomfort or uncertainty when interacting with survivors), and social isolation (because of guilt, shame, or stigma)
6. Activism, obsession with the phenomenon of suicide, and involvement with prevention efforts, which can bring a sense of meaning and empowerment to the bereaved

Note. Reprinted from *Grief After Suicide: Understanding the Consequences and Caring for the Survivors* (pp. 30–32), by J. R. Jordan and J. L. McIntosh, 2011, New York: Routledge. Copyright 2011 by Taylor & Francis Group. Reprinted with permission.

Young Survivors of Suicide

Challenges related to parental suicide seem to mirror those of general suicide bereavement, with added complications related to change in immediate family structure and caregiving needs. Psychiatric, legal, and marital problems prior to a parent suicide and financial, geographic, and child care problems following the suicide each pose significant and unique challenges to suicide-bereaved children (Kuramoto, Brent, & Wilcox, 2009). As such, they may need special attention.

Parentally bereaved children are also at increased risk for psychopathology, future suicide attempts, and death by suicide (Brent & Mann, 2005; Brent et al., 2002; Pfeffer, Normandin, & Kakuma, 1998). Childhood survivors of suicide may identify with the deceased parent and are often themselves afraid that they will have mental health issues or die by suicide (Dane, 1991; Requarth, 2006; Simone, 2008). The fear, sadly, is somewhat realistic when considering the genetic predisposition to mental illness (Jordan, 2001) and increased risk of suicide among child survivors of parental suicide. Children who experience the attempt or completion of suicide by a parent have a six-fold increased risk of attempting or completing suicide during their lifetime, a very lethal difference for children whose parents die by these means (Brent et al., 2002; Hung & Rabin, 2009; Sorensen et al., 2009). In the book *Before Their Time: Adult Children's Experiences of Parental Suicide*, the authors point out that this identification and predisposition are further complicated by the fact that from birth we are encouraged to follow in our parents' footsteps (Stimming & Stimming, 1999). Simone (2008), in interviews with parental suicide survivors, found that the age of the parent at the time of death was significant for some of the participants, giving them a greater sense of security once they had passed the benchmark age.

A number of studies have highlighted additional risk factors for children of parental suicide. One suggested that they are more likely to react with high levels of anxiety, depression, fear, anger, developmental regression, poor school performance, and lower levels of social adjustment (Mitchell et al., 2006). Pfeffer and colleagues (2000, 2002) found that children who were suicide-bereaved experience more anxiety, anger, and shame along with depressive symptoms and interpersonal problems when compared with nonsuicide-bereaved peers. A controlled study involving parental suicide survivors suggested greater levels of anxiety, aggression, or withdrawal within weeks after the suicide and a potential for future delinquency (Shepherd & Barraclough, 1976). Cerel et al. (1999) found that children parentally bereaved by suicide were more likely to experience anxiety, anger, and shame and to have more behavioral issues. In their literature review on psychiatric and psychosocial outcomes of bereavement during childhood, Kuramoto et al. (2009) found that the suicide of a parent produced increased incidence of suicide and bipolar disorder, and the risks were greater when it happened at a younger age and when it was the mother who had died rather than the father. Older children also face challenges, especially during adolescence, making them more likely to engage in at-risk behaviors, such as higher than normal cigarette, marijuana, and alcohol use, suicidal ideation and attempts, and fighting. They also have lower life expectancy, report more emotional distress, and experience decreased parent-child and family connectedness (Cerel & Roberts, 2005). These challenges may exist before the death and continue in the aftermath; thus it is difficult to tease out the effect of the suicide itself.

Posttraumatic stress has been cited as common in children following the suicide of a parent (Dowdney, 2000; Dyregrov, 2009b), and the incidence increases with level of exposure to the death (e.g., finding the body or being in the home when the suicide happened). Using the Child Posttraumatic Stress Reactions Index Scale, Grossman et al. (1995) found higher scores in those exposed to the suicide of their fathers by presence in the home, concluding that "the shock of unexpectedly discovering a loved one, dead by suicide, in the familiar setting of one's own home is a traumatic experience that leaves a unique stamp on grief" (pp. 13–14). McMenamy et al. (2008) further report that more than half of adult survivors experienced trauma symptoms at a moderate to high level.

In short, past research tells us that suicide bereavement has many similarities to bereavement of other types. We know that children who lose a parent to suicide in general have reactions, struggles, and coping strategies that are much like those experienced by peers whose bereavement stems from other causes. The common feelings experienced by bereaved children in general seem to be exacerbated among children mourning a suicide, and according to one study, their effect becomes more apparent around six months after the death (Cerel et al., 1999). We also know that the complicated grief is seen in only a small number of suicide-bereaved children, and that witnessing the suicide or discovering the body places children at higher risk. However, the literature is equally clear that suicide bereavement *is* different, and that to know those sometimes subtle differences can make all the difference when counseling, parenting, or simply assisting a suicide-bereaved child. An aim of this book is to highlight some of the subtle differences associated with parental suicide to inform professionals in their responses.

two
Challenges

To a child, losing a parent to any type of death is difficult, and a loss to suicide poses additional challenges (Dalke, 1994; Elder, 1995; Pfeffer et al., 2000). It has been referred to as "the almost uniquely inexpressible tragedy, even beyond other childhood bereavements" (Cain & Fast, 1972, p. 94). Wright and Partridge (1999) go as far to say that parental suicide could be considered a form of child maltreatment. Grief after parental suicide is sensitive to a number of factors, including the surviving parent's warmth and caregiving ability, developmental tasks, the influence of stigma, the family environment, and communication surrounding the death (Cain, 2002; Jordan, 2001; Mitchell et al., 2006; Sveen & Walby, 2008).

We know that prior research on the differences between suicide bereavement and bereavement from other types of loss is inconclusive (see Chapter 1). Our survivor stories describe challenges that are at times very much like, and at other times very much different from, those surrounding other types of deaths (see Figure 2.1 for a list of challenges and the number of participants reporting each).

Emotions

Individuals who experience parental suicide demonstrate a wide variety of emotional reactions, though previous studies have suggested certain emotional responses particular to this group. Blame, anger, and anxiety are commonly cited emotions (Cerel et al., 1999; Dyregrov, 2009b; Kaslow & Aronson, 2004; Kuramoto et al., 2009; McMenamy et al., 2008; Ratnarajah, Mcouns, & Schofield, 2008). Child survivors may assign blame to others, particularly the surviving parent, feeling

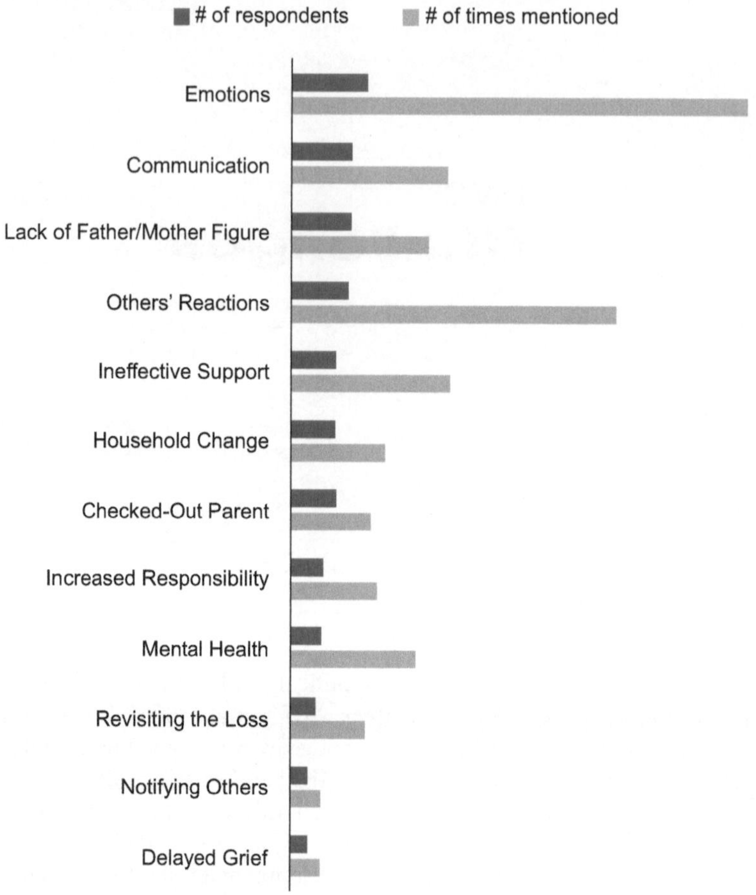

FIGURE 2.1 Challenges: Types and frequencies.

angry that they caused or should have stopped the suicide. Such anger and blame may be influenced by the coping of the surviving parent; many survivors describe parents who are emotionally and physically unavailable after the suicide. This leads children to feel responsible for the continued well-being of the family, taking on adult roles and in some instances becoming the caretakers of the surviving parents (Dalke, 1994; Demi & Howell, 1991; Dyregrov, 2009b; Ratnarajah et al., 2008). Anger may also be directed at the parent who died, though this happens less frequently because survivors seem to recognize the influence of mental illness (Simone, 2008). Guilt and shame are also frequently cited emotions by parental suicide survivors (Dane, 1991; Hung & Rabin, 2009; Kaslow & Aronson, 2004; Kuramoto, Brent, & Wilcox, 2009; McIntosh & Wrobleski, 1988; Ratnarajah & Schofield, 2007). In one study of 63 adult survivors of suicide, for example, guilt was the third most indicated of 25 issues, with nearly three quarters of the sample reporting moderate to high levels (McMenamy et al., 2008). Survivors feel guilty for their words and actions or for inattention to the signs of suicide, and they wonder whether they could have stopped the death (Cerel et al., 2008; Clark & Goldney, 1995).

Our survivors reported experiencing a wide variety of emotions in relation to the suicides of their parents. Many of the emotional challenges occurred immediately following the death, whereas some continued or emerged later in life. The range of emotions included panic, disbelief, confusion, sadness, hopelessness, loss, guilt, self-blame, fear, regret, intimidation, anger, worry, resentment, frustration, loneliness, shock, devastation, abandonment, and shame. Some survivors reported a lack of emotion or feeling detached from the situation. One person indicated feeling "*cheated that he [his dad] can't be there for me.*" Others qualified their emotions using expressions such as "*complete panic,*" "*intense, intense sadness,*" "*scared out of my mind,*" and "*a wreck.*" Many participants shared the intensity of their emotions, with one person describing how she felt as "*being on a rollercoaster, like every organ in my chest cavity fell out. That feeling times a hundred. It was this indescribable feeling of despair, loss.*"

Amber, who discovered her mother after she died by hanging, described herself as her mother's caregiver during bouts with depression, and she discussed a range of emotions following the suicide. "*I felt hopeless mostly,*" she related, "*and then panic, and then I couldn't contain anything. I was uncomfortable, lost in my own house, pacing around while on the phone with the preacher, just complete panic, panic, like, what did I do?*" Following her father's suicide, another survivor shared fears that her mother would follow the same path.

> Sometimes my mom would lock herself in the bathroom just to have 5 minutes of peace. With three kids in the house, that's probably what she was doing. I remember she was in the bathroom and I felt like so panicked. I needed to see her or hear her. I just remember screaming and pounding on the door and yelling, "Mom!" I was just afraid that if it happened to my dad, it could happen to my mom too.

Many participants described anger, especially at the person who had died. Jerome, 3 years old at the time of his father's death, described feelings of anger that have persisted over time.

> I was angry at my dad. I still kind of am. I felt abandoned by him. I just think that he left us hanging. He left my mom with two kids, all alone. I remember as a little kid, being at other friends' houses, and their mom and dad would be there, and I remember thinking, "How is my mom going to do this alone?" It is weird being a little kid and thinking of things like that, but I remember worrying about how my mom would cope with two kids on her own.

There were two participants, Jenna and Brooke, who experienced abuse from their fathers prior to their suicides. Both held anger. Jenna described the unique mixture of feelings with such a complicated loss as "*angry guilt*," adding, "*I was being angry and I was being rebellious and I was this horrible 13-year-old—angry all the time about everything.*" Brooke directed her anger squarely at her father.

> I was a pretty angry kid, angry because I still had a lot of questions for my dad, like "Why?" And now the opportunity was gone. My mom took me to counseling and all that stuff, but I didn't say anything. I was just angry. Of course I wasn't going to tell everybody that I was angry. I was going to tell everybody that I was fine.

Survivors also directed anger at others. Several voiced anger at religious institutions that were perceived to be insensitive, and others voiced anger at classmates, as in this example.

> I had friends that were strict religion kind of people. When I came back from being gone after the suicide they told me that they didn't want to be friends anymore. So all the way through high school they would make little comments to me about my dad. I had a lot of anger in high school because of the jokes about what my dad did. I had a lot of blow-outs with people. So after a while everybody was just kind of scared of me.

Survivors also expressed feelings of guilt. In most cases, the feelings of guilt came from wondering if there was something that they had done or something that they could have done differently. Trevor's guilt, present even in his adult years, seemed to stem from questions about how his behavior may have influenced his father's suicide.

> Sometimes when I think back on it, I do feel guilty. I wish I was 8 years old again, but this time, I wish I wasn't a whiner kid. I wish that I could just be happy around him, whenever he was there. Sometimes I just wonder, was I that terrible to be around?

Dirk came upon his father, who died by hanging, and spoke of regret, wondering if he could have saved his father if he had not struggled when helping to untie the rope.

> For a few years I was feeling guilty. I had dreams. It's one of the worst things for a person, guilt. It's something that comes on. It's not something you push away and not have. It eats at you one way or another. I felt like I was the reason why, but it took me until I was older to really finally realize that it wasn't my fault.

Charlotte, age 15 at the time of her father's suicide, shared her guilt in the following way.

> I feel a lot of guilt, like if I wouldn't have got pregnant, he wouldn't have been forging checks again, wouldn't have got caught, and he wouldn't have killed himself. But then I think it was obviously a long time coming, and it's not my fault, at all. It took me a good four years to not blame it on myself. It's not my fault. I know that now.

Fred, a preadolescent at the time of the suicide, also shared his guilt at somehow having been responsible for his father's death.

> What did I do wrong that made him do that? What did I do as a kid that pissed him off enough to go shoot himself? Did I not take out the trash like he told me? Did I not do other certain things? What did I not live up to as a son to have him do what he did?

Some survivors described feeling *numb* or *detached*. Guy described his inability to feel emotions. At age 6, he was the first to find his father, who died of a self-inflicted gunshot wound. His way to cope was to repress feelings, which he described in this way:

> I remember that day, everybody else was crying, and I couldn't. I ended up sitting there, pretending to cry. I just didn't feel it. I would say I just felt like a zombie. I wouldn't even eat or drink because I just didn't feel anything.

Guy further described himself as being *"emotionless, kind of hopeless—stoic"* until he entered high school. He acknowledged feelings that were repressed, saying they can *"catch up with ya . . . and then, to find out, ya know, 10 years later, it catches up with you, and you start feeling things."*

Communication and Expression

Family communication issues and other related dysfunctions are often present before the death, further complicating healthy engagement and interaction following a suicide (Cerel et al., 1999; Ratnarajah et al., 2008; Webb, 1991). Children bereaved by suicide witness suicide threats and attempts and other familial disruptions (e.g., parental mental health issues, marital strife, or legal troubles) prior to their parent's death more often than those whose parents die by other means (Cerel et al., 2000; Ratnarajah et al. 2008; Shepherd & Barraclough, 1976).

In the aftermath of parental suicide, distortions in communication are often present, including denying, evading, and fabricating facts about the suicide (Webb, 1991). Parents may try to hide information, which can be a significant source of upset for children experiencing grief (Giovanola, 2005). Secrecy and lack of open communication are common in cases of suicide and can result in endless mourning

(Nelson & Frantz, 1996). Not only does concealing information lead to distrust but also it fosters misconceptions that complicate the grieving process (Giovanola, 2005). Although the stigma that surrounds a suicide death is less prevalent now than in past generations, recent studies suggest that secrecy continues. Demi and Howell (1991), for example, found that many families use secrecy to cope, and Cain (2006) found that this secrecy can persist even into the third generation. The secrecy and lack of communication are seemingly meant to protect from stigma or rejection, but ultimately compound negative outcomes for children (Mitchell et al., 2006).

Communication is often hampered, and the grieving process further complicated, when traumatic parental death results in depression or posttraumatic stress for children (Dowdney, 2000). Communication issues can persist into adulthood, particularly related to sharing feelings and grief (Avrami, 2005; McMenamy et al., 2008). Parental suicide survivors tend to cover up personal pain related to the suicide, which can be protective but may also exacerbate closed-family communication styles (Demi & Howell, 1991). The age of the child seems to influence communication following parental suicide, with younger children receiving less open and honest communication (Ratnarajah & Schofield, 2007; Shepherd & Barraclough, 1976; Wyss, 2003). Surviving parents, particularly those with young children, may not know how to talk in an age-appropriate way about the suicide, so they often avoid discussing it altogether.

Children who have experienced the death of a parent due to suicide may be less skilled and confident in their ability to communicate with others as a result of the pre- and postsuicide issues and family dynamics. Nearly one third of the participants in our study reflected on their poor communication skills or the inability to express feelings. Often, poor communication was a result of a lack of trust in others, or because survivors isolated themselves.

Trevor, who expressed himself through fighting and bouts of anger, has always found it hard to put his feelings into words.

> I've never been real good with expressing feelings. I've never been good at talking, to tell people how I feel about something. I'm always kind of a mixture of thoughts all in one. In high school I definitely really struggled with people. I wasn't really good with communicating with people.

Lisa expressed difficulty trusting others enough to share her "*private feelings*," hoping that her feelings would go away on their own: "*I felt like these are private feelings. I need to keep them to myself, not tell anybody, and it'll go away, and it'll fix itself in time.*" After feeling abandoned by her father because of his suicide, Julie did not believe that she could trust anyone with her feelings, stating that "*in my heart I knew better, but in my head I was just like, I can't trust my dad, I can't trust my mom either, you know? I'm obviously not going to trust some stranger either.*"

Many described how feelings of isolation blocked their ability to express themselves and seek support. Brooke described how her isolation affected her behavior and recovery, which ultimately resulted in a prison sentence.

> My mom saw me as pretty isolated. She did nothing but try to support me, and she was nothing but there, but I didn't let her be there. She wanted me to talk to a counselor. My older sister tried to get me to talk too, but it wasn't going to happen. The whole reason that I went down the path that I did is because I turned everybody away from me that wanted to be there and I completely isolated myself from anybody who was thinking about helping me.

In several cases entire families struggled with communication. One family was described as a "*family where we would never talk, we would always yell about things.*" Another was described as a "*whole family of social problems that don't get along as people.*" Jake described how the suicide of his father impacted his family and their ability to communicate and to support each other, and he described the resulting anxiety.

> We all dealt with it differently. One of my brothers is pissed off to this day, and the other one is on the same street, just pissed. I don't really talk to them much. My sister, she is the same as me. She has accepted it and has dealt with it. My mom still really blames herself. I think my brother is a lot like my dad, and it makes me wonder if he'll ever commit suicide. I worry about that a lot, both of my brothers. So that sucks and that is something I think about a lot, because if they end up dying of suicide, what it is going to be like to deal with that.

A number of survivors discussed how poor or closed family communication interfered with their recovery. The most problematic dynamics were keeping the suicide a secret, lying about the nature of the death, or not talking at all. Most, like Suzanne, told of how being lied to about the nature of the death, even when understanding the loving intent, actually interfered with recovery.

> My mother chose to tell myself and my sister—so we are 8 and 10 years old—that he died by heart attack. That's a problem, when you don't tell a child about something. That makes it even worse. I never really believed the heart attack story because the kids at school immediately said, "No, no, no, no, no, he died by suicide." I even found his death certificate, and she had attempted to cross the cause of death off. The fact that my mother tried to cover it up to us about how my dad died, that meant that there couldn't be open and honest questions about it. She did it for the most loving of reasons. She wanted to save us from the pain, but it really didn't help.

Lack of Father or Mother Figure

When a parent dies, children lose one of their strongest potential supporters. Our survivors revealed how their deceased parent's absence resulted in diminished practical support, less opportunity to participate in certain activities, lack of support at important life events, and changes in personality and identity. They reflected on missing their deceased parent during important life events such as first communion, prom, homecoming, father-daughter dances, graduation, weddings, or when getting a driving license. Several mentioned missing an important role model with life lessons such as "*feeling comfortable around people of the opposite sex*," "*understanding a sport*," "*learning how to shave*," "*talking with boys*," "*having a period*," or "*learning how to be a good mother and wife*."

Rachel, who lost her father at age 7, reflected on the effect of that loss at key events in her life.

> At important events, like at prom, I would have liked both parents there taking pictures. It was just my mom at my graduation. It was really hard for my mom on that day. A couple people from the family told me, "Your dad should be here, that would have been a really proud day for him."

Rachel wondered about missing her father at future life events. "*So now I think about when I get married, who is going to walk me down the aisle? Do I want someone, or do I not want someone else?*"

Dirk and Trevor, who both expressed anger, shared how the absence of their fathers played a role in their behavioral issues. They shared the following feelings:

> When I got my license or going to that first homecoming, going to that first dance, stuff like that it was really hard because he wasn't there. He wasn't there to see me graduate, and I think that was the reason why I got in trouble, skipping classes and all that stuff. If he was there I would never have skipped, because my mom didn't discipline me. I wasn't scared of what she would say if I skipped school, so it was not having that structure that was a problem.
>
> Socializing with the opposite gender never really worked for me. I was just at the age when he killed himself that I was just starting to become interested in the opposite gender, and I didn't really know how to deal with that kind of thing. That got me in so much trouble at school. I didn't know how to handle it.

Lisa, who lost both parents to suicide, and Fred, who lost his father, shared how the absence of their parents impacted confidence and skill during important developmental milestones.

> The first time I got my period, I remember using toilet paper because I didn't know how to tell my grandmother. I actually went to my aunt, and she was like, "You didn't tell Grandma?" I'm like, "She's my grandma. She's old. I'm not going to tell her that." That was really hard.
>
> My friends did a lot of things with their dads. I wondered, am I going to be able to fish? It sounds corny, but I was like man, am I going to be

> able to learn how to do stuff like that, because I don't have a father figure to teach me. It sounds silly, but I learned to shave by myself because it wasn't like I was going to ask my mom about it or something. I just learned how to do a lot of things myself, doing laundry, how to talk to girls, and, you know, stuff that people take for granted.

Others' Reactions

The reactions of others, whether well or ill intentioned, pose a challenge for surviving children, resulting in damaged emotions and difficulty in coping. Reactions of first responders, for example, have a lasting impact on those bereaved by suicide and can greatly influence the course of recovery and the grief process (Davis & Hinger, 2005). Experiences with police, victim's assistance providers, and clergy may vary from extremely positive to very negative, and lack of communication and inappropriate or dishonest communication by formal and informal support systems can contribute to hardship (Davis & Hinger, 2005).

According to Jordan and McIntosh (2011), the stigmatization surrounding mental illness and suicide may contribute to the potential for adverse reactions from others. Some in the survivor's support network may withdraw because they assign blame or see them as "tainted" by the death. Suicide survivors seem to be judged more negatively than survivors of other types of loss (Range, 1998; Stillion, 1996). Returning to school and being subjected to harsh treatment both by teachers and by fellow students can be particularly difficult (Davis & Hinger, 2005). Peers may feel uncomfortable around someone who has experienced such a significant loss. Because they do not know how to behave appropriately, they may withdraw from the grieving peer. This sudden change in the grieving teen's social circumstances can be very upsetting, adding to the stress and grief that is already present (Auman, 2007). Survivors may self-stigmatize and withdraw from potentially supportive interactions with others because they believe they will be judged (Dunn & Morrish-Vidners, 1987). These challenges can contribute to a cycle of misunderstanding, avoidance, and withdrawal between survivors and their social networks that can complicate the mourning process (Seguin, Lesage, & Kiely, 1995).

Such reactions mentioned by survivors featured here include (a) law enforcement and medical staff performing initial postsuicide interrogations, (b) extended family and friends placing blame on the family, (c) peers bullying, (d) well-meaning people expressing pity, (e) clergy making adverse comments, (f) school personnel not knowing how to respond, and (g) people who were previously not close friends with the bereaved trying to suddenly be friendly. One surprising finding was the number of participants who were offended by the approach of key crisis personnel such as police, clergy, and school personnel.

Charlotte, whose father died when she was a teenager, described the difficulty of friends' and classmates' casual references to suicide in conversation and of her own daughter and mother casually threatening suicide.

> . . . friends saying, "I'm gonna kill myself," or "I'm gonna kill you." Shut up, shut up, you have no idea. I mean they say it just to say it, but they haven't the slightest idea. My daughter says it. "I think I'm gonna kill myself." Or my mom says it sometimes when she's having a hard time, and I don't listen, I block it out. I know that my mom would never do it, but then, I also didn't think my dad would ever do it. If my mom ever did it, I probably wouldn't make it through.

Many stories were told of friends who were cruel. Melissa and Julie, early adolescents when their fathers died, were especially sensitive to peers' comments. Their stories of rumors and thoughtless comments by friends and classmates seemed especially hurtful.

> What was not helpful was the entire school being rumorville, gossip. You could feel people staring at you. Nothing was said to my face and that's worse than actually saying something, because then you can confront that person.
>
> I remember some of my friends actually teasing me, friends of my family. And my neighbor across the street, we were in English class watching the Romeo and Juliet movie, and at the very end he shoots himself, and I started crying in class, and I remember one boy sitting behind me says, "Oh, she's just looking for attention." I'll never forget some of their comments.

Lisa and Shane shared vivid memories of feeling harassed by peers, as indicated in the following excerpts.

> I would get picked on by the popular kids, you know, "Where's your mom?" "Why isn't your mom on the booster club?" "Where's your dad?" "Why didn't he come to the activity?" They didn't know. I just had to stand back and say, "Don't hate them. They don't know." But one time I did tell one of them, "You know what? My parents are dead. Stop asking me." And he looked at me and he said, "Well, why are your parents dead? What happened?" I said, "They both committed suicide." And he said, "Well, that's not cool, are you gonna commit suicide?"
>
> More of the rude people will be like, "So I heard your dad shot himself in the head or blew his head off." At least have the common courtesy to show some politeness towards me when you ask me that kind of question. I've come close to filing a harassment report against him because he showed so much disrespect toward me.

In some cases, participants spoke of being treated poorly by the very people from whom they would have expected to receive support. Amber was clear in her disdain for the clergy after the suicide of her mother. "*I found them very hypocritical, 'cause anybody that commits suicide goes to hell. As soon as it's my mom, 'Oh, she's in heaven.' So, yeah, so I found nothing there.*"

The next quote makes clear Amber's criticisms of police and hospital staff who talked with her during the aftermath of her mother's death.

> At the hospital, it was interrogation central: "Was she depressed? What had happened? Why didn't you see these signs?" I just remember thinking it was just really cold and unwelcoming . . . I just went through this outrageously intense experience untying my own mother, thanks. And then they asked me questions about what did the knot look like, how long did it take you to untie the knot? They implied that I should have noticed her behaviors were degrading toward suicide. First it was mostly police officers and some doctors. I got it from one group of people, and then I got the same sort of questions from another group of people. I was like can't you just transcribe it for these other guys? I felt tired, exhausted, intruded upon, and blamed. The connotations and implications of how they were formulating their questions were accusatory. Instead of saying, "Did you notice?" It was more like, "Didn't you notice that things were happening?" The coldness, it was the opposite of what I needed. I needed consoling and instead they separate our whole family and get everybody's story separately because they suspect foul play, so there was this really uncomfortable, frustrating, impersonal feeling. I felt like I was just a source of information rather than a person.

Like Amber, several other participants reflected on failings of clergy. Charlotte reflected that "*I wanted to play a song for my dad at the funeral, and they wouldn't let me. I remember that clearly.*" Suzanne remembered a priest whose sermon caused her family great pain.

> The priest gave his sermon about how anyone who commits suicide is going to go straight to hell, and in doing that he pounded his fists on the pulpit thing, and that was horrible for our family. I mean you can imagine, here you are so raw in the grieving process after my dad died. When you talk about who helped and who didn't, the priest pounds on the pulpit, and harms the family so much by how he handles it.

Ineffective Support

Social support appears to be a crucial factor in determining outcomes following any type of death (Stylianos & Vachon, 1993), and bereavement via suicide produces even more pronounced needs (Callahan, 2000; Seguin et al., 1995; Thompson & Range, 1991). One study indicated that those bereaved by suicide perceive being treated differently, less positively, and with less support than are survivors of other types of death (Range & Calhoun, 1990). Bereavement by suicide can be isolating; the knowledge that resources are available is the first step in addressing the unique needs of those impacted (Jordan, 2001).

Although formal types of support seem to be effective for adults and children, adolescents and young adults may require a different approach. Dyregrov (2009a) asked 32 suicide survivors between the ages of 13 and 24 (20% had lost a parent) about their needs for help and support following the death. Many of the young people expressed frustration with help received from professionals. Some had disappointing initial encounters, which caused them to be turned off to the idea of further help. Many did not feel that the mental health professionals really cared, addressed their current problems, or had experience with suicide. Further, youth admitted that they did not know, themselves, what kind of help they needed.

Factors that interfere with potential social support received from family, school, or other sources can have direct bearing on the mourning trajectory (Cerel et al., 2008). One barrier may be that the survivors do not seek help, due to depression or a lack of information (McMenamy et al., 2008). Another related barrier involves a lack of communication with others, which may result in a lack of friendships and an "us-against-the-world" mentality within the family, particularly for those who experience blame and criticism (Ratnarajah et al., 2008). An additional barrier relates to the often passive responses from the community, which mainly involves referrals from doctors, hospitals, and churches (Campbell, 1997; Campbell, Cataldie, McIntosh, & Millet, 2004; Rubey & McIntosh, 1996). The lack of organization consistently leaves many families unaware of existing resources such as crisis centers, mental health clinics, and support groups (Hung & Rabin, 2009).

Nearly all of the survivors featured here perceived that key people could have provided better support or could have reacted in a more thoughtful manner. They discussed a wide variety of failed support, expressing criticism of people who should have been the most helpful but were not, including surviving parents, professional counselors, teachers, and friends. Several mentioned that surviving parents or grandparents were overprotective, overbearing, or not approachable. They expressed feeling that they had no one to talk to who understood, including friends and family. Professional support was also lacking in multiple instances where schools seemed ill equipped to provide assistance, counseling was viewed as ineffective, or families resisted counseling.

Amber described, for example, how her dad kept her from seeking counseling when she needed it most, indicating, "*When I did get counseling once, he came back and said that it was a crock of bullshit and he's not going to put his kids through that money-sucking crap that doesn't do anything.*"

Although several participants mentioned being helped by counseling, most spoke of its ineffectiveness, as in the following excerpts:

> There were a couple times when we went as a whole family and times when we went separately. In the state of mind that I was, it didn't help. I got really upset about things. I was just angry all the time about everything. I didn't want to go to counseling. I put up such a fight.

I went with my mom and he kind of scared me. He would ask really bizarre questions. They freaked me out. I was just a little kid, and he asked me if I had seen my dad after it happened—ghosts and things. I got scared was when I was alone with him.

It's nothing against them personally, just that I hadn't found any benefit from it. It seemed to me like it was costing money to go and talk to somebody where I very well could have just talked to a friend and that would have done just as much if not more.

My mom sent me to a psychologist. It was only a month or two after the suicide. I didn't like the guy at all, and it wasn't the questions. There was something about him I didn't like. He was condescending. There wasn't a lot of empathy, not someone you would want to open up to. You could just tell this guy really could care less.

It didn't really do any good. It never did any good. I became very attached to the woman who was my therapist. She was kind of a mother figure that I didn't have anymore. I became very attached, and then she moved to Texas, and then I had to start all over again. It was like, "Wait a minute. I can't start all over again!"

"Tell me your problems for the next hour and I'll listen, and then offer some generic advice, and then you can go on your merry way," and so, no, that wasn't helpful.

Although most school personnel were recognized for trying to help, in several cases they were described as ineffective. In one case, Fred told of a school counselor trying to "*pry answers from me.*" In another, Brooke described weekly meetings with her school counselor in this way: "*The guidance counselor would call me in every single week to check up on me and I wouldn't tell him anything—nothing—I'd be like, 'I'm fine.'*"

Household Change

The death of a parent can cause significant disruption to a child's daily life (Melvin & Lukeman, 2000). Multiple family changes may occur as a result of parental suicide, including changes in parenting style, relocation to a new home and community, remarriage of the surviving parent, and changes in finances. Such changes are often referred to as *secondary losses.* In fact, for some children, it may not be the suicide itself that leads to problems, but rather such things as subsequent family functioning (Jordan & McIntosh, 2011). Survivors featured here discussed the challenges that these family changes posed for them.

Rachel had a very close relationship with her father prior to his death, when she was 7 years old. The relationship that they shared was one of the reasons that Rachel had such a difficult time adjusting to the change brought on by her mother's remarriage. Such a reaction is not uncommon; grief reactions may be triggered when subsequent life changes occur, such as the remaining parent remarrying (Raveis, Siegel, & Karus, 1999). Rachel described feelings about her stepfather in the following way:

> I don't consider my stepdad any sort of a father figure at all. No. I really don't like him. It's not a secret. No one will ever replace your dad, and no one should ever try to. I would never, ever call him "Dad," and it bugs me when people say, "your dad." I just wanna say, "He's not my dad!"

Jenna described changes in her family that resulted from her dad's death. The first quote indicates financial challenges, and the second describes changes in her mother's style of parenting as "*unfair*" and like a second loss.

> We lived on the social security. I remember understanding money at a very young age, like understanding that you can't have everything you want, and that's just the way life goes, you know?
>
> We never had a bed time. My mom wasn't the type of parent to put her kids to bed at 8 and then stay up late all by herself. As long as she was awake, she would let us be up. And then she started going to counseling and talking to other parents, and she started changing things, putting us to bed early and a lot of, "Parents do this, and kids do this." Part of it was healthy, but part of it was very unfair, because in a way our father was gone and so was our mom. She was very, very different.

Many other survivors mentioned financial issues as among the most challenging consequences of their parents' suicides. Charlotte, a teenager at the time of her father's suicide, revealed her frustration and anger at having to go without things that she needed.

> My mom had help financially with child support. There are things that I needed and didn't have, and I always had to ask my mom, and it got hard for her. So she tells me she's pissed at my dad, she's mad at him for leaving her here, for leaving her with us. She yells at him, and I yell at him.

In Lisa's case, the death of her mother caused a chain of family challenges that she described as "*chaos and craziness.*"

> My grandma immediately said we had to move. She couldn't live in the house anymore. She hadn't slept in weeks, and over that time she became addicted to prescription medication. It was just so traumatic for her, and not a lot of support for me and my brother. Everyone was so focused on what they were going through that they kind of forgot there were two little kids that just lost their mother. My grandmother took custody of me, and a week later my brother's father—who he didn't know

> because we have different fathers—came and took him away. So he lost his mother and then a week later was placed with a stranger. There was just so much chaos and just craziness. It was hard to know that my brother was so far away and I couldn't be there to take care of him. I felt like, I'm the next one. I'm supposed to take care of him, but I couldn't. It was just too many things at one time. We were bound to self-combust at some moment.

Checked-Out Parent

While higher levels of caregiver warmth and lower levels of caregiver mental health problems protect against negative outcomes from the death of a primary caregiver (Haine, Wolchik, Sandler, Millsap, & Ayers, 2006; Lin, Sandler, Ayers, Wolchik, & Luecken, 2004; Luecken, 2008), surviving parents may not function as effectively because of their own grief, increased responsibilities, and personal problems preceding or as a result of the suicide (e.g., mental health, drug, or alcohol abuse). This may result in the child taking on more responsibility within the family or simply lacking adequate support, structure, and direction. Surviving parents may be less emotionally available to their children following suicide (Lohan & Murphy, 2002). The stigma and isolation they themselves may experience can compromise their ability to support their child's grieving process (Jordan, 2001; Sveen & Walby, 2008). The child is then left to cope and process on his or her own (Ratnarajah et al., 2008). A number of survivors featured here reflected on their surviving parent's inability to function and provide support following the suicide. Jenna coined the name of this theme by describing her mom as "*checked out.*"

> My mom was checked out. She was kind of dealing with her own stuff. I felt like I was the one holding things together, taking care of the younger ones, and so I just felt really lost. I was supporting a lot of people, but I didn't have anybody supporting me.

Two participants, Kevin and Charlotte, described vivid memories of watching their surviving parents fall apart. Kevin remembered his mom as being "*very depressed and her crying all day all of the time.*" Charlotte, who was a young teenager, shared how lost she felt when her mother checked out, in the following way: "*I hate it. I hate it. I hate when she breaks down and crumbles, because then I'm like, 'You can't do that to me, because you're everything.'*"

Julie, who was fifteen at the time of her father's death, stepped in to try to hold her family together. Julie's grades dropped, and she began smoking cigarettes and drinking as her own way to cope.

> I was this keeper. Keep everything together with my family. My mom, she lost it, went berserk, started drinking, and my youngest, second

> youngest brother, he started getting in trouble and running away, and he blamed my mom and, said, "Oh you killed him, it's all your fault, and I hate you," and all that. My youngest brother didn't understand—he was only 8 years old. He was growing up and started to realize, "Well, gee! I don't have a dad." So I felt like I was the one who was the support. I had to keep everybody together. Because if I didn't, then everybody was just gonna go off the deep end. So, in that aspect, I had to be the mom and take care of my two youngest brothers. I even had to take them on dates with me. It was really embarrassing.

Guy described the hopelessness felt by his family in the years between the time his father died when he was 6 and now as a 19-year-old young man. The hopeless feelings were made worse because his mom was "*strung out and held it in.*"

> My mom all of a sudden was a single parent and didn't really have any time, and us kids just kind of fell apart on their own, and so did she. So, I'm around my family, and we're falling apart, and no one really cares. That's when I did drugs. It's all about who you're around. And the rest of my family has their own problems, and it's easier to suppress the feelings, and that's how most of our family was. It was very stressful. My mom was always sick. She would basically just go to work, come home, clean, was just overbooked. She just got strung out and held it in, and well, let's just say everybody went their own way. We didn't go to the park, we didn't go on family rides, we didn't really do anything because everyone was doing their own thing, and that's it with the drugs, too. Once somebody gets on drugs, they don't really do anything else. They just do that.

Melissa, likewise, described her mom's inability to take charge immediately after the suicide, when she herself had to be the one to make funeral arrangements, and again later when she described having a mom who was overly permissive.

> My mom was in such shock that I helped her plan the funeral, wrote and edited the obituary, picked flower arrangements. I convinced her not to go with the cheapest coffin. My mom also spoiled us afterwards, like, "You wanna buy a game system?" Whatever would make you happy or content or provide distraction. I immediately started going out with someone, and my mom would let me stay over every evening: "Whatever you wanna do." I guess she didn't want to deal with it.

Amber, a teen at the time her mom died, spoke of taking over for her dad when he couldn't function. Her surviving parent was so out of touch with the fears of his children that he openly contemplated suicide himself. This was not unique among survivors featured in this book. Other surviving parents did the same.

> I was the only one because Dad was just gone. Just absolutely couldn't function. So I was sitting with him because I never wanted to leave him alone, and he's crying, and he hands me this suicide note, telling me that he was going to commit suicide too, and I said, "Okay, stop, let's keep it together, people," you know, so my job was to just to help, to be there, and to make sure that everything was okay. So I went out and got a job and tried to help pay the bills, getting the laundry done, made sure people ate, and made sure that everything was happening the way it was supposed to happen.

Increased Sense of Responsibility

Surviving children may take on more responsibility within the household to compensate for a deceased parent's absence and the surviving parent's difficulty functioning. It is common for a young person's role in the family to change following parental death, causing them to assume caregiving responsibilities for younger siblings, take on additional household responsibility, and perhaps even bring in additional income (Auman, 2007). This is sometimes called the *little-man, little-woman*, or *man-of-the-house* response. In fact, because many completed suicides are by persons with a past or current psychiatric disorder, some reversal of the usual parent-child relationship might have occurred prior to the death (Stimming & Stimming, 1999). As one example, Ratnarajah et al. (2008) shares the insights of a survivor of parental suicide who was expected to provide stability and take on the role of partner to her mother, even to the point of sleeping in the same bed. These additional responsibilities may cause surviving children to neglect their own needs, and to set aside school, extracurricular activities, and friendships.

Examples revealed by our survivors include managing the home, paying bills, generating income, doing laundry, cooking meals, getting everybody where they needed to be, and caring for other children. Some felt a sense of responsibility for the coping of others and described themselves as having "*grown up*" as a result of the suicide, and indicated a need to become "*the man of the house.*" Brooke stated simply, "*I guess you could say I had to grow up quick when I was 12*," and Guy, who was even younger, echoed Brooke with a terse, matter-of-fact statement: "*It forced me to mature sooner.*"

Jenna, the middle child of 9, who in the wake of her father's suicide cared for her younger siblings, felt that her sacrifices went unnoticed. As a caretaker in a large family with a new baby, Jenna didn't receive a great deal of support, adding that she often felt "*lost.*"

> I felt like I was the one holding things together. I was okay with that, but I guess I wanted recognition for it. I wanted people to get it that I was helping out. I didn't feel like people were taking notice of the things that I was sacrificing.

I felt like I didn't have any other options, because, as you know, I was a middle child. I was taking care of the younger ones, and then my mom had the baby, and a lot of her focus was on the baby again, and so I just felt really lost. I was supporting a lot of people, but I didn't have anybody supporting me.

Dirk was 16 years old, with one younger brother. Jared, age 12, the oldest boy, had six siblings. Both reflected on how their teen years turned from a time of freedom to a time of adult-like responsibility.

I kept getting the whole, "You're the man of the house now" thing. It was just me my mom and my brother. And my mom was working, so after school I would have to stay home and babysit my brother. So I really couldn't do any after-school stuff.

It was, you know, "You're the oldest boy," and "You've gotta take care of your mom," that whole spiel. "Step up!" I got a lot of that. And I did, because my mom had a lot on her plate, especially with my brother still being a baby and stuff. I worried more about trying to help Mom out and taking care of the house and doing what needed to be done, like shoveling the snow in the winter. So there wasn't a lot of, you know, go out, play, have fun, do sports and that type of stuff. And all the way through high school I never did sports or anything. I worked all the time. I don't remember really being told, "Hey, be a kid. Go have fun and play."

Mental Health Issues

As discussed in Chapter 1, survivors of parental suicide appear to be at a higher risk for a variety of mental health issues. The experiences of our survivors support and expand on this previous research, with survivors revealing mental health issues such as bipolar disorder, attention deficit disorder, and anxiety that presented both before and after the suicide. Mental health issues were often discussed in relation to other difficulties such as self-mutilation, severe nightmares, substance abuse, and suicide attempts. Nearly one third of participants described how mental health issues interfered with their recovery. The words and descriptions used by these eight participants were some of the most lengthy and riveting of the study. Guy and Trevor, for example, described, respectively, a seemingly overwhelming mix of mental health issues that included ADD, drug and alcohol abuse, depression, anxiety, ADHD, and rapid-cycling bipolar disorder.

About the end of sophomore year, I fell apart. I wanted to see some psychiatrists, and nothing really ever worked. Part of it was I had attention deficit disorder. I didn't start doing drugs until my senior year, and then I started drinking heavily, and then I started doing ecstasy, and pot,

> and coke, and then crack, and then I got kicked out of the house and tried to kill myself again. I really fell apart, really got depressed 'cause life didn't work out sober, or well, without medication from psychiatrists. And, even now I have anxiety problems and obviously depression.
>
> I definitely was overdriven big time with depression throughout my younger years in high school, not because of high school itself, just because I never really had a good day, just a bad day every day. Like for no reason. Initially I was getting treated for depression and ADHD, and when I was talking to the psychiatrist, he said, "Well, from everything that I'm hearing from you, it sounds more of like a rapid-cycling bipolar disorder."

In many cases, mental health issues were present both prior to and after the suicide; however, the issues were often described as having changed or intensified after the death. In this excerpt, Amber described how "*cutting*" herself changed after her mother's suicide.

> I was just kind of obsessed with watching myself bleed. I would rather bleed than feel the emotions that I was feeling at that time. I didn't think that it was as big of a deal at the time because I'm not committing suicide, because you have to go like parallel to the ends of your arms rather than across. Before the suicide it was primarily my legs, cutting awkwardly with razor blades. After that, just whatever knife or scissors was handy. It was the most outrageously difficult thing for me to ask for help.

Several survivors had either thought about or had attempted suicide themselves. Charlotte indicated, "*I thought about killing myself for a little while. If he can do it, I can do it.*" Shane and Guy additionally reflected on their more serious suicidal thoughts and behaviors.

> I had gotten to the point where I was getting in trouble at school. I didn't really care—my grades were horrible—and I actually didn't see a point in living. I didn't really think that far ahead to the future—my life sucked at that point—and I myself said I was going to kill myself. Understandably, my mom took that seriously, and admitted me to a hospital, and that kind of worked for a little bit.
>
> Then right at the beginning of junior year I attempted for the first time, and it just kind of went from there, and then junior year, probably barely got a 2.0, and then senior year was just pretty much bad shit. I got stuck in a psych ward three times that year and, all I did was just do it, get out, try to do it again.

Each of the three survivors in our sample who witnessed the suicide described characteristics of posttraumatic stress disorder. The most prevalent symptoms were dreams and nightmares. Amber and Guy, respectively, described them as follows.

Amber described nightmares related to the hanging death of her mother, whom she discovered. Guy spoke about how he still deals with nightmares, 10 years after he was the first to find his father, who died of a self-inflicted gunshot wound.

> And then I started having nightmares, nightmares, nightmares, like three, four, five nightmares a night, in which case I was afraid to sleep. Luckily for me, this happened during the summer, so it wasn't like I had class. But I still had to work. Then, like a month worth of I'm afraid to sleep, I can't sleep. I sleep just because I am exhausted. I'll pass out—wherever. I have for my entire life had recurring nightmares of domesticated animals convincing people I know, especially my intimate family, to commit suicide telepathically, and then I am killing the animal. That is the time when they all commit suicide. It's weird.
>
> A big part of my thing is nightmares, since that day, just pretty much regularly, at least once or couple times a week I have nightmares. I went on with life and forgot about the death, but then there's always the night. As I've gotten older I've started monitoring the dreams, 'cause they just get irritating. I've been dealing with them for 10 years.

Revisiting the Loss

Literature suggests that grief does not end for children and might be more accurately described as *regrief* (Oltjenbruns, 2001; Rosenblatt, 1996). It is common for grief to occur in episodic pangs over a lifetime, as a result of cognitive and emotional maturation and sometimes triggered by an emotional or physical event (Hung & Rabin, 2009). Grief can fluctuate over time, and may be triggered when subsequent life changes occur, such as the bereaved person having a child of their own (Raveis et al., 1999). Studies have demonstrated that a child's understanding of various aspects of death evolves with age (Childers & Wimmer, 1971; Willis, 2002) and cognitive ability (Cotton & Range, 1990; Reilly, Hasazi, & Bond, 1983). Piaget's (1973) widely recognized theory suggests that children move through four broad qualitatively different stages of understanding of death, from infancy through adolescence, involving mental operations that evolve from learning based on simple sensory and motor activity to logical and abstract thought.

Because of unanswered questions or the traumatic and sudden nature of the death, children of parental suicide may have an even more difficult time "putting the death to rest." Memories, emotions, and questions can resurface and need to be reevaluated at different points in life, causing the individual to deal with the death repeatedly. Fine's (1997) book *No Time to Say Goodbye* contains personal accounts of parental suicide survivors and brings to light the fact that mourning is without understanding. Survivors are left to wonder why the person chose to leave them, and this question never really gets resolved (Clark & Goldney, 1995; Dane, 1991). Traumatic losses may require considerable time and psychological effort in coming to terms with the perceived senselessness of the event (Currier, Holland, Coleman, & Neimeyer, 2008; Currier et al., 2006, 2007; Holland, Currier, & Neimeyer, 2006; Neimeyer, 2002, 2005; Neimeyer, Prigerson, & Davies, 2002). The focus of grief may shift as children mature from missing the deceased parent, to grieving over what the parent could have been to the child, to coming to terms with the parent's contribution to his or her own death (Hung & Rabin, 2009).

Rachel, now 21, was 7 when her father died. In the following series of quotes, Rachel reflected on how her father's suicide came up at different points in her life, how her mother's remarriage and insights about depression made her wonder about details of her father's life and death, and how she is seeking the help of a psychiatrist to reevaluate the meaning of the suicide in her life now:

> I was a 7-year-old dealing with it, and I think it just kind of comes up at different points in my life. It wasn't like I dealt with it and got past it. I kind of feel myself having to deal with it again and again and again.
>
> In my circumstance, it's a little interesting because my stepdad was his friend, and people have hinted over some years that maybe my dad asked him to take care of my mom. And those are things we would never know, but there are things you wonder: explaining how the depression is an illness, and because of this illness he felt like he wasn't a good dad, and things like that.
>
> I'm getting to a point where I want to start reevaluating, and not thinking like a 7-year-old about it. So this is why I think it is good that I actually have set up an appointment with a psychiatrist that I used to see after he died. There's just some other things, some changes that have gone on in my life recently that I feel things resurfacing, and I just want to reevaluate it and rethink about what it means to me and my life, because I really think I haven't thought about it past how a 7-year-old thinks about it. I know what happened and how it happened, and I was okay with those things, but I was 7 years old, and I think I need to understand it in a way that's fits a 20-year-old now.

Only 2 when his father died, JC "*wonders*" what his life would have been like and if he would be less "*angry*" under different circumstances.

> Mostly I wonder what it would have been like, what would be different in my life, if that had not happened. I am doing good in my life, and my family is doing good. I never really took it all that hard. I was just kind of angry, I guess, and still am.

Several survivors revisited what Charlotte called "*unanswered questions*" in the first quote ahead. Because of her religious beliefs, Charlotte wondered about the effect of the suicide on the chances of meeting her father in heaven. The most prevalent unanswered question, as in the following second quote, by Shane, is why a parent would choose suicide.

I don't know if I'll ever even see him again in another life, because I'm Catholic, and if you kill yourself, you go to hell, you don't go to heaven. Well, I'm going to heaven! So, will I ever see him? I don't know, and that sucks. I mean I'll never know the answers to my questions. So, I think that's the hardest part—unanswered questions.

And one thought that I've had ever since is, "If he truly loved me and my whole family why would he have done that? Why would anyone do that?" That is the one question I never will be able to answer.

Many participants spoke of circumstances that caused grief to resurface later in life. Suzanne, whose career included counseling suicide survivors, described how she was overcome with grief while reading another woman's story.

She was searching for that one answer for why her son committed suicide, and she finally comes to the conclusion, and I just closed the book and cried my eyes out, because I realize that I'm just like she is. I'm just like all the other people. The one question that everyone searches for is, "How could this possibly have happened? What could we have done? Why would they do something like this?" Even though in my dad's case, the mental health—why all these other people who have mental health issues don't think of suicide—why did that get into my dad's mind that it wouldn't get into someone else's mind? You have all these questions. Then you even have questions about what was bothering him that he didn't tell us about. Was there something that happened in his life? There was a parent who I worked with who went to every parent teacher conference after her son had committed suicide, and she asked every single teacher that had ever had him in class, did you think of anything since the last time that I was here that would help me to understand why he committed suicide, why he died that way? So that is the eternal question of people who are closest to a suicide. I believe they will have that question for the rest of their lives. I know there isn't a simple answer, and yet that doesn't stop me from searching. You never stop searching for the answer. It's a mystery. I know my dad did want to live, because I remember him thanking my mother for saving his life, but that doesn't help either, because you still are searching for that answer.

Suzanne also gave an emotional and philosophical account of how grief resurfaced in her own life during her daughter's baptism. Her grieving was triggered when she realized that the baptism was held on the same date as her father's suicide many years earlier.

Grieving is such a thing that it hits you when you don't expect it, and it hits you in ways that you don't expect it. Our daughter, who was 8, was baptized on the same day of the month as my father died, and

> some in my family are saying, "Do you know what day it is, Suzanne?" And I say, "Yes," and they say, "This is wonderful, now we have a wonderful thing to remember about this date." So they didn't make it that it was a bad day, but they just remembered. It is impossible not to remember a parent's death date, but when it's by suicide, of course you never ever forget. For me, that date was full of regret. When our children got to be 8 and I looked at them, and that's when it really hit me about how very young and fragile I was, and how much I needed my father.

Jared shared how the death of a close friend brought back memories and feelings of his childhood and the suicide of his father. Aspects of both deaths were so similar to Jared that it was sometimes difficult to discern in his conversation which death was being described.

> When my friend Ethan died, I was about the worse I've been emotionally since my dad died, and that brought a lot up, because we were really close. I mean he was my best friend and he was my best man. I was his best man. That brought Dad back up, because I wasn't there and I hadn't seen him for so many days before. We had seen him in the morning, went to school, and the afternoon came back and he was dead. He had been gone all week, so it was kind of almost like a continuation of that. I mean you see him in the casket, but he had left, and then it was done, he was gone. I would say that the recent death of my friend brought up a lot of the memories.

Lisa spoke of how difficult it was to accept the deaths of two classmates that occurred within only a few years of her own mother's suicide. A few years later she would lose her father to suicide as well. Lisa's story is one of tremendous resilience.

> I lost my mom in third grade, and another year later I lost my best friend, and then I befriend this girl, and she died in fifth grade, and when she died, I was asked by our teacher, "Are you going to go to the funeral?" I said, "I don't wanna go." And my grandmother and my oldest aunt asked me numerous times, "Are you going to go, do you want to go?" I said, "I don't want to go. I can't go." So they went, but I didn't. I stayed at school. And I had a really hard time that day, sitting through school and listening to my teacher, and several times he had to just say, "You can leave the room. Why don't you go to the bathroom?" Or "take a little walk," because he could just tell I wasn't there. And so that set me back another step, to try to move forward was just so hard because every time I would, something else would set me back another step.

Notifying Others

In a surprising number of cases, surviving children were actually called upon to notify others of their parent's death. This challenge was not identified in prior literature; however, there were six separate instances in our sample where the burden of having to notify others that a parent had died of suicide fell at least partially on the child. Most were teenagers, who, because of circumstances or the incapability of the surviving parent, took part in notifying others of the death. In three cases, Guy, Louise, and Lisa, respectively, all young children at the time, vividly recalled the scenes of watching and participating as an adult told other loved ones what had happened.

> My mother came home, and she walked in the door, and the cops told her what happened. And she just fell down and started screaming. And my brother went in there, and it really definitely etched the picture in his brain. My sisters, who were at after-school activities, by the time they got home, it was all taken care of, but we still had to tell both of them.
>
> So the four of us younger siblings drove to the restaurant where my sister worked and told her, and she broke down, and then she left work right away.
>
> My grandmother called the ambulance, and then she called my aunt from school. She was in seventh grade. We told my mom's sisters, both of them. It was very difficult.

Teenagers at the time, Julie, Jared, and Melissa, respectively, described struggling to tell authorities or other loved ones what had happened.

> My oldest brother didn't know yet, so I had to call him because my mom couldn't. She couldn't call him at work. She could barely talk. So I called him at work, and, actually, my friend Kristen, she actually told him, and, he cussed her out because he thought she was lying.
>
> The first I had any idea that something had happened was when we had gotten on the school bus. The school bus route is normally a set route, and for some reason the school bus driver is like, "I'm dropping you off down at the neighbor's house." I thought that's weird, because our school bus never goes past that house. It was probably about 30 minutes after we had been there they told us that Dad shot himself and that the coroner was still there and the police were still there. So after that we went to the restaurant where my sisters worked and told them. We got them, told them, and then we all went home.
>
> I had come home from school and found, well, that my dad had killed himself, that there was a lot of blood in the bathtub. I turned around and started walking for the phone, thinking, "I wonder if something's happened," and I'm beginning to see a bunch of bloody fingerprints on the

> walls and floor. I got to the phone, and, well, I had dialed 911 wrong: 119 or something like that. I went to the neighbor's house whose phone had a little display so I could see what I was doing wrong there, called the police, and called, you know, 911.

Delayed Grief

It is uncertain whether early or later loss in childhood is worse, according to the overall literature on childhood bereavement (Cerel et al., 2008). Based on what we know about child development and understanding of death, though, it makes sense that delayed grieving can occur in some circumstances. With some of our participants, the young age at which the suicide occurred interfered with the ability to comprehend, or grieving was delayed as a result of the extreme shock associated with the death. One example is Melissa, who described the delay in her grief, stating, "*I slipped into shock and couldn't think of anything. It took about four years for my brain to comprehend, for myself to feel normal, for things to register.*"

Similarly, Lisa, who, experienced the shock of waking up lying next to her deceased mother, described how her shock affected the eight-year delay before it "*sank in.*"

> To sit back, hearing paramedics, my brother and I didn't know what was going on. He thought it was a game. I just sat there scared out of my mind, because I was 8 years old, I'm like, "What's wrong with Mom? What's going on?" I just didn't think it was real. I thought it was a bad dream and as soon as I woke up everything would be okay, and my mom would be here to take care of us. It took a long time to realize it wasn't a dream; it was real. At the time I was just scared.
>
> At the age of 11 I was still acting like an 8-year-old, because I didn't really grow up. It didn't sink in until years later, at my first trip to camp. I was 16, and then I finally said, "Oh, wow! It's real." I wanted to know what happened. I was old enough then that I understood. I was old enough that I wanted to know, I needed the details. Not like when my mom died, I didn't understand that. I didn't get those details until I was 15. It was after my dad died that I finally said I need to know the details of Mom's death, and that was when I found out that she committed suicide, too. I didn't know it was a suicide!

Jake's account demonstrated the significance of developmental stage in comprehension of death and how delayed grief may result as understanding becomes clearer later on.

> I remember her telling us. I thought he killed himself, but at 4, forever seems like not a concept to you. I don't think I even cried, to tell you the truth. I remember thinking that he was just at work, because he would

go to work for a week at a time, and it would be a bit of time before we would see him again. I remember telling myself that he would be back. It wasn't until I was 6 that I realized he wasn't coming back. At 4, I went to the funeral, but it never really fazed me until I realized that it was final. When I realized he was not coming back, I was just distraught. I don't remember why or how I realized it. I think it was when my baby sister was born, and I just kind of finalized it. I don't know how it clicked with me, but maybe it was how people are born and people go. I just remember sitting in my room just bawling, and my mom came in and I was just sitting there talking about it with her and she explained how it is forever. That's when it pretty much sunk in.

CASE STUDY

Amber's Story

Renounced

Don't ask me to smile. I don't have to! And please don't pity me. Treat me like a regular person—that's all I ask.

I was 17 when my mother committed suicide. My parents had been arguing as they had before, the kind of argument where they separate so they don't say things that they'll regret later. I was always the mediator. I would talk with my dad to try to figure out what his problem was, and then I would talk with my mom to try and figure out her problem. My mom started exhibiting some pretty atypical mannerisms. By that I mean that she was huddled in a chair, much more quiet than normal. She didn't even look at me. She was really blank. She was covered with a blanket, and I sat down next to her and talked with her for a while about feeling hurt. She was so cold, so inaccessible, but I went into this long lecture about how I appreciated her. As I was talking with her a thought entered my mind from nowhere; the devil was trying to convince her to commit suicide. At the time I was pretty Christian and this idea, I knew, shouldn't be in her thoughts. "Please don't commit suicide," I told her, not thinking that she really would. I asked her what she wanted, what she needed. She just told me to go to bed.

I was raised in a family that was really disciplined, and when you were asked to do something, you did it without question. I lingered awhile with Mom, and then I went upstairs to my room. I played some worship songs and prayed, hoping that He would hear me from where I was. I heard my dad come upstairs and poke his head in my room, "Where's Mom? Have you seen her?" "No, I haven't." He turned then and headed back down the stairs. I could hear his every footstep as if our house had somehow suddenly acquired amplification. As I sat on the bed listening to his steps recede to the lowest level of the house, the most bestial noise—a noise that I would never have believed was human—pierced the air. I jumped from the bed and ran in its direction, and I knew that it had erupted from my dad. I could hear him screaming, "Help, help, help!" I ran so hard and fast to get to him. That sound—it was so frightening.

As I ran through the doorway of the basement, I saw my dad holding my mom up by the waist. He was yelling at me to "untie her, untie her, untie her," and I saw my mom with an extension cord. I tried and tried to untie that knot, but it just wasn't working. I just couldn't get it. Finally I felt it start to give and then it was undone, and my dad was laying Mom gently to the floor. He was trying to give her CPR and bring her back. I ran to call 911 and I couldn't remember the number. What the hell is the number? 4, 5, 3—no, what is that number? 911—it finally went through and the ambulance was on its way. Dad was still trying to revive Mom, and I just couldn't look. I couldn't watch what he was doing. The police finally arrived, and I hung up the phone. I needed to talk with my pastor, so I called him next. As soon as he answered, I said, "You better start praying. My mom is dying."

The paramedics placed my mom on the stretcher and took her out the backdoor. My dad and I just stood there not knowing what to do, watching them leave with her. We eventually walked out the front door and stared at the ambulance as it pulled away. It was so late, around midnight, I think, and I was holding tight to my dad. We knew that we had to go to the hospital, but as we started walking out onto the grass, Dad just collapsed and started to cry, "She's gone, she's gone—I just know she's gone." Watching my dad as he cried was the first time since the whole thing started that I actually felt something. I didn't cry. I just thought, "Wow, here we go now. I have to get my brother out of bed so we can go. I know that he must know by now what is going on." I was so scared.

When we arrived at the hospital, it was interrogation central. The police, the doctors were all asking questions: Was she depressed? What had happened? Why didn't you see the signs? The whole time at the hospital was like that. Everyone and everything seemed so cold and unwelcoming, very blank and stale and, sad to say, that continued for the next couple of weeks. Imagine just going through this intense experience of untying your own mother and having questions thrown at you: "What did the knot look like?" "How long did it take you to untie the knot?" They were cold, impersonal questions implying that I should have noticed that she was spiraling toward suicide. I felt so exhausted, intruded upon, blamed. Instead of providing my family with support and consolation, they separated us and questioned each of us individually. I guess it was because it was a suicide they suspected foul play, so they had to see if our stories would match. I felt so uncomfortable, so frustrated. Everything about their actions was impersonal. I thought, my God, my mom just died!

I remember the next morning going into that empty house that I grew up in and feeling like the house was saying, "Just stay away. You're not welcome here anymore." I just felt blank and pale, if you can imagine pale as a feeling. The rest of the year was the same. I went through the motions of my brother's graduation, but I still felt blank inside. Not really empty, just blank. It's hard to explain unless you've felt it.

My mother had been very introverted and unaffectionate my entire life. With Mom, there was always a theme to her life. First she immersed herself in trashy romance novels; later it would be computer games. She always found ways to spend time with herself and nobody else. It was a chore to be able to penetrate her alone time, and when I was successful, I really felt special. Sometimes she would head for the computer at 4 in the afternoon and not emerge again until 4 in the morning. That was the basis for the argument that day, my dad saying that she wasn't really a wife or a mother but some computer geek who found reality in games. We just couldn't figure out why we weren't the reality that she needed. I remember trying to hug her and trying so hard to hold on for that extra second or two, only to feel her pushing me away.

After her death I felt so responsible. I had to take over my mom's role, but I wasn't sure that I even knew how. My new role was to pay the bills, get everybody to where they needed to be, and to make sure A, B, and C happened. And cooking, this was all so new to me. I also felt responsible for my dad. He wasn't doing so well in the months after my mother's death. It was as if he just left us mentally. He wasn't functioning like a father, so I wanted to stay with him all the time, to watch over him and help him. As we were sitting together one day, he handed me a note that said, Amber, my God, I love you, I appreciate you, but I can't continue. He was crying and telling me that he had thought about suicide, but realized that he just couldn't go through with it. I took the booze and the gun away. I thought, my God, what is happening to my family? It has to stop! I knew that my new role was also to help heal this family. I found a job and started helping with the bills. I became a mother to my brother, making sure that his homework and chores were completed, that the laundry was done, that food was on the table. I felt so driven in this new role that I didn't have a grieving period, not until four years later.

I came from a small town of about 3,000, and my junior class was just 140 students. My mother's death was a shock to the entire system. Support was something that I didn't have a lot of. Doing nothing with my dad except being with him was one thing that was powerfully supportive to me, kind of like I was thankful that I still had him in my life. In school I never saw a counselor or anything. Really, I don't think anyone knew how to deal with this.

To make things stranger at school, two years before my mom died, I choked in front of the whole school assembly; I mean I almost died, and they had the defibrillator out ready to use on me. They took me to the hospital, and later I learned that the whole school had been silent for the rest of the day. I died right there in front of everybody, my brother included. So now my mom had died, and I think the school was thinking, "What's up with this girl?" Oh, I had people coming up to me at school, people I had never talked to, and I thought, "If you're my friend, then be my friend, and if you're just my friend today then be that friend from afar. Don't ask me to smile. I don't have to! And please don't pity me. Treat me like a regular person. That's all I ask."

I had a couple of friends, one or two, who just sat and did nothing with me. They didn't demand anything of me, just sat with me, and I appreciated that. My softball team showed up for the funeral, and I thought that was great. They stayed in the back of the room, and that was what I needed, just knowing they were there and I could go to them if I needed to. My friends provided indirect support, such as making little cards that showed they were thinking of me, but not standing right in my face.

Feelings of guilt surfaced later, guilt that I felt myself, and then the guilt that others put on me. I blamed myself because I was her last outlet. Maybe if I had pulled that blanket off her I would have seen the extension cord, or maybe if I had just stayed with her instead of going to bed, it wouldn't have happened. Remembering that day now, I think, "I had an opportunity to change things, and I didn't do it." There was also a lot of blame from one half of the family. They said that my dad murdered my mom, and then the people who worked with my mom started saying the same thing or that it was his fault. I became so protective of the males in my family. I took on the guilt of not defending my father to everyone and not saying, "No, he didn't, 'cause I was there and this is what happened and how dare you say that about him, 'cause he is all I have left." They wanted to put him in jail for no reason at all, and then, great, my brother and I would have had no one.

My brother's experience was different from mine. He stayed in his room during the entire suicide event. He didn't talk about Mom and didn't want to talk about her or her death. He stayed very private throughout. We sided together after a while, because our dad became so angry and would cuss out our mother, calling her a bitch and saying, "How dare she do that to us?" She was our mother, and it hurt to hear him say those things. My brother and I just wanted to avoid his anger, and we really didn't talk about the death.

I was so preoccupied with my dad that I didn't know what to do with my brother. As he got older, I noticed that he began to save people, especially females. If there was a female who was down and out and said anything about suicide, he was there to love them and save them. He became their rock, their grounding device. And that has gotten him into trouble, especially with law enforcement. He is so passionate about everybody else; he lays out his cards to them and doesn't have a hand to play for himself. He says that he finds comfort in someone else finding comfort. I really try to encourage him to do something, anything, for himself, but he is really selfless in an almost unhealthy way.

Camp HOPE was the first time that I dealt with my emotions. The onslaught of emotions was overwhelming. It was like I was an entire campus of network cables, cut in half, and sprawled everywhere, still live. Then the nightmares began. I had three, four, five a night sometimes. I became afraid to go to sleep. I had this recurring nightmare of domesticated animals telepathically convincing people I knew, especially my immediate family, to commit suicide, and while I was killing the animal, the member of my family would commit suicide. If I could have forgotten about the damn animal, I could have saved my family!

Actually, the nightmares began long before Camp HOPE. I was 7 when I had my first nightmare. I can't remember who was in it, but I remember that it was a brown owl with a white belly. People think brown owls are fat and cute, but they scare the crap out of me. This owl was like Poe's "The Raven," you know, you'll never get it, you'll never get it, and then it's gone. That's weird, an impending sense of doom brought on by the presence of a usually comforting sort of animal. These dreams were sporadic, maybe a couple in a row and then maybe one more during the year. There are two themes to these dreams: first, domesticated animals convincing someone to commit suicide, and, second, a sense of impending doom in which I have to save everyone's life and I can't.

Most of my life, I have been self-mutilating. Before the suicide I would primarily cut my legs. I was obsessed with watching myself bleed. I could justify the blood by thinking that I would rather bleed than feel the emotions that I was feeling at the time. I didn't think that it was a big deal at the time; it wasn't like I was committing suicide. Then after the suicide I began to cut my arms. First I started with razor blades, then knives, and then anything that was handy. I couldn't ask just anyone for help, but when I was riding in a truck with my boyfriend one fall day, I pulled up the sleeve of my shirt. He shrieked, "What the hell happened?" It took the whole truck ride just to tell him that I needed help. I was crying, and admitting that I needed help was the most difficult thing in the world. So I went to counseling, and this woman starts to psychoanalyze me. I remember that my boyfriend was in the counseling session too, and I kept thinking, "Why is he here?" Then the therapist told me that my cutting was because of our relationship, but I told her that it started way before we became a couple. I lasted a few months with her, but I'm not sure that it helped.

After Camp HOPE my dreams became very intense for about a month, a month of two or three dreams per night. It got so I couldn't function anymore, and I knew that I needed to get some help. I was so afraid to go to bed, so scared to close my eyes. Other than being cold, I hate being scared the most. But I met this woman at Camp HOPE. She was a psychotherapist and she really helped me. We talked about a different kind of therapy she felt would really help me which involved watching lights that made a little pattern. I can't remember what it was called, but it wasn't as intense as talking and going through all the emotional stuff. The therapist gave me some things to think about while watching the lights. It took care of my nightmares; once I started the therapy they were gone.

When I first attended Camp HOPE, I thought that I had to do everything possible to help the kids who like me had experienced suicide. I would seek them out specifically and let them know that I was there for them. Then I realized that I was doing the same crap that people used to do to me. So now my way of helping is much more subtle. Camp HOPE is really intense, but at the same time it's therapeutic for me and I hope it is for the campers as well.

I regularly attend camp as a counselor. At first I felt an unwillingness to tell my story, even unsure of how to say my story. This was supposed to be a fun camp, so how do you focus on death and grieving? That's hardly fun! The veteran staff members, who are there all the time, were very helpful as they know everything that is going on, so they become the counselors for the new counselors. This is a minicamp within the camp that many people don't know about.

Another aspect of Camp HOPE is the candlelight ceremony. This is where the counselors and the children sit around a campfire and talk about the person they lost. My first candlelight ceremony, I bawled my eyes out when I told my story. Nobody had ever wanted to hear my story before; nobody genuinely cared. I went on and on that night with my story. I think it was the hardest that I cried since my mom's funeral. I remember going up to her at the funeral and touching her arm and it was so cold. I knew it would be, but it still was a shock. I remember falling on my knees in front of everyone and crying and crying. It was the same thing at Camp HOPE. I cried and cried, and I didn't have to care about who was around. I had my cry at the funeral, and then I went and sat back down on the pew with the family. I didn't feel that I needed to escape or anything. That's the way it was at Camp HOPE. I knew it was going to be intense, but I also knew that I didn't have to run away or be a rock.

Today my dad has remarried, and we all have excellent relationships with each other. I am very at home with my family now. I don't think about the suicide, necessarily, unless someone brings up my mom, like someone will ask where my mom is and I just tell them that she is dead. When they ask how, I say suicide. I feel more confident now in my ability to respond to what people think they want to know or should know. I am much more available to talk without getting offensive. I am much more forgiving of myself now, more apt to feel a sense of independence from the issue. Because of my mother, I am very academic. My father made me accessible, and my stepmother has brought out my spontaneity and my playfulness.

I want to be a professor of creative writing. Suicide was a big theme in my writing earlier, but now I have lightened a bit, writing more about dreams and nightmares. I wrote a poem titled "Renounced" that was trying to explore the separation of my mom and me, and my dad's anger. Do you know that even after all these years he still calls my mom a bitch? I wish that he could get past the anger.

If I had to advise a child who had just lost a parent to suicide, I wouldn't know what to say. A child isn't going to believe it's not her fault or that with time it will get better. I guess I would tell that child that she's not alone and that people genuinely care about her well-being and to please ask for help if she needs it. I would want her to know that she's loved and that she'll be cared for, and just that death happens and that it was not because of her.

CASE STUDY

Fred's Story

Dad's Right-Hand Man

"You're the oldest boy and you've got to take care of your mom." I got a lot of that.

The first moment that I realized something was wrong was when the school bus driver dropped my siblings and me off at the neighbor's house down the road. Because the school bus route was usually a set route and we had never been dropped off anywhere but our own house, I remember wondering what was wrong. There was "stuff" going on at our house, the neighbors told us. They took us in and told us we would have to stay there for a while. It wasn't until about half an hour later that they told us what had happened with my father.

Mom had been home sleeping and woke to the sound of a gunshot. She found my father's body on the back deck, along with a suicide note he had written.

After some time, the neighbors took us kids home to be with our mother, and then they stayed with us for a while. They were religious people and really wanted to stay and comfort my mother as much as possible. Being the one who found him and all, she was hysterical from the whole thing. So, we kids kind of did our own thing by sitting around and trying to find comfort from each other. That was the way we were programmed; whenever our parents would fight or if we ran into any sort of problem, we would always go somewhere to sit down and talk it through together. It kept a close sibling bond. This time I was not sure if the younger siblings really understood much of what was going on, but they sat with us too.

Looking back on it, I know there were warning signs with my dad that we all saw. Once, as a child, I can faintly remember walking in on him attempting to commit suicide, and there were rope burns around his neck from another attempt that he had made. He had sought help through the hospital, but that must not have been enough.

During the following days, our close family relatives showed up to help my mom with the funeral and the wake. We kids stayed home from school for a while to help out our mother and to grieve. The first viewing was in our hometown, for all of my father's friends from around the area. Dad was a real people person, so we did that in order for his friends to have closure and to pay their respects. After that, the whole family headed out to my dad's home state, where he would be buried. The cost was too much to have the casket driven in a hearse, so my uncle decided to drive him there in the back of his suburban, with my younger brother riding shotgun.

When we got back home, things were kind of hard. My mom was dealing with her own grieving, and it was tough for me to find someone to talk to about my father's death. There wasn't really anywhere for me to find support or anything like that. Instead it was more of a, "You're the oldest boy, and you've got to take care of your mom," sort of thing. I got a lot of that. Everyone was telling me that I had to take care of the family and help my mom out and everything like that. It was tough.

School was tough, too, because there were a lot of people who tried to tell us how sorry they were, but it really didn't mean a lot to us. You see, we had been homeschooled for most of our lives, and at the time of dad's death had only been going to that public school for a year. This meant that there weren't many people who actually knew us enough to say they were sorry. Teachers would tell us that they were sorry to hear of our loss, but there really wasn't a lot of emotional support from them. I remember the first day back at school I had a meeting with a counselor who belittled the situation by telling me, "This is hard to deal with, but it happens, and if you need further help come back to see me." I really didn't seek out any help after that.

My uncle offered for me to stay with him for the summer. His son was in baseball, so I spent most of the summer playing ball with them and going to all the baseball games as well. We did a lot of just hanging out. It really made a difference for me, because I am the type of person who doesn't like to deal with the emotional side of things. Getting away from all of that at home really helped take my mind off of everything. Time spent with my uncle sort of replaced the time I would have been spending with my dad.

Growing up as the oldest son, I was always Dad's right-hand man. Everything he would do, I would do, and everywhere he would go, I would go. I was always there with him, which is why it made his death so hard on me. Sometimes we would even go on trips, and he would show me off to all of his friends. My dad and I had a huge bond, and his death was a huge loss. There are still times that I want to show him how far I have come and what I have done. We just always had that relationship where we would show each other our accomplishments.

Because there is a history of suicide in our family, I worry. I have had great grandparents who have committed suicide. My father committed suicide. And so, where does that leave me? I have sought help through counseling, but it has been a long process. The first time I sought out help was when I came home from Iraq, where I served in the Iraq war for about a year. All of the emotions and issues of Iraq that I was dealing with, along with one of my best friends being killed in a motorcycle accident, made me decide to get some help with my grieving by seeing a counselor. It was through counseling that I realized a lot of different things about myself and even about the way I dealt with my father's death. I still have things I need to work out, but I am glad that I went to counseling.

My family is great support to me too. The death of my father brought us closer together in a way, and we all try really hard not to let that go. We still get together for the holidays and visit each other when we have time. My mother has a gentleman that she sees now as well, so that is a new addition to the team, and a good support for her. Thankfully he never tried to step in and replace my father or that sort of thing. The way he acts is really real, and he has always just been that background person who is there to help my mom. He never really interfered with us kids, which really helped us to accept him. After all, he came into our lives very shortly after my father passed away. I mean, he would help out, but I was still the one, the go-to person when stuff needed to get done.

We all still have our issues with what happened with my father, but most important, we have moved on. There is only one thing that I would change about the way we dealt with my father's death—the way I had to step in as a child. I never really got a chance to do sports in high school or to go out there and just have fun like all the other kids. I had to work all of the time so that I could buy my own car and do stuff without having anyone to help me out with any of it. I don't ever remember being told, "Hey, be a kid, go have fun and play." I was always being told to help out instead of have fun. Families who go through a loss like mine need to make sure that the kids still get to be kids. Kids should not have to grow up too fast.

For now, I just do the best I can to be the best person I can be. I have a wonderful wife, a great family, and things seem to be going really good right now. All I can hope is that my father somehow knows how far I have come with my life and how much I try and make him proud. For now, that's more than enough.

CASE STUDY

Dirk's Story

The Man of the House Now

I am now a father myself, and being a parent makes me very aware of my dad's struggles. I definitely don't want to make the mistakes he did.

The day of my dad's death, my mom and dad got into a huge argument, and my mom left the house. After she left, I called my dad some stupid names because he was threatening to leave and drive drunk. He said good-bye to my brother, but didn't say a single word to me. He just left. When my mom returned home, she took my brother and me to a family member's house for a planned get-together. We returned home from their house, opened the garage door, and found my dad. He had hung himself moments before we got back. I tried to get him down, was trying to pick him up, and if I would have only thought clearly, I would have tried cutting him down. My mom rushed my brother and me into the house and called 911.

My mom's sister, who lived in the neighborhood, happened to be driving by just as the cops were getting there, and when I ran across the lawn to her, the cops pulled guns on me and told me to get down on the ground. My first experience with the police was not a good one, to say the least, and my mom was really ticked about that. I'm sure they didn't know what was going on yet, and then saw someone running in front of the house, so I probably alarmed them.

It was not long after that when the ambulance arrived, and we all made our way to the hospital. We were all crying, and I remember my aunt saying, "We don't know what's going to happen. He's tough." All I could think about was, "What's going to happen if he dies? What's going to happen if he lives? How's it going to be then?" What strange thoughts for me to have. After we got to the hospital waiting room, they came in and told us he was gone. I was 16 and my world had just been turned upside down.

We left the hospital and went back to my aunt's house, and funny enough, we sat and drank beers. We just sat—in shock—talking about everything, talking about my dad. We reminisced about him, trying to get our minds off of what had happened. My little brother wasn't there, and I don't think he went to the hospital either. My cousins, who were in town visiting, took my brother, who was only 7 at the time. And my brother was with them at the hotel. It was just me, my aunt and uncle, and my mom. So, the four of us just talked, and none of us could sleep. What was being replayed over and over in my mind was coming home and finding my dad like that.

We didn't go back to the house for about a month after the funeral because it was just too hard. Even just going into the breezeway of the house was difficult because it was attached to the garage. It definitely wasn't lonely in the days following the funeral. There were plenty of people to lean on. We stayed with relatives and had a lot of food, which I couldn't eat because I wasn't hungry. I kept getting the whole, "You're the man of the house now" thing. It was hard to hear, but I think they were saying it more in reference to my brother. They were saying to be an example to him, and that's something I really tried to do. Although, looking back, maybe I was better at leading him in the way of what *not* to do.

My dad had said stuff before about ending his life. He had had a temper and a drinking problem for a long time. I learned that before my parents were even married, he had taken a whole bunch of pills. Even before they got married he drank, and it just got worse over time. Then, after an injury at work, he began drinking heavily and taking Vicodin for his back pain. I think he also battled depression. My mom said that he battled demons, so I guess there is more stuff that I and my brother don't know about him. He did leave a note, which my brother and I have never seen. I asked about it once, but part of me didn't want to see it because he had been drunk and might have said some things I don't really want to hear from him. He always favored my brother, who is built more like him and was athletic just like he was, so I'm sure he said things directed toward me and my mom in the note. I know he was drunk, so I wouldn't take anything he may have said to heart. At the time, though, I might have taken it to heart, so I'm glad my mom never let me see it. I'm sure if I wanted to see the note now, I could get it, but I don't need to see it. I guess I really don't want to know what it said. I'd rather not hear his words, because even though I know better, it would still hurt.

The night he died was like the tip of the iceberg between my mom and him, which my mom feels a lot of guilt about. They had been fighting a lot, and I think my mom decided that day that she and my dad were going to split up again. Because my dad had been drinking, he just overreacted to some stupid little thing, and then it blew up, and they got into the fight. I'm sure my mom was feeling like, "Okay, I can't do this anymore." Then we came home and found him. It was not how any of us wanted the fighting or drinking to end.

His death brought financial issues, which we eventually worked out, and my mom started doing better. She still had her moments with being sad and stuff, and she struggled keeping the house and everything together, but her boss was understanding and let her work part-time. One of my biggest challenges was taking care of my brother. There was just the three of us now, so I would have to babysit and watch over my brother.

My dad died two weeks before school started in my junior year. I never really had a lot of friends before that year. Of course, there were a few people who I talked to at school and two who I talked with on the phone, but no one who I hung out with outside of school. I really didn't have a lot of friends to lean on. At school, I received some support from a couple of teachers who knew me through student government, and I received a couple of cards, and some of the teachers seemed more lenient with me. I remember in one of my sociology classes, I said something about my dad passing away, and some girl was saying, "You're lying, shut up and quit making things up." The teacher stuck up for me and told her I wasn't lying.

My counselor was really nice too. He had helped me because I have ADHD, so I had a lot of problems in school. He was the only person from school who came to the funeral. He always looked out for me, and if I needed anything I knew that I could go to him and he would help me out. I talked with him about my dad, and when I was skipping a lot of school, he said he understood what was going on with me and that I needed to hear that things were going to be hard. He also said that there would always be someone to help me. He said, "You have to remember that there are things you have to do. You have responsibilities, and you need to get done with school, otherwise you are going to be in a lot of trouble." After graduation, I worked at a tire shop, and that same counselor would come in and talk with me, and he was just very nice, always asking how my family was doing.

My mom also sent me and my brother to a psychologist, but I didn't like the guy at all. I really don't know what it was. There was just something about him I did not like. He seemed condescending and that there was not a lot of empathy there. He was not someone you would want to open up to. You want to feel comfortable opening up. Before getting anything out of someone, that person has to feel comfortable saying it. It can't just be forced out of you. So, I saw that psychologist just once and then told my mom that I wasn't going to go see him again. A couple of close friends I was able to talk with were more help than him.

I would say that making friends did help me cope with my dad's death, but they also caused me some guilt feelings. This is because most the friends that I had made were because of my dad's death. I would have dreams that my dad came back and that I didn't have any friends anymore because he was actually alive. Guilt is a big thing. It's something that comes on, and it's not something you can push away and not have. It eats at you one way or another. Having friends really helped me. I had a hard time opening up about how I felt to any of my family members; it was so much easier with friends. I definitely dealt with a lot of sadness there for a while and mostly tried to push it away instead of dealing with it. I shut down at first, but after a couple of months opened back up again.

Over the years, there were times, like when I got my driver's license, or went to that first homecoming dance, that were really hard because my dad wasn't there. He wasn't there to see me graduate, and I think a lot of the reasons why I got into trouble with skipping and all of that stuff was because he wasn't around. If he would have been there, I never would have skipped school. I was too afraid of his wrath. My mom, on the other hand, didn't discipline me enough. I wasn't scared of what she would say if I skipped school. I guess not having that structure was a problem for me.

Until I was 9 years old, it was only me and my dad. I was his namesake and was everything to him. Then, through middle school, I got into a lot of trouble, and that got me into trouble with him. With my dad, it could be really bad, or it could be really good, especially with his drinking. As my brother got older, the worse it got for me. My dad never had a problem with my brother, but with me, sometimes he would be really nice when drinking, then something would happen that would make him mad. It was a strained relationship. He was definitely the disciplinarian, and I think my mom was so lenient toward me because he was so strict. Most of the time he was in a good mood while drinking, but lots of times, he was not.

What I felt after my dad died was a lot of guilt and sadness. I missed him despite all of the problems we had. I would sit in school and think about him. I never really got angry at him for leaving, and I don't know why I didn't. I mostly just felt guilty about it, like I was the reason he died. For a while, I felt guilty about my problems with school and not being the son he wanted. I wasn't the one who was really athletic like him, and my brother was his spitting image. I just felt like he really didn't like me sometimes, and I always felt like everything was my fault. It got to the point where I thought that if my mom hadn't gotten pregnant with me, they wouldn't have gotten married, and he wouldn't have been unhappy. It really does take a lot of talking about it with people and a lot of thinking about it. You definitely do a lot of analyzing of yourself to get over that stuff. It took me until I was older to really finally realize that it wasn't my fault.

I think my dad's suicide has made me more aware of myself. It doesn't really hurt anymore. There is a little sadness on his birthday or the anniversary, but it just makes me more aware of my own feelings. Sometimes things get so frustrating or overwhelming for me that I can understand why he did it. He was overwhelmed with life in general, and then when drugs and alcohol are added, I can understand why. When I'm feeling depressed or overwhelmed, I try to remember my dad and remind myself that the feeling will pass. So, I guess that dealing with his suicide has kind of helped me. If I hadn't gone through that, I wouldn't be able to recognize and work through my own issues. His death has made me more aware of how I feel and how to fix how I feel. I understand that it is a feeling and it will pass. Some people don't know why they feel a certain way. I know why and work through it.

My dad's death has also made me, my brother, and my mom really close. My brother and I are very close, and he sees me as a brother more than anything. I'm not really an authority figure or surrogate dad. He was out partying recently and just got real sad and called me. It was like the first time we had talked about Dad's death in a long time. I am now a father myself, and being a parent makes me very aware of my dad's struggles. I definitely don't want to make the mistakes he did, but I worry about it as my daughter gets older. I worry about being too strict or that maybe, at one point, I will lose control. Like maybe I will have a drinking problem. I'm very aware of that, and if I do have a couple of drinks after work, I'll wait until the kids have gone to bed so they don't see me like that. I'm very aware of that kind of stuff, living through it with my dad and seeing what happened to him.

Here is what I would tell kids who face this in the future. I have been exactly where you are. You are going to have a lot of mixed and different feelings, lots of anger, sadness, and you are going to blame yourself. All of the feelings are natural. Just remember that it was their decision and there was nothing you could have done to prevent it. Your parent was going to do it one way or the other. There is nothing that you could have done, or any way you could have acted, or anything you could have said that would have stopped it from happening. Sometimes people just cannot handle living anymore. They can't deal with the stress, their feelings, or what's going on in their heads. It will get a lot easier as you get older, and one day you will understand why they did it. The first couple of years after are going to be tough, but it will get better. It will definitely get better! Talk to your friends or talk to someone about it. One day, you will definitely understand why and how they could have given up. Use that knowledge to keep yourself from giving up.

CASE STUDY

Brooke's Story

On My Way Out

Sometimes you just can't believe your own life, you know? It seems like something you should be watching on a television show instead.

I remember that day very well because I was in gym class when the guidance counselor and another teacher pulled me out of class and asked to take me home. At first I thought the whole situation was weird. I hadn't thought to panic because I figured that most emergency situations didn't involve the school taking you home but rather your parents picking you up. When we pulled up outside of my house, and I saw some of my family, some neighbors, and the cops, I worried that maybe one of my grandparents had died. Apparently my mother was so hysterical that the school volunteered to take my siblings and me home for her. I was 11 years old when my dad shot himself.

I felt numb when my mother told me. I knew I was supposed to be feeling sad and lost, but the feeling that actually stood out the most was relief. To be honest, at that point I didn't even shed a tear. The whole situation with my father was such a mess. He was being prosecuted at the time for abuse against me, and to make things worse, the whole situation was being blown up in the papers. When I was a young child, my father had never paid much attention to us kids, and so when he finally did start to show us some attention, it was the wrong kind. He was actually only two days away from his court hearing when he shot himself. And I felt numb for a long time after his death for not feeling the way I was supposed to when it happened. But with the circumstances surrounding his death and me being 11 and all, it was really tough for me not to feel numb and angry over his death.

I really don't remember the weeks following his death. I suppose I blocked a lot of it out, feeling that it wasn't a good thing to remember anyway. My return back to school was overwhelming. The newspaper published an article on my father, and although they hadn't mentioned my name specifically as the girl he was abusing, they did mention that she was an 11-year-old girl. This of course sent the questions flying when I came back to school. I told people that I wasn't sure of the circumstances surrounding that article, and I tried my best to avoid the whole situation. As if things weren't hard enough for me, the school started doing more and more assemblies on sexual abuse, and they really seemed to downplay the whole thing. The assemblies featured sayings like, "All you have to do is say, 'Don't touch me there,'" and "Just say no," which really frustrated me because things are never as simple as that when it comes to abuse. But it wasn't like I could just stand up and tell the whole school that that is not how things go. Instead, I had to sit and listen to the constant reminders of my father's death and the abuse that I had endured.

I still had a lot of questions for my dad that now I will never get to ask him: "Why did you do those things to me? Why did you kill yourself?" Now, I will never get the answers to my questions, and to me that is the saddest part of losing my dad.

As a kid, I didn't really want to deal with any of the emotions that my dad's death caused me. I tended to just bottle everything in and chose anger as my most aggressive emotion. That was hard on my mother, because all she wanted to do was help me to feel better. She sent me to counselors, hoping that I would open up to them, because I wasn't opening up to her. Unfortunately, though, I was a very stubborn kid and wouldn't give them the time of day. My thoughts at the time were that I didn't want to explain my life to someone who was getting paid to listen to me. Instead, I isolated myself from others, bottled up my anger, picked fights with my mother, and eventually started skipping school. I felt like if I couldn't trust my father, then I couldn't trust anyone. And that mentality stayed with me for quite a while.

I never really planned on telling my mother about the abuse in the first place. We were sitting down one day, and the words just flew right out of my mouth. I didn't even realize what I was saying. My mother kicked my father out that same day and told him never to bother coming home. That all happened within four months of the day he shot himself. Sometimes you just can't believe your own life, you know? It seems like something you should be watching on a television show instead.

It wasn't long before the kids at school moved on to the latest gossip, and the teachers began to expect me to get back into the swing of things. But that isn't really how things work when a parent dies. I was still feeling really overwhelmed by the whole situation, and it wasn't going to go away anytime soon. At age 11, it seemed as though everything was happening so fast, and I couldn't control any of it, so I completely shut down. The only thing I remember that actually helped me to cope was art. One of my counselors told me to draw and express my feelings through art, and that actually did help me quite a bit. I may not have felt like talking, but this was something that I could do without talking, and I could still express how I felt. It was something. And something was better than nothing. In my heart, I knew better than to keep silent, but my head just kept telling me not to trust anyone. I couldn't trust my father, so I certainly couldn't get myself to trust a stranger. There was a whirlwind of things going on in my head, even guilt over the fact that I believed for a short while that I could have prevented my father's death. I *knew* I should have shared that with someone, but I just couldn't.

When I was 13 I started to skip school. My mother would drop me off at school, and I would pretend to wave good-bye, but as soon as she left, so would I. At first I just wandered around town until school got out, but eventually things got worse. Before my father's death I was an A and B student, honor roll and all, but afterwards I lost my ambition, and so I lost my grades. I started to see a boy who was into drugs, and I skipped more school and began smoking weed. I saw in him someone who could be my best friend, even though I didn't feel like talking about things. He knew that I had been sexually abused, but he never pushed me to tell him about it or to talk about how I felt, and I liked that about him. I finally found someone who wasn't going to make me talk!

My mother and I argued a lot, and I'm sure she knew I was on drugs but when she asked, I would just keep telling her no. It was bad.

At age 16, I ran away from home for about a month and a half and didn't tell anyone where I went. I knew that my family must have been worried sick about me, but I also knew that I was with my friends, and I thought that they cared about me too. Eventually I decided to call home one day when I knew that my mother wouldn't be there so that I could talk to my brother and tell them that I was okay. After hearing his voice telling me to come home and crying, I just couldn't take it anymore, and I decided to come home.

Soon after I came home, a fight between my boyfriend's friend and another friend of mine led to a death that changed my life forever. My 911 call started a long string of lies, and when the lies finally caught up with me, I was the one in jail. I was charged with first-degree reckless homicide, party to a crime, because my boyfriend's friend had died when my friend hit him. I did nine and a half years in prison for that. But to tell you the truth, prison was a good thing for me. I can't tell you how much I have learned because I went to prison or how much my life has turned around because of it. I don't even know if my life would be in as good a position as it is now if something like that hadn't happened to me. I think I needed something big to get me back to reality and into a better way of living. In fact, I fear that my life would be much worse if that never happened. In prison there is a lot of time to soul search, if you will, and that is exactly what I did. I came to terms with my feelings and my life, and now I am a lot better off because of that. I took advantage of every program and schooling event that I could so that my time there wouldn't be a waste.

I want to do what I can to prevent others from going down the road that I did. I regret the situation that happened, but I don't regret prison. It helped me. It was a long therapy session for me, if you will. I talk with a lot of kids now and always tell them that if their parents or anyone is willing to be there for them, then they should take advantage of that. They need to understand how quickly it can all get ripped away. Take advantage of support while you have it, because you just never know what is going to happen. Every decision has a consequence, whether it is good or bad. But no matter what happens, you always have to deal with the consequences.

The whole reason that I went down the path that I did is because I turned everybody away from me who wanted to be there for me, and I isolated myself. So, instead of holding it all in and releasing anger on someone else, my advice is to keep a support system, whether it's family, friends, or even counselors. Even if there is only one person who you trust, everyone needs at least one person to talk to when they are feeling down. A situation like the one I have been through affects everyone differently, and that is okay, but you still need someone to trust in and someone to talk to. My mother has told me many times that she doesn't excuse my behavior, but she understands where I am coming from, and you know what, that means a lot to me.

I have my own place now and a good support system. I plan to go to school and find a job that I enjoy working at. I know that won't all happen right away, but I also know that I am on my way there eventually, and that's what matters.

three
Support

To navigate challenges following parental death by suicide, survivors utilize various types of support. The literature suggests that social networks and social contexts have an impact on reactions to stressful experiences such as death (Belle, 1988; Silverman & Worden, 1993). Surely, changes in the child's daily life, available support, and parental coping styles are all part of the context framing the lives of bereaved children. A strong social network can provide an atmosphere of support and care for children, and can promote the use of other available resources. Our study participants described use of six forms of support in the hours, days, weeks, and years following the suicide of their parent (see Figure 3.1 for themes and the frequency with which they were reported).

Family Support

Suicide often takes place alongside mental illness, life stress, and family chaos, and, as such, suicide-bereaved families seem to have higher levels of chronic turmoil and stressful events, such as marital separation, trouble with the law, or domestic violence prior to the suicide (Cerel et al., 2000). Poor communication and strained relationships often exist within families prior to a suicide and can complicate recovery (Grossman et al., 1995; Ratnarajah & Schofield, 2007; Webb, 1991). Family stability and cohesion may be lacking following the suicide, with such families being involved in fewer family activities both before and after the death (Cerel et al., 2000). Suicide may challenge a family's entire belief system, including their own sense of existence as a unit. Further, children faced with parental suicide are

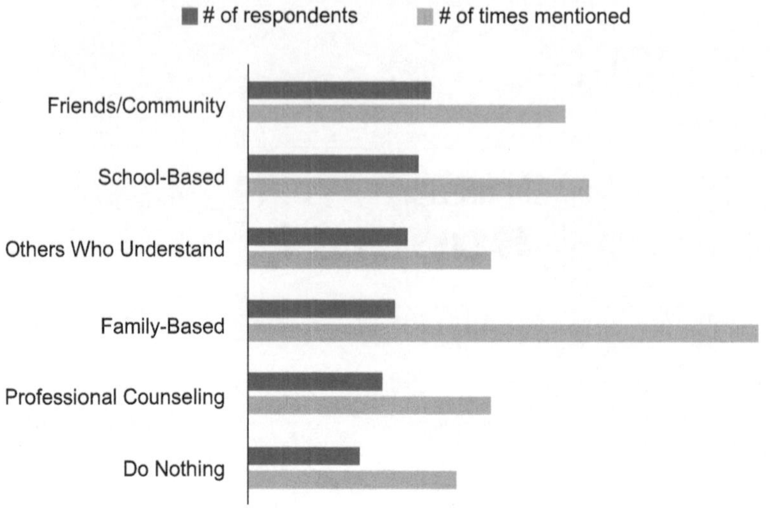

FIGURE 3.1 Support: Types and frequencies.

at risk for complicated grief and may become preoccupied with the deceased parent, making it more difficult for the surviving parent to respond to their emotions (Gray, Prigerson, & Litz, 2004; Provini, Everett, & Pfeffer, 2000; Shneidman, 1996).

Even so, family support has been identified as a critical factor in recovery from parental suicide (McMenamy et al., 2008; Provini et al., 2000). Though children bereaved in this way generally come from families with a history of psychopathology and family disruption, surviving parents do not typically exhibit higher rates of psychopathology than do other bereaved parents, and many have positive relationships with their children that can be important to the recovery process (Cerel et al., 2000). Broader research in the area of childhood trauma suggests family relationship quality as an important influence on whether a child can "bounce back" when trauma occurs (Mandelco & Peery, 2002). In fact, some research suggests that when suicide-bereaved individuals do not seek professional help, it is often because they are relying on support within their immediate families (Provini et al., 2000).

Because some suicide-bereaved children rely exclusively on family support, this domain is worthy of significant attention. Survivors featured in this book described family members as being strong sources of support in a number of ways, including assuming parental or "father figure" roles that were lacking because of the suicide, serving as positive role models, providing emotional support, and offering practical support (e.g., a place to stay, meals, laundry). Surviving parents, stepparents, siblings, and extended family were highlighted as being significant to the recovery process.

The tendency for families to band together has been highlighted in previous studies (Clark & Goldney, 1995; Ratnarajah et al., 2008; Requarth, 2006). One participant spoke eloquently about her family providing such a reprieve.

Suzanne was 8 when her father died by suicide. She was interviewed at age 50, two years younger than her father had been at the time of his death. Suzanne came from a large family with eight siblings and talked about how she coped by banding together with family.

> We would have never been able to endure that and be that strong family that we were, if we weren't a really strong family before that happened. And it also caused us to band together, especially when the kids at school were teasing us. The family became the refuge. We were all hurting together.

Consistent with previous research, a number discussed the significant role the surviving parent played in their recovery. Louise, for example, discussed how her mother's sensitivity and attention, in spite of Louise's resistance and adverse behaviors, were instrumental to her healing process.

> I didn't really see any good as to putting me into shelter care or that psychiatric ward for a week, but it worked. It was her way of saying, "I'm here and I'm not going to abandon you like he did." She was always trying to talk to me. She did nothing but try to support me, but I didn't let her be there. I was very defiant about that counseling thing. She wanted me to talk to somebody because she didn't know really how to handle it either, when there are two issues, losing your dad and sexual abuse there. I would come out of a counseling session and I would talk to Mom about it. "This is what we talked about and this is why I acted this way." And I of course apologized a lot for the way I acted, because she was only trying to help. She says, "I understand that you were angry and you didn't want help." So she doesn't excuse my behavior, but she understands what was going on.

Missy described the central role her mother played in deterring her own suicide and providing ongoing support that she felt no one else could offer.

> I thought about killing myself for a little while. If he can do it, I can do it. My mom stopped me. I don't know what I would do without her. My mom was my counselor. I don't need anybody else. It all comes down to my mom, really strong, and holding me together. My mom is both my mom and my dad, and she always has been even when he was alive. So when he went, she was strong enough to hold it together. I'm not perfect in any means, but I graduated from high school, and I went to college, and I work, and I have my own apartment, and that's all because of my mom. Nobody knows me like my mom knows me, and nobody's there for me like my mom's there for me. She's my best friend, she's everything to me.

Lisa, who had not had a significant relationship with her father prior to her mother's suicide, discussed how reconnecting with her father afterward was significant to her recovery. She stated, "*I was probably 12, and my grandmother had me baptized, and my dad showed up as a godparent. And having that relationship with my dad was great.*" Rachel and Suzanne both discussed their mothers' strength as being instrumental to their recovery.

> Just try to make the most of what life is now, that's what my mom tried to help us do and see. She's very inspirational to me because for her it was losing a husband, and the father of her three kids. So I kind of think, well, if she can deal with it and live a normal life, I sure can.
>
> My mother had so many talents, and she loved us so much and dedicated her life so much to her children, both before and after, but I would say she would have run herself down health-wise, just to take care of us kids, to do the very, very best that she could.

Stepparents may also be significant in the surviving child's recovery. Stepparents may include those who were married to the surviving parent prior to the death, those who were married to the parent who died by suicide, and individuals who married the surviving parent following the suicide. Jerome discussed the significant role that his mother's second husband played in the recovery from his father's suicide.

> My father left us hanging. He left my mom with two kids all alone. I have a lot of respect for my stepdad, who did a really good job filling in a big part of my life. My stepdad was a very positive gain in my life. He did a lot for my mom and for us. He got us into good schools. He stepped in and did what he could. He was a friend and kind of a father at the same time.

Lisa, who had a different father than her brother, discussed the impact her brother's stepmother had in advocating for her and her brother following their mother's death.

> They would bring me along with them on camping trips, and I remember one night my brother came on the top bunk with me, and we were talking about Mom, and his dad came in—and he was a real jerk. I disliked him so much—he came in and he yelled at us, and he said, "You never ever mention her name in my house again. Don't ever do it," just like yelling, and I'm just sitting there sobbing, and my brother's stepmom comes in, and he had actually started to call her Mom, and I was resenting her for that. And she came in and yelled at his dad and said, "No, these children have right to know who their mother is. I know that you put all her pictures away. You need to get them out. We are getting them out so that that young boy can know who his mother was." After that moment

> I no longer resented her, I had the upmost respect for her and knew he's going to be okay.

Lisa's father later died from suicide as well, and Lisa benefitted from the support provided by her own stepmother, when she attended his funeral.

> I walked in a little bit further, and I could recognize from some pictures my grandparents were sitting in the front, and I was walking down the aisle, and my grandmother turns to me and she said, "You don't belong here." And I stopped, and I was already in tears because I felt like a pariah in the room. I was trying to be strong, and it helped a lot that my stepmother was there, standing there with me. And I said to her, "I belong here! That's my father. He meant just as much to me if not more than he meant to you, and you made the choice to not be a part of my life. I didn't make that choice."

A number of participants discussed the important supportive role that siblings played in their recovery process. Charlotte discussed the importance of time with her siblings, closely following the death of her father when she was 15. She said, "*After the funeral, we got a hotel room, me and my brothers, and we hung out, and we talked about all the different times with my dad.*" Jared talked about an ongoing relationship with his older sister and how she helped him relieve stress and manage his own suicidal thoughts.

> We talk quite a bit about it. I'll talk to her, and she'll say, "Yeah, well, I spent a lot time today just thinking about Dad." It's kind of the same way for me. We've talked some, especially more recently. We normally talk about it when we are getting stressed and our stress gets piling up. We kind of go back to it, because I guess that's just the natural thought, you know, "Man do I really want to do this anymore? Do I want to, you know, keep going?" That's what Dad did. He went back to it and apparently said I can't do this anymore, and ended it. So that's when the stress gets up there, those thoughts kind of come about, and we end up kind of talking to each other, and see where each of us are at, and kind of support each other.

A number of study participants discussed extended family as being a significant source of practical and emotional support. Rachel discussed how helpful her extended family had been immediately following the death by saying, "*We had relatives staying with us and helping out, and lots and lots of people dropping off meals and things like that. And people helping with laundry and everything.*" Somewhat unique to death by suicide, though, is the fact that surviving family members may not want to be in the home in which the suicide occurred, for a period of time following the death. Jerome recalled the support of extended family in providing alternate places to stay.

> My mom has a very large family. They were always there for us and they helped us out a lot. We stayed with family members because my mom did not want to be in the house. I remember staying in a lot of different places afterwards. I had cousins my age and just kind of keep everyone's mind off of everything.

Jared conveyed similar sentiments, further commenting on the importance of distraction and separation that extended family provided.

> I stayed with relatives that whole summer. So that helped a lot because that completely removed me. I wasn't at home. I just did stuff with my cousins and my aunts and uncles. When I look back at it, there wasn't that being around every day and being around home without Dad being there. I would say it was good for me because I wasn't sitting around home thinking about it all the time. I was like, I am gone for the summer, I am spending time with the relatives, and not I am spending the summer at home without Dad being there. When I went back home, it was more of an easier transition. I didn't have to deal with the thought of it every day.

Although stepparents can certainly serve as role models or parent figures, other family members often step up to assume such roles with the child. Trevor's comments highlight the importance of certain family members stepping in to assume a father figure role.

> A few of my uncles really stepped in as kind of being the father figure. My oldest brother, I was always intimidated by him, but he kind of tried to take over the father figure of the house. He would do all the outside chores, he would do everything and come down on us if we did something wrong. So it was really nice to have my other uncles and aunts to be in there, and really take us all under their wing, and really help us out in the growing process as well. Just take us places that my mom couldn't afford to take us or wouldn't be able to take us to, and they brought me up deer hunting and all that other stuff I would have done with my dad. That was definitely beneficial to have family. My uncles really filled in with a lot of things, like when I went through hunter's safety, my uncles were there and went through it with me—father-son things.

Lisa also discussed the importance of various older relatives stepping in to offer encouragement and take on parental roles.

> My grandma, who was right on top of it, said, "Alright, it's time to start going back to therapy. You need to do this." Two of my aunts kind of took on the roles, for me and my brother, of helping to raise us. One aunt took on my brother and just kind of coddled him and carried him

> through. And the other took on me. There are traits that didn't come from my mom. They came from the people who stepped in and took care of us, and they will never know how much I love and appreciate that. It's been rough, but I've had a solid support system. And taking care of me and making sure that I'm headed in the right direction. Grandpa was there. He would come over, and he would play with my hair, and tell me how much it felt like my mom's, and how pretty I was, and how much I looked like my mom when I was growing up, and it was a good relationship. My aunt would tell me, "That's a bad kid. His brother's in jail and he's headed down the wrong track." I wanted to be the first person to go to college in my family, and get an education, and truly make something of myself. And my aunt's husband was a huge presence in pushing me to go to college, and he was like, "You can do it! Your mother would want you to do this. Your dad would want you to do this." And having him there to push me along was phenomenal.

Family support may involve carrying on with traditions, family activities, and special events. Children remember special days and can hold onto those memories when they are aching for their parent. If the surviving parent is unable to provide this, extended family members or trusted friends can step in to help children cope by creating those special moments. Suzanne shared how her family supported her in this way when she had her first communion.

> I remember still today how hard my family tried to make that day special. We had a big family dinner like my mother would have always done, and then in the afternoon, an uncle took really nice pictures of me. I think just being the youngest child, I even got more special treatment because everybody was so concerned about how young I was and losing a father, and then losing by suicide.

Support from Friends, Faith, and Community

Children do not recover if they are isolated from others. Supporting them, therefore, must involve their families and communities (Kaslow & Aronson, 2004). Though much research has addressed the role of friends in preventing suicide (e.g., Wyman et al., 2010), little has touched on the role of friends in recovery from suicide (Dalke, 1994; Provoni et al., 2000). Because of the stigma, social difficulties (Hung & Rabin, 2009; Pfeffer et al., 1997), and self-esteem issues (Cerel et al., 1999) that may manifest following a parental suicide, support from peers and family friends should not be underestimated. Children, and especially teenagers, often feel more comfortable discussing feelings with friends than with a parent or other adult, and support from family friends and neighbors may be significant in filling part of the void left by parental suicide.

Although some research has investigated the role of religion and spirituality in bereavement from suicide (e.g., Houck, 2004; Vandecreek & Mottram, 2009), no studies have specifically looked at the role of faith networks in responding to parental suicide. Studies of clergy responses to suicide in general suggest that clergy do not feel prepared to respond (Malikow, 1991) and are not viewed as helpful (Flarity, 1993). Because clergy and others in the faith community may have contact with those who are bereaved by suicide, attention to their skill development in this area is appropriate (Resnick & Rozensky, 1996).

Our survivors reflected on beneficial support received from friends and friends' families, clergy, neighbors, and members of the larger community. A number of them discussed the importance of support from close friends, hinting at the importance of a small friendship network in the recovery process. Several mentioned being selective about whom they discussed the suicide with, as noted by one who stated that the "*people I'm close with . . . the ones that matter, know.*" Mirroring that sentiment, another shared the following:

> I really didn't talk to too many people about it outside of a really close friend. I don't really want people to know about it because I don't want people to feel sorry for me, like I am weaker than somebody else.

The caution with friends continued, for some, into adult life. Rachel was 7 when her father died in their basement. In college at the time of the interview, Rachel was meeting many new people and discussed how she gained support through confiding in new friends.

> There usually gets to the point in a new friendship, and some it's sooner than others, but that it comes out. And I always feel good after that point. I think just that they know. Just that it's out there and it's not like there's any secret or something that they don't know then.

Guy, Dirk, and Shane, respectively, also shared comments about the significant support that close friends provided.

> My roommate is really, probably pretty much my only friend. We've been friends probably for a decade. He's always been there, and pretty much that's just the way I am. I only like one friend.
>
> I did have friends, a couple close friends I was able to talk with when I was feeling down. I talked to them about it and that helped me through it.
>
> I've got a few friends in my high school, a few of them in my classes, and they're enlisted in either the army or the marine corps, and they understand where I'm coming from, especially since we're on the same page with where we're going with our lives and they're just—they help me through the winter.

Immediately following her father's death, Charlotte benefited from the kindness of close friends, which she found more helpful than outside intervention:

> My friends gave me a lot of support. My friends found out probably like two days later. They called me. I got flowers sent to me, sympathy cards, and I had a lot of support. That's all I ever want. I don't want these people who don't know me to come and tell me, because I don't like that. I'll deal with it on my own. But my friends supported me a lot. I had so many flowers coming to my house, it was crazy.

Melissa also reported a preference for the use of friends as support instead of professional counseling when she spoke of the supportive role her current boyfriend plays:

> I've sort of substituted counseling for just talking to him. I mean he's never been through anything like this, but he at least has some appreciation for how difficult this may have been, and he does try and put himself in my shoes and think about how he would have reacted, and that definitely is helpful.

Julie, whose father died when she was 15, commented on her friend's parents taking on a parental role for her following the suicide: "*My girlfriend's mom was like a second mom—her stepdad too. They were all like family. They were real comforting, and I mean they were just as upset.*" Lisa discussed the important role that her best friend and her friend's mother played, with the mother facilitating support when Lisa not only lost her mother in the third grade but also experienced the death of another friend. This support was able to continue into later life.

> My best friend since kindergarten had just moved all the way across town. Her mom brought her back to that school so that she could be with me. And we could be together, and she stayed for the remainder of our third-grade year. She knew that we both needed that. Especially in high school I was afraid to tell people about my mom's death. The only person that I could talk about it with in high school, friend-wise, was my best friend. After they moved, we lost touch for a while there in fourth grade, fifth grade, but then, about sixth-seventh grade, we got back together, got in touch, and we were inseparable to this day. Our children are all the same ages, but she was the only person that truly understood what I had been through and what suicide was.

A number of participants talked about older family friends who were supportive following the suicide, when the surviving parent could not manage. Louise, whose father died when she was 9, shared the following:

> My mom couldn't take care of us, and one of my father's best friends, him and his family ended up moving over here for a while because she

> just couldn't take care of herself or us. We had some other people come over and cook us supper or make sure that us kids were being taken care of. It took her a long time to finally accept it.

Some participants spoke of the supportive role that the church or clergy played following the death of their parent. Rachel reflected on this source of support that began in her childhood and continues today, indicating, "*The church that I grew up in. I have a lot of friends from there. I got a lot of support from there, or even like my own faith that I have today.*"

Suzanne also spoke of the support clergy provided starting before her father's death and continuing afterward.

> The priest came to the house all the time, and was checking on us after my dad's death, and we never had television, and he eventually was the one who got us a television, and he would get all these games, and he did this even before my dad died, because I remember him coming over with some puzzles, you know.

Though the African proverb "It takes a village to raise a child" may seem cliché, this notion is of particular importance to survivors of parental suicide. Neighbors and others in the community may serve as natural sources of support. One participant felt supported by a peer neighbor who had experienced a different type of parental loss, "*. . . being next door neighbors, we talked. His mom and dad had got a divorce. It was kind of like the same thing. His dad didn't come around a lot.*" Fred and his brother Jared, whose father died by suicide while they were at school, also spoke of the significant supportive role neighbors played immediately following.

> We got dropped off at our neighbor's house because we live out in the country and we were like, "What's going on here? Why are we getting off the bus? We have, like, another mile to go." Our neighbor, who was kind of a pastor, was trying to explain it to us what had happened I guess in a more gentle way, a more of a softer way—that your dad chose to go to heaven and everything. He never really went into detail. We kind of realized that he was no longer with us and everything. Probably the biggest thing was having that neighbor, a nice guy, great guy, explain it to us.
>
> The neighbors who helped actually ran a Bible camp that we had gone to a couple times, and they weren't like real close friends but they were an older couple, so they were home, and that's where they had us dropped off at. They stayed for a while and, well, of course for them being, I guess, religious people and they stayed around and tried to comfort my mom as much as possible at the time.

Suzanne, whose family was living on limited income before and after the suicide, talked about the importance of support from the broader community:

> Other people reached out as you would for any death, any child. That part of it was still there. People still felt really bad that we were that young, and probably myself being the youngest got extra consideration. So that allowed my life to be a very good quality family life, and a good community. There were people reaching out to us—the president of a bank in town—they had a lot of money. They had a huge house and they were just wonderful, wonderful people in those years after my dad died. So it's those little things that people do to reach out that mean the world.

School-Based Support

With school being one of children's most critical domains outside of the home, teachers and other school staff inevitably play an important role in supporting those who experience the suicide of a loved one and are in unique positions to intervene (Dyregrov, 2004). When a child returns to school after a parental death by suicide, other children can be very insensitive (Ratnarajah et al., 2008). In addition to handling reactions from peers and school personnel, children who survive parental suicide may have trouble concentrating, causing grades and overall performance to suffer (Cain & Fast, 1972), and may experience overall school adjustment problems (Pfeffer et al., 1997). Teachers often witness such negative effects in students and are in an optimal position to intervene. School can be a significant place of healing by injecting routine and a sense of normalcy back into a child's life (Requarth, 2006).

Survivors in our study talked about various aspects of school-based support that were beneficial to them following their parent's suicide. Although seemingly simple to outsiders, phone calls and cards may be significant to children who experience a death that often carries shame, stigma, and guilt. A few participants discussed the impact that kind gestures from peers had on them, as indicated in the following excerpts:

> I remember I missed a couple of days of school, and then I got back, and everyone was sad for me. They made cards and everything.
>
> I was in a peer leader's group in middle school, and the counselor—everybody that was involved with the group—signed this book for me and for my brothers. So that was really nice.
>
> A couple weeks after we went back to school, I remember a casual friend called and she was on a three-way with another friend, and they had called to say they were sorry about my dad. That was nice. I really didn't have a lot of friends, no one I had hung out with outside of school. I really didn't have a lot of friends to lean on.

Suzanne recalled a peer who stuck up for her on the playground when others were teasing her about the suicide, a gesture that she felt influenced her recovery:

> We were playing on this old merry-go-round, taking turns, and then you're standing on the sidelines waiting for somebody else to get off, and then you get on. During the process, a bunch of kids are teasing me. They are saying, "Your family is going to lose your farm. You're not going to have any food to eat. Your dad died by suicide." Of course, I'm disagreeing with them because my mother told me he died from a heart attack. So there is one girl who is probably two years younger than I am, and she's defending me, and she's doing what any wonderful kid would do when somebody is being bullied. She's sticking up for me, and she's going back at the kids and saying, "Get out of here. You don't know what you're talking about. She's going to be just fine. Her mom is going to take care of her." She was doing the thinking for me and defending me, and I mean it to this day, I pray for her. I'm thankful for her.

Two participants shared examples of school personnel supporting them outside of the school environment, and the significance of such gestures to their recovery.

> My teacher sat with me for some of that day at the funeral, and my mom really to this day really remembers that and appreciates that, and she's always been one of my favorite teachers.
>
> I had an elementary school teacher who offered to give me piano lessons. That really helped me.

A number of participants discussed how school staff accommodated their feelings in and out of the classroom following the suicide. Zach, whose father died when he was in grade school, discussed his teachers' understanding expressions.

> The teachers were understanding. They all told me if I needed to go out just to tell them and they'd let me go out in the hallway and just do whatever. I know one time on the playground I just sat down and cried for a while there. My friends saw me and they tried to talk to me, but then they eventually got a teacher and they took me inside.

Kevin, who was 13 and in middle school at the time of his father's death, reflected on how the writing prompted by a teacher helped him deal with his feelings.

> I had this one teacher. She told me if I wrote about it, it would probably help me out. And I actually did write it all. I wrote it all out, really, really detailed.

Julie, who was 15 and in high school at the time of her father's suicide, recalled a particular teacher who accommodated her emotions.

> There was an English teacher, and she was very, very helpful. She pulled me aside one day in class, and gave me a big hug, and told me if I ever needed to talk to her I could. And so I remember talking with her after class one time and crying on her shoulder like a big baby.

Lisa, who lost her mother to suicide at age 9 and her father at age 15, reflected on her school's accommodating support.

> The teachers were absolutely amazing. When I was in third grade, the year that she died, we had a student teacher, and she actually ended up being my fourth-grade teacher, and she was a huge support because she was there when I experienced the loss and then to guide me through that next year. And all of the staff at the school knew, because the school had never had a student experience something like that in years, so they didn't really know what to do and how to handle it. And the principal was there if I needed anything. There was the guidance counselor. And my godmother, thankfully, later on, was right there in that school when I needed her, so she was easy to go to and find.

Participants discussed the benefits that *school-based support groups* had for their recovery. Rachel, who was only 7 when her father died of suicide, discussed her involvement in such a group:

> I started being part of a group of kids at school who had also lost parents, and so I remember I would get taken out of class, which was kind of exciting. It must have been with a guidance counselor, and we would talk or listen, and it was just a group of kids who had all lost parents. They read this book to us, and it was about life and death. It had to do with, like, trees, and the changing of seasons, and the leaves falling off the trees.

Other participants discussed the significant role school counselors played in their recovery. Trevor's dad died when he was 8, and school counseling services benefitted him:

> I would go once a week, and talk to the school guidance counselor, and just kind of say what was on my mind, and what I was thinking, and it worked, as well with coloring to express myself and round my thoughts out, and what I was thinking. It was definitely nice to know that there was somebody there that kind of cared. It was nice to have people to say, "You know what, you need to go and talk to the guidance counselor."

Dirk, who was 16 when his father died, reflected on the involvement of his school counselor in not only assisting with his learning disability but also providing support in and outside of school:

> My counselor was really nice, a really good counselor. I have ADHD, so I had a lot of problems. He just kind of helped with me and my classes and with teachers. He always looked out for me, and anything I needed I would just go to him and he'd help me out. I did talk to him a little bit about my dad. It was towards the middle of the first semester when he died and it got worse towards the end of the year. I was skipping a lot of school, and so we had to meet, me and my mom and my counselor, and he understands what is going on with me. I really needed to hear that things will always be hard, but there is always someone there to help you, but you have to remember that there are things that you have to do. He was actually the only person from school who came to the funeral. I used to work at a tire shop on the north side of town after school, and he used to come in all of the time for stuff, and I talked to him then, and he stil was very nice, asked me how me and the family were doing and everything.

Professional Counseling

Professional counseling is a commonly reported source of help for those bereaved by a family member's suicide (Provini et al., 2000). The support of individual or family counseling has been used effectively by parental suicide survivors to heal, but often not until much later in life and often following a personal crisis (Demi & Howell, 1991). Bereavement from suicide is an ongoing process, and offers of assistance may need to be repeated at many points throughout bereavement (Provini et al., 2000). Participants highlighted here discussed the benefits of individual or family counseling. Although our participants may recommend a certain therapeutic approach, we caution counselors to conduct additional research before utilizing any approach mentioned.

Amber, who was present when her mother's body was found, discussed how the use of Eye Movement Desensitization and Reprocessing (EMDR), an information processing therapy, helped her deal with the effects of her mother's suicide, particularly nightmares:

> We had time to do bits of discussion at the end, but most of it was this different kind of therapy that she thought might be really helpful. You're not exactly going as intense into your emotional stuff, but it's real silent, and you watch these lights as they do this little pattern. I just watch them, and they give you some things to think about when you're doing the lights that help you bring about these things. There's something

> about the visual thing that it recalls the emotional response with it. It's apparently break-through therapy. So I did this for quite a long time. My nightmares decreased drastically, and hopefully it was because I was dealing with these things during the day. That was really helpful.

Rachel's therapist used systematic desensitization, a behavioral treatment that is used to treat anxiety-causing behaviors, and to help her cope with her suicide-related fears, after the death of her father when she was 7.

> Mom had us start seeing a psychiatrist pretty soon after. I went for, like, a year or two years. I remember playing games with her. We'd play board games or bean bag toss. I remember one issue that I had. I was really afraid to be alone in any sort of room, even if I was down here and my mom was upstairs. That was too scary. So I remember one thing she worked on with me was I had to pick a room that I was afraid to be in, and I said my mom's room, if I stayed in her room by myself, not like a time out or any sort of like bad thing. I'd sit in there and watch TV, but I was in there alone. If I could do that for 15 minutes, she let me pick what kind of reward I wanted, and I picked candy, so I got a piece of gum. At the time, I probably didn't even realize what sort of help it was giving me. I'm sure it put my mom just a little more at peace just knowing that we were getting some sort of help. So, did it help? I'm sure it did.

Some participants shared how later life events were complicated by the suicide of their parent. Lisa, for example, discussed her use of counseling for postpartum depression and how her struggles were linked to the loss of her mother to suicide.

> It really didn't hit until after my second child was born, and it got really bad, and it was approaching the time where I was turning 25, which my mom was 25 when she committed suicide. So, for me, I always knew that that year would be a hard year for me because I was afraid. It was something that I would do, and my husband finally realized that and said, "You've got to go to a doctor." And he went with, and spoke up and said, "She's laying in bed all day. She doesn't want to talk, she doesn't want to take care of the baby, she doesn't want to touch the baby, she doesn't want to do anything, for anybody." I went for about six months to a psychologist, and I felt phenomenal after six months, and they wanted to give me medication. I said, "I don't want medication. I can work through this. I just need to be confident that I can trust you with my feelings and my emotions." And she had to do a lot of convincing in the first months that I saw her that it was okay to feel the way I did, and it was okay to talk about it to her. And we had a couples session—after about three months—and my husband said, "She's a brand new person." And the psychologist said that a lot of it was with my first child. I was living with

> my grandmother. I had somebody there to kind of help and take care of me and take care of the baby, and then when we moved out of her house we moved right in with my mother-in-law. So she was there. So there was always kind of a mother person around to kind of guide me and help me. Then I was on my own and I didn't have that mom growing up, like a normal woman does, to show you and teach you how to be a mother and a wife, and she said that was my biggest problem, that I just needed to be confident, that even without that guidance I could do it and I would be okay.

Jared, whose father died when he was 12, discussed how traumatic experiences later in life led him into counseling and how discussion of his father's suicide surfaced.

> The first time I sought help was while I was in Iraq. I was having a rough time dealing with some of this stuff, and I sought help there. I don't know if it was a psychiatrist or psychologist. And then more recently my best friend was killed in a motorcycle accident when I was there, and I went back again. And I am still in the process right now. And the suicide had been brought up on that, of course, regarding the stress and anxiety from this other stuff.

Dirk, who received counseling during his time in prison, revealed the importance of such interventions to his recovery and success:

> Prison is the reason that I'm where I'm at today. I have no idea where I would have been. I probably wouldn't have gotten the help and counseling that I needed. I was about 19. I knew then that the way I was living wasn't working. But there are good people out there, and not everybody's going to hurt me, and I obviously have a lot of anger issues that I have to fix or I'll be right back in there, and staying angry and all that wasn't going to help me get through the prison sentence. I took advantage of every single program and all the schooling I could to make it not a waste, I guess, just sitting time to sit time.

Other participants spoke more in general about the benefits of counseling to their recovery not only immediately following the suicide but also into later childhood years and adulthood:

> Me and my psychologist have known each other for three years, and we have a great relationship, and he's been through, not exactly but somewhat some similar things, and it's just someone to relate to, and obviously in the last few years it made a big difference.
>
> Mom had us in counseling from the time that it happened until, I don't even know. Anything that popped up, it was we need to go see a counselor. It was years of counseling mostly just for the suicide, until I was

> about 8 or 9. Then I quit going for a while, and then she thought we should get back into it just as we were getting older, just behavioral things I guess. Counseling helped.

"Do-Nothing" Support

A theme not discussed in previous studies that emerged here is that of "do-nothing" support. Several survivors discussed the benefit of such indirect support, in which others simply spent time with them doing ordinary or fun things, maintaining a sense of normalcy, and not forcing discussion of the suicide. Amber discussed the importance of this type of support, coming from both her father and her friends. She had previously revealed her need to maintain the household because her father was not functioning well.

> My best support was just being able to do nothing with my dad, lie down and do nothing and be just absolutely lazy and being in his presence. It made me feel better that I still had this half support. I had a couple of friends who knew just to do that sit-and-do-nothing thing with me. My softball team all showed up to the funeral, which was really nice, because they were way in the back, and it was the best for me when people were just back there, but I could go to them if I needed them and if they did things not right to me. Indirect sort of forms of support were the best at the time. And they got together and made all these little cards, and that was nice to know that you're thinking about me over here, but that you don't necessarily have to be fixing me in front of my face. People didn't do anything different, there wasn't any kind of extra effort by most people who knew me, and I appreciated that in which they just kept the same things. So I guess it was supportive in that it was the same.

Amber also reflected on this form of support being an important part of her Camp HOPE experience.

> You have most activities that are just fun and just creating an atmosphere of we are supportive and we are a community together. And the coolest thing about camp was people need to know that they are not alone. When you are the only kid in town that has experienced something like this, you think that you are the only kid in the world 'cause kids are really egocentric. So that was the main thing, but mostly we just play games, do crafts, go outside and play, play, play and there are a few key things that we do to give an opportunity to start talking about it. And it's not like, "Tell me about it, tell me about it, tell me about it." It's, you know, "We're going to do the candlelight ceremony." And you just basically say, "I'm here for this person." And then you can talk about whatever.

Dirk also talked about the do-nothing support he received at Camp HOPE.

> I remember at nighttime when we were all supposed to be in our bunks, it wasn't like we were causing trouble, our counselor let us go, me and two other guys and three other girls, we just hung out on the pier. We all just talked. We talked a little bit about our losses, but also we just kind of hung out.

Jenna, who was 11 when her father died, talked about the supportive presence of the people she babysat for following the suicide.

> The biggest thing that helped my recovery was babysitting. I had started babysitting for people. I wouldn't have to talk to the people I was babysitting for about the whole situation, but it's just like you know they were there.

When asked for advice to others who have experienced parental suicide, Guy suggested the importance of doing ordinary activities.

> Activities are definitely another important thing—just having fun with groups of friends and definitely having their parents doing things with them, taking them to the movies or going to a park, and still doing things. That makes a big difference.

Jared, who was 12 when his father died, stayed with extended family for the following summer and benefitted from this form of indirect support.

> I stayed with my uncle, and his boy played baseball in high school, so pretty much that whole summer they were playing baseball. I would go to all the baseball games with him. I actually started running the scoreboard at the games and just did a lot of hanging out. It was nice because they actually had a pool at their house, and so pretty much every other night all summer friends were over for them and just like hung out, and it really made a difference with the way I am. Just hanging out going camping and baseball games helped a lot.

Melissa discussed the role her friends played in helping her maintain a sense of normalcy following the suicide.

> They didn't know what to say. I mean, we were all 14, and the usual thing for people to do at that time was, go out, see a movie with my friends. There wasn't much to do other than try to return to a sort of normal routine.

Support From "Others Who Understand"

Although people who have lost someone to suicide can provide a depth of understanding unlike any other, connecting children to those who have lost parents to other types of death can be as effective (Brown et al., 2007; Requarth, 2006). One study revealed that suicide survivors experience substantial difficulties in the social arena (e.g., talking with others about the suicide), and though they view professional help as beneficial, informal sources of support are also valued (McMenamy et al., 2008). Connection with "others who understand" may occur in person, or through books and websites. Realizing they are not alone, children feel less like an oddity or a weaker individual. Sharing such an experience with another who understands is especially important to suicide survivors because it normalizes the experience, neutralizes feelings of stigma and isolation, and allows for open expression of the loss (Jordan, 2001; Pietila, 2002).

No studies have captured the significance of this form of support to parental suicide survivors. Survivors featured here benefitted from the support of others who were perceived to understand due to having had difficult experiences themselves, having gone through the suicide experience with the surviving child, or having known the deceased parent and being able to provide a realistic perspective on them and the suicide. Rachel, whose father died when she was 7, discussed the importance of friends who understood what she'd been through:

> There's like three close girlfriends. Two of them I've known since first grade and one of them I met in fourth grade. The two even knew my dad, and then I have my next-door neighbor I kind of grew up with, too, and she went through it with me as well. It's not like I need on a daily basis really specific support or something, but just the fact that they do know what I've been through and what happened is really comforting and supportive to me.

Rachel further went on to describe how her family, who understood how her father's mental health issues resulted in suicide, was able to help her understand the realities of suicide:

> Explaining how the depression is like an illness, and because of this illness he felt like he wasn't a good dad and things like that. I think they did a good job of kind of helping me through that and realizing that he felt this way. It was the sickness that caused the suicide. He really was a great person.

Similarly, Suzanne discussed the importance of her mother helping her understand her father's strengths and struggles:

> My mother never made him out to be a perfect person. She made him out to be a real person. He was a wonderful father. He didn't have an

> alcohol problem, he wasn't abusive, he wasn't a gambler, he didn't mismanage his money. There were all of these positive things that he did in his life that were easy to talk about, but my mother did not deny the mental health issues. She would say, "Daddy didn't think about that right, Daddy didn't understand, he didn't realize that he thought this way, but this is the way it would be." So she also pointed out his weaknesses of not that he died by suicide, but that he would be depressed, that he would worry about things that he didn't have to worry about. So she made him to be a real person. That kept other people from wanting to emulate him so much.

Three participants talked about being able to relate more easily to others who had experienced challenges in life, even if the challenge was not the suicide of a loved one.

> I would babysit for people that went through a divorce, and so it was like, well, just kind of understood. And I don't know that I really thought about it at the time, but I think looking back at it you can see it. It's like if they can get through stuff, everyone else can. We're all dealing with the same thing at the same time.
>
> I had a friend whose father died also later on in life, and it was like we could talk to each other, and we knew what it felt like.
>
> My wife's brother was killed in a car accident not too long after we met, so there's a kind of understanding there, and one of her friends from high school committed suicide. So I'd say we'd pretty much understand how the other feels.

Because almost all of our participants attended Camp HOPE as children, camp experiences pertaining to this theme emerged frequently. Camp HOPE seemed to be one way to bring people together who understand.

> I didn't know that so many other people and kids my age were going through what I was feeling—to hear other people's stories and then I could talk about mine—and it was a big relief.
>
> It was really nice seeing other people with similar experiences, being able to talk about it freely.
>
> A lot of it is bringing in people that are open to talking about what they have been through—similar experiences. There's a lot more than you realize. When I stood there that first camp, I looked around, and I'm like, "Really? All these people have had somebody close to them die? Are you serious?" It is a lot of people. So it is very, very powerful.
>
> Other people who understand where you are coming from makes a big difference. That was good to be around a whole bunch of people that are going through the same thing. It was good to talk to other people, so I knew that I wasn't the only one. I was still angry, and I was still sad,

and still upset. There was a lot who lost their parents to suicide, and their sisters or brothers or whatever, and then just ones in general who had lost their parents. It's hard either way losing a parent at all, much less to suicide.

One counselor gave me her number, and she was like, "Honey, you got to stay in touch." She was like a big sister. We stayed in touch and she broke into my high school graduation without a ticket to see me graduate. It was phenomenal because that was probably the next hardest experience for me—high school graduation. I'm standing there in my cap and gown, and I'm looking and there's all of my family. Everybody was there, but there were two faces missing, and that was killing me. I didn't know how to deal with that, and then I look up and I see her, and she was like my representation of my mom and my dad, and at my wedding. She was at my wedding as well, so she was my representation of my mom and dad. I needed that on those important moments.

CASE STUDY

Lisa's Story

It Is So Powerful

Everyone was so focused on what they were going through that they kind of forgot about us, two little kids who just lost a mother. They needed to focus on us.

When I was 9 years old, my mother committed suicide. It was very hard on my whole family. The combination of sleeping pills and late-night drinks after her shift at the bar put an end to her life. At the time, my grandmother was living with us. It was my mother, my 4-year-old brother, and me in the small house that my mother was renting.

The morning following my mother's death started out as a typical one for my brother and me. I woke up to him watching cartoons, and we both decided to crawl in bed with my mother on the cot she slept in. At that point, we kids still had no idea that she had passed. Well, that morning happened to be the morning that the landlord had come to collect the rent, so when my grandmother came to my mother to ask for the rent money and my mother didn't wake up, my grandmother just froze.

She then took my brother and me immediately from her cot and put us in another room. The paramedics came next, and my grandmother called both of my aunts to the house. My brother and I rode in the back of the ambulance, with my brother thinking that it was a game and me scared completely out of my mind, only to be told later that my mother was gone and not coming back. To me it felt like this rush of events all happening way too quickly to perceive. None of the true meaning of the situation had even begun to sink in. It was just too much for my brother and me to handle. The next time that my brother and I got to see my mother was at the wake. We weren't even allowed to go to the funeral.

About a week after my mother's death, my brother's father took custody of him. It was extremely difficult for my brother to have to lose his mother and move in with a complete stranger, all in one week. It was just too many things at one time. We were bound to self-combust at some moment. Thankfully my brother and I had visitation rights to see each other, but it was just never enough. One positive thing that resulted from all of this was that my father actually became a huge presence in my life. I actually became baptized when I was 13, and he was one of my godparents. It was too bad that it took such a loss for him to become a presence in my life. That was hard.

I just remember the chaos of that time, and as if it weren't enough, my grandmother decided to move us because the house reminded her too much of my mother. It became so traumatic that she wasn't sleeping anymore. Then, my grandmother became addicted to prescription pills that she was getting from her therapist to make herself feel better. I was probably 11 or 12 when she finally got un-addicted and got her life back on the right track. Even that took a lot of effort from all of my aunts and me helping her.

What I don't remember is a lot of support for my brother and me at that time. Everyone was so focused on what they were going through that they kind of forgot about us, two little kids who just lost a mother. They needed to focus on us. I did, however, go to counseling about a year after the fact. I became very attached to the woman who was my therapist because she became that mother figure that I longed for but didn't have at home anymore. So when she moved away, it was very difficult for me. I didn't want to have to start all over again. I felt like my life was a soap opera, and I didn't want to have to tell it to a complete stranger all over again.

After my grandmother came back into my life, she became my mother-like figure, very protective and overbearing, always trying to overcompensate to make my life much better than it ever was. But it was never going to be so much better because there was such a loss already. Thankfully around age 10 or 11 my grandmother let me visit my father more often. He started to take me for weekends, which was a huge help because I really enjoyed building a father-daughter relationship with him. I knew that was what fathers and daughters were supposed to have. It was phenomenal.

I still didn't really grow up in those next few years, but I did start to feel a bit more support as time passed. People in school, for example, were very sensitive at first. I had gone to the same school since kindergarten, and they had never dealt with anything like this before and didn't know what to do. I ended up befriending one girl with a disability and taking care of her, which I believe was my way of trying to move on. I felt as though being motherly to someone else would help me cope with my own loss of my mother.

By the time I got into high school, I had started to crawl out of my shell. I started to grow into myself and become my own person. My dad ended up getting married, and I went to his wedding. I was excited for him, and his wife turned out to be a great woman. She had a daughter who was a little bit younger than I was, and we got along great too. But that dissipated too, because my dad just wasn't a stable person emotionally. He was just putting on a façade that he was happy, but he was so emotionally unstable and so unhappy that it ruined his marriage, and my stepmom ended up leaving him too.

Shortly after my stepmother left my father, I came home from school and there were these all-too-recognizable cars of family members in my father's driveway. We all thought that my father was doing okay. I was so confused. So I went up to my aunt, who was sitting on the steps, and asked her if everything was okay. I remember walking into a kitchen of stone-cold faces. My stepmom walked up to me and told me that my father was gone, and I responded by asking where he went. It was then that I realized that he was dead. I fell to the floor with absolute hysterics, and it took hours for them to calm me down. When I calmed down, I wanted to know exactly what happened. Until that point, I had never even gotten the full details of my mother's death. I never knew my mother's death was a suicide until then.

On that day in June, my father had pulled his truck into his garage, closed the garage door, turned his truck on, and began to write letters to everyone he knew. The paramedics who found him said they believed he had changed his mind after writing the letters and decided he wanted to live, because he was found outside the car. But he was already so consumed with carbon monoxide that when he opened the door, he actually fell out and snapped his neck.

One of the reasons that my father's funeral was so hard on me was because his parents wanted nothing to do with me. My grandmother actually tried to tell me that I didn't belong at the funeral and that I should leave. Thankfully, with the help of my other grandmother, godmother, and Dad's best friend, I worked up the courage to tell her that I belonged there just as much as any other person, because he was my father and I loved him very much.

Shortly after my father's death, I went to grief camp with my younger brother, Joe, who was about 12 at that time. His father had also remarried, and Joe's stepmom was actually the first one to hear about grief camp. Joe's guidance counselor actually had recommended the camp for Joe because he was having some issues with sitting in class and concentrating, and they were starting to think it was because he had never fully dealt with the death of our mother.

I kicked and screamed all the way to camp. I thought the idea of sharing feelings and all that other kid stuff was absolutely ridiculous. I wanted no part of it. But it ended up being a life-changing experience. Neither my brother nor I had truly dealt with the death of my mother, and Camp HOPE helped a lot with that. The biggest memory I have of camp was when all the campers sat in a circle around a campfire and shared the stories of how they had lost their loved one. The circle went around, and everyone started to tell their stories, and almost immediately following each story everyone started to cry, everyone but me. I started wondering what was wrong with me. I just didn't want to cry in front of people that I didn't know. And that was when the circle came around to my brother. He looked down at his candle and then he began, "Well, my mom died 8 years ago, but I don't remember anything," and that is when I jumped up and was at his side within seconds, and we both started sobbing. It was a huge breakthrough because we just needed that cry together. We needed to grow up a little and come to terms with our feelings and share them with each other instead of bottling them up like we had done for so long. I finally saw the light at the end of the tunnel. It was like a big weight was lifted off of my shoulders. I knew I wanted to help my brother remember my mother forever, but I also knew that he was going to turn out okay without one.

Before camp, I used to be a rolling ball of emotion. I understood that it was okay to cry, but I wouldn't do it in public. Instead, I would cry privately, in my bedroom, by myself. Occasionally, at school I would go to the bathroom and I'd just cry, and that was my old outlet. But after camp, it was like, wow, I can do whatever I want to do. I can cry when I want.

Another thing that I noticed about Camp HOPE was that I went out of it looking at my family in a different light. Up until that time, I had grown up thinking that I was alone and that was why I was failing. I tried to do it all by myself because I thought I was alone. But the truth was that my family was there all along. They were there for me a lot more than I thought and more than I noticed. I am so thankful for everyone who was there for me through the rough times. I even had a counselor from camp who attended both my graduation and my wedding. It meant a lot to me, because she was there when my parents weren't. She filled the hole in the crowd that I would have noticed at those special times if it weren't for her. I am a very lucky person.

I have three kids of my own now, and I love it. I still have my ups and downs, but I know how to handle them better after everything that I have gone though in my life. One way I cope with my own depression is through exercise. I really enjoy going to the gym after a long day, and I don't deny myself *me* time. I love to go out for lunch with friends or even just spend time alone, as long as I am enjoying myself. I have found that it is really important to release emotions instead of bottling them up. I think it has made me a better mother. I would never change my life, because I don't know if I would be in as great of a position as I am today if it weren't for those obstacles in my past. If I could give my advice to a child who was going through the same thing as I did, it would be to be as open as possible. I wasn't open, and it made me feel lost and insecure, with no confidence for so long. I wish I would have been more open to talking about it, and about my feelings. I especially recommend talking to people who have gone through the same sort of things you have. It is so powerful.

CASE STUDY

Shane's Story

My Family, My Support

I made a promise to myself that I will never ever commit suicide and leave my family the way that my father left us. I don't understand how he could do that to us and I never want to do that to anyone else because I know how it feels to be left behind.

My father was the kind of guy who always believed that the man of the family should be the one to provide for the family. So, when he lost his job, he started to go downhill fast, into a deep depression. It even got to the point where my mother admitted him to a psychiatric ward for about a week. I had no idea where he had gone or why he had gone away, and all I remember at the time is being so glad to see him home. After that, my father no longer told jokes or smiled as much.

I was in the sixth grade when my father committed suicide. I remember riding the bus home from school that day and seeing a black van and three police cars parked outside my house. My first thought was, great, what happened now? Originally I wondered if someone, or even myself, was in trouble with the law. My family hadn't had a lot of trouble with the law, but we had had some, nonetheless. I knew it was bad when both my sister and the police officer failed to answer my questions about what was going on. When my sister finally told me that my father was dead, I didn't react at all because I couldn't believe it. The funeral was really hard. My grandmother was torn apart over his death, and that was the moment when I truly realized the reality of the situation. He was gone, and I was never going to see him again. I was left in a state of complete speechlessness.

After only the weekend, I returned back to school, and when I did, it seemed like most people wanted to avoid me completely. They wanted to avoid the subject of suicide so they chose to avoid me. I was deemed the "creepy" boy from then on, and, as you can imagine, that made school hard. I did have a couple of really close friends, though, and they stuck by my side throughout schooling. They made it clear that I was always welcome to hang out with them, and if I needed them, they were always there to talk to. I still hang out with them now, and it is such a joy to have them around, because they are the type of people who make me laugh and give me a reason to live.

It wasn't until about a year later that I was told that his death was a suicide. I thought to myself, "Why would he do such a thing?" I knew that ever since he lost his job, he had changed, but I didn't realize how bad it must have been until he was already gone. After his death, I felt lots of anger and hate towards him, because we were just starting to get close, and it felt like he abandoned me at an age where I needed him the most. If he truly loved me, he wouldn't have done that.

One thing that was especially hard for me was socializing with girls. That is actually what got me into a bit of trouble when I first started high school. Since my father was the one who taught me how to make friends and how to socialize, and I was at that age where I was becoming interested in the opposite sex, I had a hard time figuring out how to act around them. I was actually kicked out of school at one point and sent to an alternative school because of problems regarding the opposite sex.

It took me two years to get back to my normal high school, but I did it and am so thankful that I will graduate with the rest of my class. I have also found a couple of teachers who are there for me when I need them. That really helps. School comes first now. Everything else is on the back burner while I focus completely on graduating. One thing I will never forget about my father is that he taught me that school comes first. He might not be proud of some of the things I have done, but I know he would be proud of me for finishing school the way that I have. I want to make him proud.

There are still rumors about my father, but it is a lot easier to deal with them now that time has passed. I've become very open whenever anyone asks me anything about my father. If they ask politely, I will answer. Some people completely disrespect me by asking about "my father blowing his head off" or something of that matter, and that really gets to me, but the ones who ask and are polite about it, I tell them straightforward what happened. I would rather have them know the truth than keep the rumors floating around.

Coping has been a struggle. The first way of coping that my sister and I tried was seeing a psychiatrist. We both saw psychiatrists for about two or three years, but I didn't really talk with mine all that much, and the only help was that it gave me time to socialize with someone and take my mind off of the death. There were a couple of times that my mother, my sister, and I all went in together, but most of the time it was just me and the psychiatrist. Eventually, we stopped going, because we all felt it just wasn't helping us any further.

My mom also tried the Big Brother Big Sister program, but that didn't really work either. I remember really hoping for a big brother who was close to my age, but instead got an older man in his 60s or 70s whom I really didn't have much in common with. I did find comfort in being around my friends' fathers. I looked up to them and even envied my friends because I felt that they were lucky to have fathers. A lot of times, my friends would fight with their fathers, and I would think to myself, "Wow, they should really just appreciate the fact that they even have a father to fight with." I think it made me more appreciative of the family that I still had.

My aunt has been of great help as well. She lives in another state, but she still has been there for me through all of this. She has made it clear that I can call her at any time, even on the weekends if I have to. After I graduate high school, I want to go and stay with her for a while.

Another form of coping that I like to use is to write things down. I try to have scratch paper on hand so that if something has been bugging me or if I have a dream that I can't quite understand, I just write it down. I also have times when I just have to cry. It is a hard thing for a man to admit, but it is the truth. I will excuse myself from class or stop whatever I am doing and just sit and cry because that is all I feel like doing. In the end, it feels really good to get those emotions out rather than to bottle them inside. I have to do something to cope with my feelings because I made a promise to myself that I will never ever commit suicide and leave my family the way that my father left us. I don't understand how he could do that to us, and I never want to do that to anyone else because I know how it feels to be left behind.

My family is my support. It is all about give and take in our family. Sometimes you need someone to comfort you, and sometimes you need to be there to comfort them. I know there were many times when my sister and I had to put all of our feelings aside and be there for my mom, the way that she had been there for us as well. There are times when I still get depressed, but I just take it one day at a time. That's all I can do.

I am thankful for all that I have learned, and I would tell anyone who is going through this that it will always be with you and always affect you, but try as hard as you can to stay out of trouble and find some sort of outlet, whether it be boxing, running, music, writing, video games, anything. Whatever takes your mind off of it and helps you to cope with your feelings and keeps you out of trouble is perfect. I personally took on taekwondo and guitar, and I believe it really helped. Overall I believe that the suicide has influenced me more so in a positive way than a negative way. I have grown up so much because of the situations I have had to face. I am a stronger person from having to go through it all.

CASE STUDY

Kevin's Story

Every Time I Look Above

Although I still miss him, I can understand why he chose to take his own life. I regret not being able to spend more time with him, but I know that his suicide made the rest of our family closer and shaped the person I am today.

My father was diagnosed with Parkinson's disease in the summer of 1996. Parkinson's, a motor system disorder, causes slowness of movement, trembling, and imbalance, and it affects coordination. It's a very progressive disease, which meant that my dad's symptoms would get worse and worse over time. He would eventually have trouble even walking and talking. The diagnosis was hard for him and our family to cope with.

I grew up on a farm, which meant hard work, but my dad and I absolutely loved it. The Parkinson's meant that my dad wouldn't be able to do the work needed to keep the farm alive, and I was only 12, so I couldn't do it alone. The realization that we wouldn't be able to carry on was devastating to both of us. The day after he was diagnosed, Dad put the farm up for sale. Within what seemed like hours, and much to our dismay, the realtor and a tall, thin man knocked on our door and talked with my dad. We returned to our afternoon chores, as always, but by the next day that tall man had bought the farm. Within three days, what we loved the most was no longer ours. Over the course of a few weeks, the young man brought his cattle and household belongings to the farm, and my mom, my dad, and I moved into a house in town.

Moving off the farm was very stressful for my family. Dad became unhappy, and nothing we tried helped. He started making comments about suicide, which scared us. I never thought he'd actually do it, but one sunny, bright, summer day in August, while we were visiting my sister's farm, my nephew and I went to play up in the hay mounds in the barn and found him hanging there, dead. I was shocked and scared. The only thing I can recall is running to the house to tell my mom and my sisters, and my mom running to him right away. The sunny, bright day was suddenly dark, gloomy, and sad. There was a lot of crying that day. I was so wrapped up in my own thoughts and feelings. My mom kept herself very busy, but I knew she was taking it hard. We moved on, day by day, and learned to adjust. We came to the conclusion that Dad had committed suicide so that we wouldn't have to see him suffer.

My family and friends were very supportive. One of my teachers encouraged me to write out my thoughts and my feelings about the suicide. Probably the best thing I did was to write my story about our farm, my dad, and his suicide where I recalled everything that happened on that unfortunate August day in great detail.

Not a day passes that I don't think of my father. Every time I look up at the stars I think of my dad, and once in a while I even talk to him. One evening stands out in my mind. I had just finished college and decided to have a little fun with a few friends, so we threw a party. That night happened to be a full moon, and the stars were gleaming with light, and I broke down right there at the party because I missed my dad so much.

Although I still miss him, I can understand why he chose to take his own life. I regret not being able to spend more time with him, but I know that his suicide made the rest of our family closer and shaped the person I am today. I know my dad would be very proud of me. I've had the opportunity to finish college. I have a great job, a beautiful wife, and a comfortable home in the country, where I'm able to look out and see the stars anytime I want.

CASE STUDY

Guy's Story

Finding My Way Back

My family and I have been through something that tore us apart. Slowly, we are finding the way back to each other and to ourselves. . . . None of it is easy, but it is worth it. It's hard, all of it, but it's good in the end.

At the age of 42, my father was diagnosed with schizophrenia. He was also addicted to morphine. His illness had progressed so far by the time he was diagnosed, that he committed suicide two years later. If you would have asked anyone else in my family, they would have said it was a good thing that he was gone. Not me, I felt sad, and I missed him.

My father became disabled by his schizophrenia. He was unemployed, but he badly wanted to work. He drank about a bottle of brandy a day. He shot guns in the house and pulled all sorts of other crazy stunts. He didn't hurt me. I was too young. He was abusive, however, to everyone else in the family. He hit my mother, but my brother was his main target, putting him in intensive care one time after almost killing him. Usually, the cops came quickly enough to get my dad off of him. Around the time of my dad's suicide, my mother was planning to leave him.

My dad hadn't always been that way. He had gone to college and was number one in his class. He had his bachelor's degree in nursing and had a really good job. He was just a regular guy. He went to work, earned a good wage, and was a good father. The first 15 or so years of Mom and Dad's marriage were good. It had been just in the last five years of his life that things had gone downhill.

The afternoon of his death, my dad had asked my mom to stay home, but she had to go to work. At that time, he could list 60 different demons who talked to him, which must have been a living nightmare for him. There was a 12-gauge shotgun in the house, and that is what he used to shoot himself. Later that afternoon, my brother and I came home from school and started playing on our trampoline in the backyard. Neither of us went in the house until I had to use the bathroom. That's when I walked in and found my dad. I ran back outside and got my brother as quickly as I could, and we called our mother and the police. The cops met my mom when she got home, and they told her what had happened. And as soon as she saw my dad, she just fell down and started screaming. My brother went in to be by her, and like me, he still has that picture permanently etched into his brain. By the time my sisters got home from their after-school activities, everything was all taken care of. We still had to tell both of them what had happened, but because they didn't see, they didn't handle it too badly. I lay in bed that night, knowing that my life was going to be different.

I don't remember much about the funeral, except that everyone else was crying and that I couldn't. I only pretended to cry because I didn't want to look like I didn't care. Everyone else was hysterical, and I just did not feel it. I remember staring at him in the casket, and all I could think of is that he probably had a hole in the back of his head. I thought of a big chunk of his brain on the floor and the massive puddle of blood. From the front, you couldn't see the monstrous hole in back, but his eyes were sort of bulging. I remember looking at him, and I just felt different. I was surprised, but pretty emotionless and kind of hopeless. That hopelessness stuck.

Nobody talked to me about what had happened. I just stopped feeling anything and for a long time. I wouldn't even laugh. I simply was not there, and it was very hard for me. I started having nightmares. I had walked in on a blown-up head and a whole room covered in blood. I was only 6 years old at the time, and it was a sight that I could not forget. The nightmares happened nightly. Most of them were about the event itself. It was like reliving it over and over again.

My mom was suddenly a single parent and didn't really have any time to spend with us. We kids just kind of fell apart, and so did she. She was only working a part-time job when he died and now had to support everybody and take care of the house on her own. She just got really strung out. As a result, everybody went their separate ways.

None of us really had any friends because our house was already looked on as the crazy place on the block. You know, they would say that Dad was a crazy drug addict and that the cops came plenty of times because he would start beating his son, or something. We couldn't really hang out with anybody else in the subdivision because parents didn't want their kids around us. So, there weren't many people who really were there for us, and there surely was not anyone there for my mom. She was alone and didn't have support from anyone. Most people in town just looked the other way. As far as family, my mother has two brothers and a father who was still alive at the time. They all lived 3 hours away. My dad didn't have many relatives, and his dad was dead, so the only one in his family was his mother, who lived in a different state. We didn't really have any relatives, and surely none who lived in the area. The only visit that I can remember was my mom's brother, who came maybe once. We dealt with this whole thing alone for many years. None of us had counseling or friends to talk to, and we did not discuss it as a family at all.

I decided to care about school and make that my focus. I was still the good child back then, and still doing well in school. I seemed so normal. In grade school, I tried to live up to my sister, "Miss 4.0," and I got straight *A*'s. It was expected of me, and I even got money if I had good grades. We were all expected to go to college. My first two years in high school, I had a 4.0 grade point average and was at the top of my class.

It wasn't until I was about 16 that I started to have problems. The end of my sophomore year is when I fell apart. My whole family felt hopeless, and I was getting used to that feeling too. When you're around a family that's falling apart, and doesn't care, and has their own problems, it is just easier to fall into that too. My oldest two siblings, who were in high school when my dad died, began taking drugs after his death, and still did. My family was falling apart, and I followed. At the beginning of junior year, I attempted suicide for the first time. I had the sleeping pills pumped out of my stomach and stayed in the hospital for two weeks. I stopped drinking and using drugs for the rest of my junior year, but I barely got a 2.0-grade point average. Living was just not worth it to me.

My senior year was just as bad. I went into the hospital twice for suicide attempts. Once was with alcohol after drinking an entire liter of vodka and a half liter of Everclear. Again, my stomach was pumped. The other time, I drank antifreeze. That's no good either. I remember feeling like I was insane. It felt like I was crawling on the ceiling, and it did some serious damage to my kidneys. I was put in a psychiatric ward three times that year, always at the same hospital, which was a long trip from where I lived. All I did, basically, was just get out and try to kill myself again. I probably attempted suicide about a half dozen times throughout a two-year period, but I always got caught. Once, I was handcuffed right in front of the school. They have to do that if you say anything about suicide, and they have to take you in on a 72-hour hold. I was "cuffed" right there in front of school in the parking lot. That's tough. Oh, well, people knew about me before that and half of my teachers hated me anyway because I never came to school and I didn't have any friends.

It is almost like there was a reason that my attempts weren't successful. I think maybe the first one was impulsive and some of the others were just impractical. A lot of people attempt suicide for the attention or just as a call for help. Most don't necessarily want to die; it's just their last resort. I never really wanted to die. I was just asking for someone to give me counseling and help fix some of these things in me. For so long, I was the perfect child, and nobody really noticed my pain. I flew under the radar because I didn't draw attention until I started trying to kill myself.

After getting into drugs again and another suicide attempt, I was sent to a halfway house. For years I never felt emotions, and if you read my writings while in the psych ward, you would see I described myself as a zombie. I just didn't feel a thing. When I got out of the halfway house, I don't know why, but something changed. Life became worth it again, and I started to feel things so intensely. I started to feel my emotions and wasn't shoving them back anymore. I couldn't hide that stuff any longer, and facing it made a big difference. I stopped using drugs, left home, got my own place and—for the first time—I felt free.

I'm going to college now, and things should be good from here on out. I have goals; I want a good degree and to make a lot of money. Now I have hope. Back then, I was focused only on the past, but now I know that there is so much more in today. I've gone through many challenges in my life. Now I'm just a regular guy. I've got my nice little apartment, a regular roommate, and a regular job. I am not the same person I once was, and I don't expect perfection of myself like I did before. Now, I get an A- or B+ and that's okay. I'm just doing the best I can and I'm satisfied with that.

Activities have been a big part of my healing. I remember being bored every summer. I didn't have friends, and I didn't try to get involved in anything. Now, I go biking. I also like going to concerts and many other things—enjoying my time rather than wasting it.

Life is good now, but not necessarily easy. I still have anxiety and depression, and I am on medications. I still have nightmares at least once or twice a week. I think a counselor could have helped me when I was young, but now I write the dreams down, and bring them to counseling, and talk about them. It seems like a pretty easy thing to do, and the counseling does help to make them go away.

Asking about dreams is a good way to start talking to children. When you dream, it is often a reflection of what is going on inside, especially for a child. Instead of having children try to explain their feelings, have them tell you what they're dreaming about. You might get a little more insight into what is going on. The things they are dreaming about are probably the things that should be talked about. When I was young, I did not really think about my dad's death, except through nightmares. During the day, I just went on with life and forgot about it, but then it was always there at night.

I never told anybody about the nightmares when I was young, and nobody asked. When you are that young, someone should come to you. You should not have to ask for help. Feeling alone is not such a good thing. Friendship and someone to communicate with is important. Having people there to talk to is the key. There were not many people my age who I could talk with at the time when I needed someone the most. Providing children with opportunities to talk is very important. Back in the day, I did not have any friends, so there wasn't much to lose if I killed myself. Our family did not have a good relationship back then either, so I was pretty much alone. Having friends and a functional family now makes a big difference.

After one of my last suicide attempts, the counselors set up a circle of people who volunteered to be there for me. Some of them were teachers and some were friends, but they were all people I could get together with and talk with. There was always someone either at school or at home who I could call. I figure someone should do that for every child while they are still young, before they attempt suicide. Why couldn't someone have done this for me when I was 6? I'm sure that if you asked, there would be someone willing to be there for a child who has gone through something like I did. Nobody really did step up for me when I was young. I have to think people saw that I was hurting. Then again, maybe not. If I wasn't showing any emotion, I always got good grades, had a perfectly cleaned room, did all my chores, and never argued. I was a good little boy, but having a parent die by suicide should not be left to kids to deal with by themselves. It is way too big of a thing to handle on your own. Communication is vital. Do not let children be quiet, even if they look okay.

Think about the rest of the family too, because they have such a big impact on a child. The other family members need to get help and need to try to be good examples, especially for the younger children. Try to help the kid get through it and be more positive. Everyone should not just be doing their own thing. Talk! I know that counseling has made a huge difference for me in the last few years. I have definitely come back from where I was last winter. I think I have dealt with it now. My psychologist and I have known each other for three years and we have a great relationship. He has been through some similar things, is someone who I can relate to, and is always there for me.

My family and I have been through something that tore us apart. Slowly, we are finding the way back to each other and to ourselves. Each of us is in a different place, but all continue to learn and grow. I have learned that living in the present is crucial. I now know that goals are important, but striving obsessively is not. I have found that being active and having people to talk to are key factors in recovery. My hope is that children who experience this have someone willing to step up and surround them with support. It is a lot easier than trying to figure it out alone. None of it is easy, but it is worth it. It's hard, all of it, but it's good in the end.

four
Coping

The ways people cope with any life crisis are highly individualized. A strategy that helps one person may not help another, although there may be similarities in coping within a specific group. Survivors of parental suicide use a variety of coping mechanisms when dealing with the unique challenges they face. Our participants identified eight coping strategies that they found helpful (see Figure 4.1 for strategies and the number of participants reporting each). Similar strategies have been found in previous research (Clark & Goldney, 1995; Demi & Howell, 1991; Kaslow & Aronson, 2004; McMenamy et al., 2008; Requarth, 2006), and our findings offer unique insights into common coping mechanisms among parental suicide survivors.

Writing and Art

Parental suicide survivors often use writing to preserve memories, to tell their loved one's story, or just to cope with the myriad of feelings (Demi & Howell, 1991). Some survivors write letters directly to the deceased and may physically bury the letters in representative places to settle unresolved issues (Clark & Goldney, 1995). Creating the "suicide story" and understanding why the parent may have taken his or her life can be helpful in coming to terms with the death, minimizing family dysfunction, and combating stigma (Kaslow & Aronson, 2004). Sharing such personal narratives of loss with others helps survivors create meaning from the event and heal (Mitchell, Gale, Garand, & Wesner, 2003). Helping a child keep

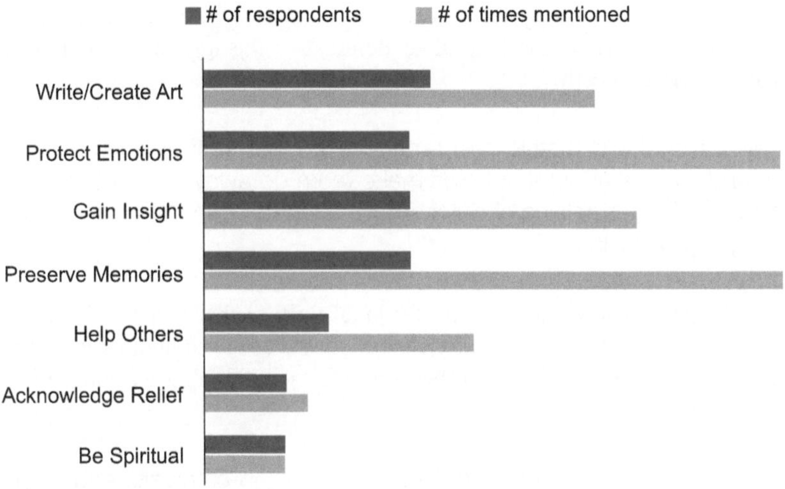

FIGURE 4.1 Coping: Types and frequencies.

the memory of a parent alive may be one of the most important ways a caring adult can impact a child. Drama likely surrounded the death, but there were also likely good times and great memories. Providing the child with memory-keeping tools, such as writing and drawing, is essential to helping a child cope with loss (Requarth, 2006).

Many percent of our participants coped through writing or creating art for themselves or for others (e.g., class assignment, counseling), with the majority indicating a preference for writing. This included penning letters to the deceased, journaling, poetry, writing about the suicide, documenting dreams, and writing professional pieces. In the days following his death, Charlotte felt the need to write to her deceased father and ask him that ever-impending question: "*Before the funeral, I wrote a letter to my dad . . . it was really long . . . but I think I asked why, probably . . . a hundred times . . . like . . . I love you, I miss you . . . but why . . . why would you do that?*"

Several participants mentioned how helpful journaling was and, specifically, how they first became introduced to such writing at Camp HOPE. "*I guess the biggest thing that helped me at Camp HOPE was the journaling. They gave us all journals and I still write in that journal to this day.*"

One participant shared how stories written through counseling or school helped him cope at the time and even now today.

> I'll find projects that I did in school in the attic or with my counselors, little stories that I wrote, things that I would write or there are the things that I still remember doing with him—I'm realizing now—that's probably why they had us do them. I mean, it probably was therapeutic then to just think about him and the good things.

Others talked about writing down dreams as a way to cope and heal. Guy, for example, found it particularly helpful to de-escalate the nightmares that had started after his dad's death.

> They [psychologists] start telling me to write that stuff down and bring it in and we talk about it. It helps make them go away. It's almost like a good way to start talking about it. That's a big reflection of what's probably going on inside.

Two participants had engaged in professional writing that helped with their coping. One created educational materials for work that talked about the myths and misconceptions of suicide. The other wrote for a children's grief publication and shared the following.

> Being able to have that regular kind of scheduled catharsis, and to be able to write for the kids, and knowing that I'm probably really helping somebody, I feel better.

Two participants mentioned *artistic expression* as a coping strategy. A young boy who had witnessed the suicide of his father at age 3 described how art had been helpful to him as a child. Perhaps it was the only thing that got through to him.

> When I did go to counseling, art is about the only thing that got me to express anything. The counselor would ask, "Why are you drawing that?" or "Why are you expressing that?" So art was a good thing, as close to communication as far as that went.

Similarly poetry was used by another participant and seemed to be a vehicle for understanding and expression.

> I wrote a poem that was trying to explore the separation of me and my mom. My original goal was to try to feel the anger that my dad did and try to represent that and be like, "Why is he so damn angry? Like, how can he even after 14 years, how can he call her a bitch, you know? Ouch! She's dead. Give it up."

Another participant, who aspires to be a writer, shared how her writing evolved throughout her recovery.

> Death is still a theme in my writing, more so now. It just kind of keeps getting lighter a bit. It went from suicide to kind of like death, and now it's into actually—dreams and nightmares. Weird, huh? It seems to be following quite the progression, and then maybe someday I will write really funny stuff.

Protecting Emotions

Intense and varied emotions can follow the death of a parent to suicide, and how they are dealt with is influenced by a myriad of factors, including the development and maturity of the child, existing supports, and the responses and needs of others. Protecting emotions serve as a coping mechanism by allowing survivors to not feel the associated pain. Demi and Howell (1991) used a grounded-theory approach to examine the perceptions of 17 adult parental suicide survivors who had lost their loved one prior to the age of 30. These authors coined the term "hiding the pain" to describe how survivors coped with the loss by suppressing emotions through use of denial, avoidance, and fleeing from family or reminders of the parent. Survivors generally were not allowed any shared grieving experience with other family members following the suicide and were expected to hide their pain associated with it. They coped by not dealing with the pain born from the death. Many pursued the socially acceptable way of hiding by becoming workaholics, and a few admitted to the less socially acceptable coping mechanism of addiction.

A majority of our participants used emotion-protecting measures to help them cope. This included lying about or minimizing feelings or downplaying the effects of the death. Many told of blocking out memories or emotions related to the suicide, and a few talked about avoiding situations, people, and places to get through difficult circumstances. In some cases, they used distraction through family, recreation, or increased involvement in school to cope.

Three participants spoke specifically about lying to the professionals (counselors and school personnel) who were supposed to be helping them. One of them, Brooke, was 28 at the time of the interview and had already been through a lot in her life. She had been sexually abused by her father, who took his own life after Brooke told her mother and the police and courts became involved. She really struggled as a result of the abuse and her father's suicide when she was 12. Brooke was angry all of the time and isolated herself from everyone.

> Of course I wasn't going to tell everybody that I was angry. I was going to tell everybody that I was fine. Mom put me back in counseling and, once again, that didn't go over so well. I'm not going to tell somebody who is getting paid to listen to me how I feel about anything, you know?

Another participant shared a similar experience with his guidance counselor.

> The guidance counselor would call me in every single week to check up on me, and I wouldn't tell him anything—nothin'—I'd be like, "I'm fine." So lying, just lying.

Rachel creatively lied to her therapist to protect her emotions as the therapist tried to desensitize Rachel to the trauma of the suicide.

> I remember one thing she worked on with me. I had to pick a room that I was afraid to be in alone. I didn't even want to tell her it was really the basement where my dad died because I didn't want her to make me go there. So, I said it was my mom's room.

A number of participants talked about burying memories or emotions. Most did not remember much about the funeral or the days after. They sort of went through it all in a fog, and many were surprised that they could not even cry at the time. This participant noted the emotional block that occurred for him following the suicide: "*After that [the suicide], I pretty much severed all ties with my emotion and buried it.*"

Burying emotions can have lifelong implications, as shared by this participant, who reflected on the impacts on his marriage.

> I am not a real emotional person, and because of that, get a lot of grief from my wife. My whole emotion, like everything I got, is buried. And I mean, it's hard for me to show it, I guess. Especially hearing it from her, she'll say, "Well, you don't do this and you don't do that." But I don't see the issue there.

Participants discussed avoiding people, places, or things to help them cope. Dirk was 16 when his father died. He poignantly described his need to avoid paternal reminders. He did not want to see the suicide note his dad had left, because he was afraid it might say something hurtful. He could not face going back to his home for a couple of weeks after the death. Entering the breezeway was difficult for an even longer amount of time because it connected to the garage, where they had found his father. He shared how even family can be difficult to face 11 years later.

> My uncle Jim lives nearby, but I don't like seeing him. He looks like my dad, he sounds like my dad. I spent the night there once a few years ago, and I woke up, and he was in the kitchen, and I thought it was my dad. Uncle Jim actually just called me and said, "I have your dad's class ring here. I'm gonna give it to you." But I still haven't gone to get the ring. Still too hard.

Distraction was another coping strategy for protecting emotions. Putting the focus on school, work, or anything other than the suicide and the related emotions seemed to help, as indicated by this participant: "*I work. I mean basically just keep myself occupied. If I'm sitting at home and it pops into my head, I go for a walk or I, you know, I do something.*"

If an entire family is protecting emotions by not discussing what happened, children will often follow suit. This participant also coped through the distraction of school:

> As a little kid, my mom was busy. Nobody really talked to me about it, and it just kind of stayed that way, and all I ever cared about was school, and that was just, like, my focus. I got really serious and just focused on it [getting straight A's].

Gaining Insight

Parental suicide survivors may look for information and insight into the suicide as a way to cope. Clark and Goldney (1995), for example, found that suicide survivors may benefit from talking to law enforcement, doctors, and the coroner's department to help answer questions about the suicide and the state of mind of the person before his or her death. Some suicide survivors, particularly children, may not have seen the body after death and need that tangible information to aid in recovery. For that reason, funeral directors are encouraged to keep photographs on file for family members' possible future requests (Clark & Goldney, 1995). Gaining insight into mental illness and the deceased person's destructive behavior can facilitate coping by generating a greater understanding of what they may have been going through (Clark & Goldney, 1995). Cain (2002) insists that telling about the suicide must not be an event but a process, with experiences being retold at different points in the child's life. As children mature, they continue to grieve in stages and will need new information about the death throughout their development to understand the loss (Mitchell et al., 2006).

Because death by suicide may violate much of what we believe to be true about our lives, the quest to make sense of that which seems to make no sense often becomes a central healing task (Sands, Jordan, & Neimeyer, 2011). It is common for bereaved individuals to question why and to try to reach some understanding of the meaning of the event (Wertheimer, 2001). The grieving process includes attempting to make sense of the loss, to fit it into one's assumptions about the world or, if necessary, to modify those assumptions (Parkes, 1998).

Our participants talked about gaining insight as a way to make it through the experience of parental suicide. They coped by reexamining the suicide from a more mature perspective to gain understanding of what it meant for their lives and how it had shaped them as persons. Participants enhanced their understanding of the realities of suicide, including mental health, substance abuse, and other issues that may contribute to it. Some tried to understand family history and where the suicidal behavior originated. Often during their discovery, they came to understand how a person could be driven to take his or her own life. Through the process, others came to realize that they were not to blame in any way for the death and were able to forgive themselves. Some participants had completed their search for answers and meaning related to the suicide. For others, the journey had just begun.

Many participants placed at least part of the blame on themselves for their parent's death. They felt badly that they had argued or did not do what they were told. They felt as if they may have missed the signs or should have been able to stop the suicide. Some found that reevaluating the suicide from a more mature perspective helped them to cope. Amber was 17 when her mom died by hanging in the family's basement. Amber knew that her mother was depressed, and she had tried all evening to console her. Shortly after Amber went to bed, she heard her dad screaming. She raced down to the basement and helped her father get her mother down off of the rope. Amber describes her guilt and how she overcame it.

> I used to just cry and cry and cry and say that I was her only hope and no, ah, I wasn't her only hope. She had tons of other hopes lying around that got crushed before that, and so I'm just more objective about my thoughts about it. I'm much more apt to feel a sense of independence from the issue.

Rachel was just beginning to have a lot of questions about how her father's death had impacted her life and was starting this reevaluation process. She wondered about the effects on a girl growing up without a father, specifically when suicide had been the cause of death. She wondered about the feelings of abandonment and wanted to discover what "baggage" she might bring to future relationships.

> I'm just getting to a point where I want to start reevaluating and start not thinking like a 7-year-old about it. There's just kind of some changes that have gone on in my life recently that I feel things kind of resurfacing, and I just want to reevaluate it and rethink about what it means to me and my life. I think I need to understand it in a way that fits a 20-year-old now. I don't like to think of myself—or my personality—as just determined by the result of this thing that happened in my life, you know? But I think there has to be some truth to it. I mean, I can't get away from the fact that it has had a big impact on me.

After finding the reasons why her father may have taken his own life, Melissa knew that she was not the cause and could not be the cure, with what she knew at the time.

> A lot of people say, "Well, do you feel like there's something you could have done?" And, looking back on it now, he was showing these symptoms. He would act psychotic. He had just gone into these fits where he wasn't able to think clearly. And now that he's gone, I'm able to say this. Hindsight is 20/20. There was nothing at that time I could have done.

One participant expressed frustration that the need to reevaluate throughout life had not been addressed with her earlier on.

> [My mom told me the psychiatrist] said that I will have to reevaluate this at different points in my life. And I'm just like, "No one has ever told me that before!" I just kind of feel like, "Why couldn't you have told me that before? Why do I have to come to this big breakdown?" It's just frustrating.

Some survivors found that understanding mental illness and its connection to the suicide was helpful in their coping, as with one participant: "*I view depression as an illness. I mean, like cancer is an illness and a heart attack or something. I mean depression was his illness and it is what killed him.*"

For Rachel, seeing a college roommate with depression helped her understand her dad's mental illness in a way she never could have otherwise. All of her memories were of a happy, successful businessman. Realizing that her perception of his life was not at all the life he lived helped her to cope with his dying.

> I understand that everyone's depression is different. People deal with it differently, and it manifests itself differently, but just thinking like, wow, this is what my dad lived like. It was very sad to see because I think you can go day to day. Like I'm sure if I just saw her [my roommate] in class, she would be fine, she would look normal. But to actually see her just not be able to get out of bed and not wanna come have dinner with us—and to think about, like, he [my dad] had this really dark, horrible, sad illness that he lived with—I don't have depression. I don't know what it's like to feel depressed. I don't know what that's like even though I know a lot about it.

Some participants found that researching about suicide and about their families helped them cope with this experience. Suzanne read over 150 books on this and related topics, and made a career of educating her family and community about suicide. She never stopped learning and felt obliged to share what she had learned. One such important discovery made her go immediately to family with the information.

> Like when I discovered in my reading that if you have a parent that commits suicide that you are in the highest risk category. I made sure that all my siblings and their spouses and their children knew, so that if there would be somebody in the family that would be suicidal, family members would know not to ignore it.

One participant shared how her sister's quest for information helped her in her own pursuit of insight.

> My sister recommended a book called *Adult Children of Alcoholics*, and she bought a copy for the other three kids. It describes my mom to a T. It describes our whole family to a T. And it's exactly the way it is. A lot of hidden things, not wanting people to look down on their family. I'm not the only one out there dealing with this. It's sad, but it's still neat to hear that I'm not the only one.

Melissa was 14 when she found her father's body after school in a shed on their property. She found that digging into family history helped her cope with the question of why.

> It's just this history of abuse passed on from parent to child. So, I guess something that helped me with the healing process was to try

> and understand why it was that my father did this, what events in his childhood made him predisposed to do this.

A few participants admitted that they gained insight through contemplating suicide themselves. This gave them unique insight into why someone might choose this route because they understood the immense pain and how it could seem like the only option. On the other hand, they knew what it felt like to be left behind and did not want to cause that kind of pain for anyone. Having concrete knowledge about the desperation of suicide, as well as the aftermath it creates, helped participants to cope with their own depression and suicidal ideation. Charlotte was 15 when her father died by asphyxiation using his car's exhaust. She was interviewed seven years after his death, and it was still obviously very painful for her. She had been raped close to the time of his suicide, and he had agreed to take her to have an abortion, but died the day before they were supposed to leave. So Charlotte was dealing with her dad's death, a rape, and an abortion, accompanied by her mom, who was against it. She described times when she was very depressed, and the thought of suicide would cross her mind.

> I think about it like a couple times a year, how easy it would be just to do it and leave all my problems behind, but, I don't want to put people in that circumstance. So I guess what I really take from it is because I know how it made me feel when he left. I don't want to make other people feel like that.

Preserving and Sharing Memories

The need to maintain a connection with a deceased loved one is historically well documented (Cohen, Mannarino, & Knudsen, 2004; Glass, 1991; Howarth, 2011; Stroebe & Stroebe, 1993; Worden, 1996). As such, efforts to keep the memory of the parent alive in the child's world has been shown to be a protective factor in recovery, yet secrecy surrounding suicide is common in many families (Ratnarajah & Schofield, 2007; Ratnarajah et al., 2008; Simone, 2008). This takes form in families not grieving together at the time of death or not reminiscing about the deceased. Some children are not allowed to attend funerals to say good-bye or keep items belonging to the parent. The tendency to stop all talk and remove all material items pertaining to the parent who died by suicide is detrimental to children in the long run.

Silverman and Worden (1993) found the children in their study devoted considerable energy to connecting with the deceased in some way. They did this through dreams, by talking to the deceased, feeling the deceased parent was watching them, keeping the deceased parent's belongings, visiting the grave, and frequently thinking about the deceased. According to Requarth (2006), "Continuing to talk about the parent who has died, telling stories, looking at pictures, and giving children mementos to treasure, are essential to helping a child cope with loss" (p. 130).

Adults should encourage children to talk about the deceased and involve them in rituals surrounding the death to ensure the best possibility for recovery (Kaslow & Aronson, 2004). Simone (2008) agrees, indicating that "to deny children and young people the chance to talk and remember their dead parent is denying them the opportunity to heal within a loving and supportive network. Sharing memories also allows for the children to re-construct their relationship with their dead parent" (p. 46).

Our participants mentioned preserving memories of the deceased parent as a way to find comfort. They did this through talking with others, becoming the link to memories, and performing funeral and graveside rituals. Building remembrances of the deceased parent helped some participants by giving them something solid to hold onto.

Some participants preserved memories by reminiscing with others. Rachel believed that memories of her dad would have been lost had she not actively preserved them. She credited caring adults with helping her keep his memory alive. When she was young, counselors and teachers encouraged her to draw and write about things she remembered doing with her dad. As she got older, family members and friends of her father shared stories about his life and the circumstances surrounding his death. She felt that with each year, more and more people started coming forward to share things they remembered about her dad or ways that he was involved in her life that she would not remember.

> I'm thankful to have those memories now, and I think I've been able to really hold onto those memories because they're things I've talked about, and people have helped me remember. I think it probably would have been pretty easy to lose those memories if they had not been reinforced.

When searching out and preserving memories, survivors wanted to emphasize the good things about their parents. They did not want to dwell on the death and the dysfunction surrounding it, but on the good times and the well person. Guy reminisced about one Father's Day when he invited his mother over and they went for a walk in the park behind his house. He wanted to talk about his dad because he did not remember much about him except for the few years before his death.

> The last four years he was drinking and beating and, I was like, "Did he ever do anything good?" And then she was like, "Oh, yeah, half of his life he was a pretty good person." I've just had to straight up tell her, like, I want to hear the good. I finally forced her to remember some of the early years and how good they might have been.

Unfortunately, not all surviving parents were able to overcome the grief or animosity felt toward the parent who had died. Some children were not given the chance to remember the parent they had lost. Melissa desperately wanted to preserve memories of her dad, but did not have people who would discuss him with her. She still longed to know him.

> What I'd wish for would be impossible: to know more about my dad. That's the only thing I wished, and, you know, still wish. I've toyed with the idea of trying to create a blog and find some of the people he may have known.

Secrecy not only hurts survivors, but also erases the legacy of people's lives that were important, no matter how they died. Some spoke of how keeping the legacy alive for others was important for their own coping and that of others. Two mentioned wanting to be able to preserve memories for their younger siblings or their own children. Lisa, who lost both of her parents to suicide, illustrated how important she felt it was to pass on memories of her parents to other family members. She also felt the need to carry on the names of her parents as a tangible way to help her own children know their grandparents.

> To keep those memories alive so that I can pass it on, not only to my brother—but then I've got three kids—and my brother and his wife are trying to have kids. And I got two younger cousins, and there are people that I need to be able to tell if my mom comes up. I need to be able to share that with them. My son has my dad's middle name and my daughter has my mom's middle name. So they all have a piece of their grandparents to carry on with them. And they know that, and they've been told that over and over, and there are pictures everywhere, and the boys are always asking, "Tell me a story about Grandma or Grandpa," and I can sit down and talk to my kids about it, and not cry. I can tell them a good story, and they'll be able to remember that and take that with them.

Amber talked about the healing that came from recognizing that she was a vessel. She had shut down emotionally after her mother's suicide. At Camp HOPE, she discovered that she was the link to her mother's memory for her younger brother. That realization allowed her to open up for the first time and begin to cope with the loss.

> At the camp fire, one person starts burning their candle and telling who they lost. We go around, and I'm like, this is so lame. I said, "I lost my mom. Whatever." And all these people around me are just sobbing as they're telling their stories. I'm like, God, what's wrong with me? Something's wrong with me because I don't wanna cry. And it gets around to my brother and he's real calm, he's looking down at the candle, and he's like, "Well, my mom died eight years ago, but I don't remember anything." And at that, I was out of my seat. Then I was at his side, and we were both sobbing. That was our breakthrough. Now I can wake up

> and see that there is light at the end of the tunnel. It was all bottled up and just needed to explode.

Performing rituals is another way to honor and remember the deceased loved one. One participant identified the importance of this and how it helped her to cope with her dad's death.

> Every Father's Day we go to the cemetery, to his gravesite, and we bring a picnic. We get his favorite foods, and usually bring a photo album, and sometimes will listen to some of his favorite music. I think we've done it pretty much every year. It still, like, feels good to do it and to know we're not forgetting him or anything.

Helping Others

Helping others to heal themselves has been cited in the literature as an effective coping mechanism (Mitchell et al., 2003). Twenty-three percent of the individuals featured in this book found it beneficial to help or reach out to family members and others who had experienced suicide or other hardship. Participants were "strong" for their siblings, comforted friends who lost parents to any type of death, befriended people with disabilities, served as pen pals to children who lost parents to suicide, and spoke publically about their experiences. They found they could really help others by sharing their strength and their stories, and it was therapeutic for them as well.

Some survivors, particularly oldest siblings, focused on their sisters and brothers instead of themselves. Making it about a loved one helped them to have purpose and to heal: "*My focus became more on helping them get over it. Taking the focus off of me and putting it on them helped me in a way.*"

Having experienced a similar death, they knew how to approach others who lost someone to suicide, and found meaning in doing so. Suzanne explained her advantage.

> Don't approach them at the funeral when there are a million people around. Wait until almost everybody has left and, you know, help them out with the dishes from the church luncheon or whatever, and wait until the time is right, and then go to them.

Two participants "paid it forward" by serving as counselors for Camp HOPE. One described how her experience helped her reach a young girl who would not open up to anyone else.

> The last few times that I've been at camp, I've been put in with 8- or 9-year-olds, the age I was when my mom died. There was one girl—her mom had died, then her dad committed suicide—[she] was living with

> Grandma. She would not talk to Grandma or anybody about anything, and I just came and told her what I had been through, and she just started talking and just going and going, and she wouldn't stop till, like, two in the morning. Her grandmother actually sent me an e-mail and said, "My granddaughter talks! She's blossoming, and I couldn't thank you more."

Another participant related how her involvement in being a pen pal to a young girl was therapeutic for her as well.

> It made me feel amazing. I've never met her—just been pen-paling, e-mailing, and letters. And her dad said, "She's grown so much, and I owe that to you." And I think that a lot of it is bringing in people that are open to talking about what they have been through—similar experiences.

Our participants also coped by helping those who had not experienced suicide. Lisa consciously made the choice to assist a young girl with a disability in her class. She healed herself by giving to someone else.

> I did befriend a girl at school who had a life-threatening illness. I took care of her. She was in a wheelchair, and I would help her. I think that was my own way of kind of trying to move on.

Some participants eventually became comfortable telling their stories to wider audiences. Brooke self-destructed after being sexually abused by her father and experiencing his suicide. She started fighting with her mom, skipping school, and hanging out with a dangerous group of friends. She ended up going to prison at the age of 17 for being present when a murder was committed. Out of incarceration for barely two years at the time of the interview, Brooke said she was actually thankful for prison. She was angry and isolated as a youth and believes that she might not be alive today without time behind bars because prison helped her deal with feelings and learn about herself. Brooke now speaks to young people who are starting down the wrong road, even if it helps only one person. Telling her story has also been personally healing: "*I've told my story so much that it's therapeutic. I mean, telling it over and over again—in speaking at assemblies and stuff like that—each time I tell it, there's some kind of release to it.*"

Just as Brooke made it her mission to help troubled kids, Suzanne made it hers to educate the community. Having gone through similar experiences to those they were helping, survivors had credibility and special connections with their audiences.

> Who wants to be an expert in a topic like this? I didn't, but because it is such an emotionally charged topic, having the audience know that I also knew the pain of this is important. People who come to the program,

either they have lost someone years ago, they have a teenage son or daughter who's exhibiting warning signs, maybe even attempted. There is always a tie in for people, and at first I thought it was only for me. Why is it okay that I do all of this for my job, when it is obviously serving a personal purpose? I've come to that understanding. Everyone says, "You're perfect for the program." And that's really what the audience has said. I was going to do one program and end it, and here it is over 20 years later, and I still can't end it, you know?

Acknowledging the Relief

Families experiencing suicide have been found to be less stable before the death than families bereaved by other causes, experiencing more divorce or marital separation, mental health treatment, and other stressors (Cerel et al., 2000). Exposure to such stressors and the accompanying suicide threats has been linked to problematic responses in surviving children, particularly posttraumatic stress and anxiety symptoms (Cerel et al., 2000; Grossman et al., 1995; Pfeffer et al., 1997). Though the potential for such outcomes exists, Cerel et al. (2000) found that suicide-bereaved children experienced fewer psychosocial stressors than did their nonsuicide-bereaved counterparts in the month after death. This suggests an initial period of relief following suicide. In fact, one study found that there was relief for some survivors knowing that the threat of suicide was no longer present, that their parent was at peace, and that family dynamics had been made better with the greatest source of stress removed (Clark & Goldney, 1995). For some families, the challenge of losing a parent to suicide is tempered with the removal of a volatile individual.

Being able to acknowledge a sense of relief, without guilt, may be important for healing. Some of our participants found comfort in the sense of relief they felt not having to deal with the challenges of the deceased parent anymore (e.g., mental illness, abuse, alcohol use, violence). They felt released from family conflict and parental illness and found peace knowing a parent's suffering had ended. These realizations helped them cope with the loss. Guy talked about the solace that came after his father's death.

I was free. He'd shoot guns in the house and all sorts of crazy things. I think he was drinking about a regular bottle of brandy by himself a day. So, it was a pretty tough situation. It was getting to the point where he was gonna kill somebody. My mom was about to grab all us kids and go to a homeless shelter. We were gonna have to leave him anyway. He had let that disease progress for 20 years without doing anything about it.

Another participant shared how his father's volatile behavior and subsequent suicide resulted in feelings of relief, as well as guilt due to the relief.

> He abused my mother and my big brother. He almost killed my brother once but usually the cops came quick enough to get him off him. My father was gonna go to jail for assault or something. If anything, I felt guilty about feeling that way.

For some, the relief was felt above all else. Jenna was 11 when her father died. Her parents were separated at the time of his death, and at the age of 20 she discussed how the relief clouded everything else.

> I also understood that he was the source of why we weren't together, the source of why Mom was upset. I was much closer to my mom. I was much closer to my sisters than I ever was to my dad, so it was almost relief in a way because I didn't understand the long term effects of it, like: Nothing bad is going to happen. We are going to move back home. And I didn't think about financial issues. I didn't think about none of that.

Some families were thankful that their loved one was no longer suffering. Cassandra was 13 when she found her father's body. She noted that her family felt like he had chosen to take his own life to spare the rest of them: "*We all had the assumption of, he did it for us, because he didn't want us to have to deal with him being so sick.*" Another participant acknowledged that her father's life was not good, and maybe he was better off. "*I'm relieved, that if he wasn't happy, you know, if he had to go, he had to go and if he's happier.*"

Spirituality

Religious and spiritual beliefs can provide meaning and purpose in times of crisis (Beavers & Hampson, 1990), and people tend to turn to their faith communities for support when they experience loss. People generally want to believe that there is something more after death and that a higher power is ultimately in control. Spirituality can provide a sense of meaning, inner wholeness, and connection with others (Greeff & Human, 2004). It serves as a fundamental form of resilience in that it helps the individual understand and overcome stressful situations (Angell, Dennis, & Dumain, 1998). Religious and spiritual beliefs and activities have been reported as facilitating successful adjustment to the death of a parent in general (Greeff & Human, 2004). In examining the role of religion and spiritual beliefs in the grieving process in general, Frantz, Trolley, and Johll (1996) found that 77% of participants in their study reported their religious and spiritual beliefs were significantly related to positive coping and future outlook, and were of considerable help in their grief. The relationship between coping through religion and a reduction in distress has been identified in other research examining bereavement in general (Park & Cohen, 1993; Sherkat & Reed, 1992).

Literature specific to religious and spiritual beliefs and parental suicide bereavement is sparse, and our participants reported spirituality as a coping strategy to a minimal extent. Perhaps people are more reluctant to openly discuss spirituality than other topics. For Amber, though, reaching out to her pastor was one of the first things she thought of after calling 911 following her mother's death. "*and then I call my pastor and say, 'You have to start praying.'*"

Some families joined together spiritually and prayed together. Suzanne's large family was religious and turned to God to cope with their father's death: "*We got strength from praying. We prayed every night for my dad—the rosary. We were Catholic.*"

For some, spirituality was evidenced by a specific event. Charlotte came to believe that her dad was watching over her and attributed his presence to the reason she survived a really horrible car accident.

> The really ironic thing is, I got into a car accident, rolled my car like three times. Should've died. It was Good Friday, which was my dad's birthday that year. So, like, do I think he's out there watching me? Yeah. And protecting me? Yeah, he's out there. I don't really believe in that kind of stuff, but I think a little bit, in a way, I do, because of the car accident.

Others were comforted by the belief that their loved one was in a better place. Melissa shared her view of life after death.

> I'm not really that religious, but basically my stance on that is, if there is an afterlife, if there is a heaven and hell, I don't think he would be something of their concern, all the people he saved in Vietnam, and just how much of a nice person he was.

CASE STUDY

Rachel's Story

Reevaluating

I want to reevaluate it and rethink what it means to me and my life. I have not thought about my dad's suicide beyond that of a 7-year-old. At 7 I knew what happened and how it happened, and I was okay with that, as I understood it at the time. I just think that now I need to understand it in a way that fits a 20-year-old.

I feel like a lot of what I remember of my dad has been formed by what others have told me. I was only 7 years old when he died, and it is hard to decipher what I actually remember. I'm sure I remember being close to him and spending time together, and I have been able to hold on to those memories by writing and talking about them over the years. Many people in my life encouraged me by asking questions, talking about him, and providing projects that helped keep his memory alive in me.

I remember feeding seagulls with my dad when we were on vacation in Florida, riding on his shoulders, and swimming in the pool. He enjoyed golfing, and I took golf lessons and played miniature golf with him. We even had a little putting green that we rolled out, and when we made a shot with our little putters, my dad would give us candy. I remember biking around the arboretum with him, and when the weather was nice, we always stopped at the ice cream store on the way. Those are the memories I have of him, and they are all good.

I know that my dad had bouts of depression throughout his whole life. The day he died, my mom had gone to the grocery store shopping, and when she returned home she found him in the basement. All I know is that it was with a rope, but I don't know if that means he hung himself or not. What I have always thought is that he just tied it so tight that. As a 7-year-old, I never really thought it through. He left a note, but I don't know what it said or if we still have it. I think it just said that he loved us. My mom always explained that he felt like he was not a good dad. I've learned that depression is an illness, and because of the illness his reality was distorted. I have good memories of him and do not think of him as a bad father. He was a successful lawyer, and there were many good things about him. I now realize that he felt one way, while reality was another. It was the sickness.

I believe that people have memories of things, kind of like snapshots of traumatic events. I have those memories, but I am sure the main reason I do is just because I have talked about them and written about them. I think that is a good thing, even if the memories got there because of stories that people told me. However the memories got there, I am thankful to have them.

My first memory of that day is of seeing my grandparents, who had walked to school to pick me up. I was in second grade at a neighborhood elementary school and thought it was strange that my mom wasn't the one picking me up from school. My siblings are both younger than me and were not old enough yet for school, and they were along as well. I just remember my sister saying, "Dad's dead." I did not believe her and wondered why she would even say something like that. We just kept walking, and walked home. That is the memory I have of that day, and then it just kind of ends. I have no idea what happened after I arrived at home.

The next real memory I have is of the funeral. Again, it is just like a chunk of memory, and then nothing on either end. I can picture the church and kind of picture his casket up there and remember wanting to put a drawing I had made in the casket with him. The drawing was of a bunny and some grass and a tree. I do not know why, but it is just the memory I have. Something that I do not remember of that day, but my mom told me, was that my teacher sat with me for some of that day. My mom really appreciates that to this day, and that teacher has always been one of my favorites. One final memory that I have of that day is of my mom's friend who always has a smile on her face, and it is the prettiest smile I have ever seen. I remember looking at her, and she was crying, but she still had that smile because that is just who she is.

My mom had us seeing a psychiatrist soon after my dad died. I am not sure for how long, and I know there were individual and family sessions, but I just can't remember. It is so funny how much I cannot remember. I do remember a specific issue I had at the time. I was really afraid to be alone in any sort of room, even if I was downstairs and my mom was just upstairs. One time my mom was in the bathroom, and I felt so panicked and needed to see her or hear her. I just remember screaming and pounding on the door and yelling, "Mom!" I was afraid that if it happened to my dad, it could happen to her too. Later, my mom told us that sometimes she would lock herself in the bathroom just to have 5 minutes of peace. With three kids in the house, that is probably what she was doing at the time. I am not sure why, but that memory sticks out for me.

Being in a room alone was just too scary, and I remember the psychiatrist worked with me on that. I had to pick a room that I was afraid to be alone in, and I chose my mom's room. I think I probably was more scared of the basement where my dad had died, but I did not even want to tell her that because then she might make me go down there. So I said it was my mom's room. She made a deal with me. If I stayed in that room by myself for 15 minutes, I would get a piece of candy. It was not like a time out or any sort of bad thing. I would sit in there and watch TV, and if I could do it, I would get the reward I had chosen, which was always candy. I can't remember how long it took, but I did get to the point where I could be in a room alone.

The psychiatrist is the one who recommended doing projects and talking about things I liked to do with my dad. She encouraged memories. One time we cut paper into pentagon shapes and put them all together to make a globe. Each pentagon-shaped piece of paper had a picture and a word on it pertaining to my dad. The things I wrote on there are the things that I still remember doing with him. At the time, I probably did not really realize why we were going to see this woman or if she would help, but I am sure it gave my mom peace of mind knowing that we were getting some sort of help. It would have been pretty easy to lose those memories, and it was probably therapeutic to think good things about him. Even now, I am really thankful to have those memories and to be able to say something when people ask me what I remember about him.

There is kind of a gap in information from the time that I was 7 until I was about 16, when people started coming out with more things about my dad. They would tell me how they remembered him and would share things they had done together. I really appreciated that. It was nice to hear about the ways he was involved in my life and other things. Maybe I would not remember them otherwise. It is just amazing to think that if people did not tell me these things, there is no way I ever would have known.

Sometimes people will ask how my dad died. It would just be so much easier if I could say "cancer." When you say "suicide," you see this "Oh, my gosh" look on their faces. I am sure they are wondering things like, "How?" But they probably won't ask. I guess I just have to be okay with the situation, and I think I am. It is not like I feel the need to tell every single person my whole life story or anything, but when they do ask point-blank, there are a couple of different answers that I give. When they ask how he died, I will say that he had depression, and sometimes I leave it at that. I let them think what they want to think. Sometimes, I will say that he died of suicide. I would never phrase it like, "He killed himself," because that is kind of disrespectful to me and has a negative connotation. I view depression as an illness. Cancer is an illness, and a heart attack is an illness. Depression was his illness and *it* is what killed him. Usually, people stop asking at that point or they give the typical, "I'm sorry." It is not a big deal when people ask. They don't have to feel bad for asking or feel like I am going to break down. I can go through daily life and mention it without distress. I do not want people to feel like they have to tiptoe around that subject with me.

Although the small things in life remind me of my dad, important events are when I miss him the most. At prom, when all the parents were taking pictures, it was just my mom. At my high school graduation, a couple of people from the family told me that my dad should have been there and that it would have been a proud day for him, and so my graduation was a really hard day for my mom and for me. At these times, I was just sad that I could not show off to him or have him be proud of me. I was sad that he chose, essentially, to not be there. So, maybe there is a little bit of anger there too. Most of all, I was sad that he was missing out on my life. I guess I am sad more because he missed out on it than I am sad that he could not be there for me.

Despite going through such an awful thing, my mom was able to move on with her life. About seven years after my dad died, she got remarried. It was hard for me, being the oldest. The psychiatrist once told me that no one is ever going to replace your dad and no one should ever try to. My brother was only 2 when my dad died, and he has no problem calling our stepdad "Dad." I would never ever call him "Dad," and it bugs me when people refer to him as my "dad." I just want to scream, "He's not my dad!"

There usually comes a time in a new friendship when my story comes out. I always feel good after that point. I think just that they know, just that it is out there and there is not any secret, is a relief. Once I share my story, I feel like people know the real me. The real me has been affected by suicide, and those effects continue. I think it makes me more alert to things I see on television about suicide or when I hear of other people dying of suicide. It also makes me more aware of depression. I do not like when people talk about suicide in a careless way. Some people say they will themselves if—fill in the blank—does or does not happen, like it is a joke or something. To me, it just has a completely different meaning. There is a whole lot attached to that phrase, and it is not something you say without thinking about the impact of your words.

I like to think that I am more sensitive to loss and depression in general. Even though the death was so long ago, it still influences my life. I cannot believe it has been 14 years since my dad died. I am just getting to a point where I have started reevaluating the death and its impact on me. I want to stop thinking about it like a 7-year-old. As hard as it is to talk about, I think it is good. I recently set up an appointment with the psychiatrist that I saw after my dad died. There have been some changes that have gone on in my life recently and I feel things kind of resurfacing from the suicide. I want to reevaluate it and rethink what it means to me and my life. I have not thought about my dad's suicide beyond that of a 7-year-old. At 7, I knew what happened, and how it happened, and I was okay with that as I understood it at the time. I just think that now I need to understand it in a way that fits a 20-year-old.

Ending a long-term relationship has also caused me to reevaluate myself, and I'm curious to know the effects on a girl growing up without a father when suicide is the cause. Is it abandonment? Do I hang on to relationships because of what I have been through? Do I hang out with guys more than girls because I did not have a father figure in my life? I just wonder how not having this male figure in my life has shaped me. What am I because of this thing that happened to me versus what would I be without it?

CASE STUDY

Melissa's Story

A Journey of Self-Discovery

It took me the longest time to remember, and when I finally did, it felt as though every organ in my chest cavity had fallen out, like the feeling of being on a rollercoaster, but one hundred times worse. It was this sort of indescribable feeling of despair and loss that took my breath away.

My father's suicide impacted my whole life. I was only 14 when I found him in the shed after school that day, and it has taken years for me to clear my head of the chaos. I remember feeling nothing because I had slipped into complete shock. Thoughts of my father just continuously ran through my head. I couldn't think of anything else, even if I tried. It was only a matter of time before I figured out that I would have to start distracting myself from the memories if I wanted to get anywhere with my life.

My father had just lost his job, and I believe he felt that everything was going wrong in his life. He always had this 1950s idea in his head that the father should be the provider for the family, and the thought of not being able to provide for his family eventually led him to take his own life. He had even been talking to my mother about a divorce because he felt so terrible about not being able to take care of our family. Of course my mother thought that was completely irrational, but to someone who was depressed and believed everything in his life was going wrong, there was nothing she could have said that would have changed his thoughts and feelings. He also had a lot of leftover feelings from Vietnam that added to his depression, and his own father had been abusive towards him in childhood. There were things my father never shared with me that he carried around with him. Overall, his depression lasted a few months, and during that time he was in and out of a mental institution, receiving treatment. Predictably, the autopsy report explained that without anyone's knowledge, he had been off his depression medications on the day of his death.

I slept at a friend's house the night after I found my father, and when I woke up the next morning I had this terrible feeling that something had gone wrong but I couldn't figure out what it was. It took me the longest time to remember, and when I finally did, it felt as though every organ in my chest cavity had fallen out, like the feeling of being on a rollercoaster but one hundred times worse. It was this sort of indescribable feeling of despair and loss that took my breath away. I felt like things would never be the same.

The loss of my father was particularly hard on my mother. She felt that my dad was the only one for her, and she loved him very much. It didn't help that my grandmother, my father's mother, blamed her for the death. Since my mom was going through so much stress, I felt the need to help in any way that I could. My mom was in complete shock, so I helped her pick the flowers for the funeral, write the obituary, and even pick out a good coffin. Mentally, she was so exhausted that she couldn't even tell the difference between the practically cardboard coffin and the others. My mind, on the other hand, couldn't stop rethinking the whole situation.

School didn't help the situation at all. It seemed like everyone knew about my father's death, and that meant multiple rumors and gossip continuously circulated throughout school. I felt like people were staring at me all the time, but thankfully no one actually came up to me and said anything. I tried to distract myself and keep busy so that I wouldn't think about it. It was so hard because my mind sort of naturally just stopped thinking. I just wasn't really able to have a decent or deep thought for a long time after my father's death. I often felt as though I had no one to talk to. The community where we lived was religious and fairly conservative, so suicide was looked down upon, and many people pegged my father and our family as bad people.

At the same time, my memory was more or less the same, if not slightly better, because I wasn't really thinking about anything else but the suicide. I even had issues about going home for several years following the suicide, because every time I went home I would have the reenactment and same terrible feelings I felt when I came home that original day. I struggled with grades and homework as well when I came back to school, but really nothing out of the ordinary. My dad had always stood over my shoulder while I did homework and continuously asked me if I was done yet. It used to drive me nuts. I hate to say it, but my grades sort of improved because he wasn't there. He was so overbearing and such a helicopter parent when it came to school. My mother even mentioned that she believes I benefitted from the independence that I gained after my father's death, unlike my brother, who needed the exact opposite and would have benefitted greatly from someone like my father always being there for him.

Since my mother struggled with depression too and knew that my father's father may have died from suicide, she believed that my brother and I needed help from a professional counselor. She sent us to the hospital for help and tried a few different counselors before finding one that worked for us. Our counselor was someone who I enjoyed seeing and seemed to really connect to me rather than being one of those therapists who listens to your problems for an hour and gives generic advice before sending you on your merry way. Counseling was really important for my brother as well. Before my father's death, I was the problem child, who always lashed out, but after his death my brother and I sort of switched roles. He spiraled into this constant state of anger and frustration, which he took out on my mother and me, whereas I tried to look back in family history to figure out why my dad did what he did and what his thought process was, rather than choosing to use my time and energy on lashing out at people.

I quickly became very interested in my father's life and in understanding why he did what he did, whether it was hearing stories from my mother or trying to dig them up on my own. I wanted to know everything I could about him, and I found out some information that I think was very important for me to know. For instance, when my dad was young, his father, who had grown up on in orphanage and was abused himself, began abusing my father. This sort of messed-up style of parenting that I had been angry with my dad for before his death had actually been something that had been passed on from parent to parent. It was something that he had learned rather than something he had created himself. Knowing that was something that helped me cut my father slack for the way he treated me before his death. Trying to understand why it was that my father did this and what factors besides losing his job contributed to him doing this was a big part of my healing process. It is hard enough just growing up and being an average teenager, but I felt as though I had an even harder time trying to find myself after something like that happened. It was a difficult journey of self-discovery, if you will.

My first year in college was a challenge. I struggled to figure it all out without a parent over my shoulder, and I put things off to the last minute. I did fill out forms explaining to the school my situation so that they had a general idea of what was going on in my life, which to me was a bit discouraging, with my father's death still following me around. I also struggled with making friends. I wasn't really into the party scene, and that was what most students my age were doing in their free time. It was also really hard to see other students doing stuff with their parents on parent weekends or to have someone ask me what my parents do for a living and to have to try and explain the situation to them. But as time went on it got a bit easier, and I am still going to school and can't wait to graduate. As many times as I have wanted to just walk away or to even take my anger out on someone, I am so glad that I have kept it together and stayed in school.

Nowadays, I still have times when I wake up in the middle of the night with my heart racing, with no clue why and thinking something horrible has just happened. Then I have to battle those irrational thoughts and tell myself that it is just adrenaline, pure adrenaline, not that something just happened. I tell myself that adrenaline is just a chemical and is something that I can control if I just calm myself down. I currently sleep better through the nights, and by eliminating panic attacks and paranoid thoughts, I am trying not to be the person my dad was.

My boyfriend really calms me. He has helped me heal and has been a positive person to turn to when I need someone to talk to. I have noticed that he is my substitute for counseling. He has never been through anything like I have, but he is able to sit back and try to put himself in my shoes. With his help, every day gets better.

CASE STUDY

Zach's Story

My Life-Defining Moment

My dad's death did not have to define my life. It would affect it, but I had a choice. I could decide how much.

Everyone has life-defining moments, and these experiences influence and alter a person's future. My moment arrived on one specific year and day in October. He left us—my mom, sister, brother, and me—five days before my eighth birthday. Even though I was only 7 years old at the time, I remember the day very well. I woke up to the sounds of my mom crying in the living room. There were two policemen standing there who would not let me or my brother or sister go into the room. They kept us away by telling us to go and watch television. About thirty minutes later, my grandma picked us up for a soccer game we had that day. My siblings are both younger, and I knew, we all knew, something was wrong. We just did not know exactly what it was, and so we played our soccer game.

I remember being so excited and specifically wanting to tell my dad that we had won the soccer game. I came into the house yelling, "Where's Dad? Dad?" But I never did get to tell him. Through our large windows facing the lake, I could see my whole family was gathering—grandmas, grandpas, aunts, and uncles—everyone from both sides of our family. My siblings and I went outside, and they told us what had happened. I started crying, but did not really believe them at first. Then everything kind of slowed down. I felt like I could see everything going on around me in slow motion. I saw everyone, including my mom, who was sitting down near the swing, on the ground, while people held her.

My dad had taken his own life.

I would say that my feelings initially, like right after I was told, were indefinable. I felt so many things at once—sadness, anger, disbelief, and guilt—that I wasn't really sure what I felt. All I know for sure is that I was crying. I felt really sad. I guess I also felt bad. I did not feel like I had spent enough time with my dad recently. He always wanted to do things after school with me, but I always wanted to do something with my friends or just watch television and relax. I didn't know he was sad. I thought everything was okay. I did not really blame myself at the time, but I wondered if I might have been able to spend more time with him. I felt a little guilty, like maybe I could have changed something, and I felt like he wasn't happy with our family.

I don't think my brother understood right away what was happening; it took him awhile. A couple of hours later, after I had stopped crying, I saw my uncle talking to him. Then he started to cry. The next day, I slept until about 3 o'clock in the afternoon. I remember I missed a couple of days of school. There were so many people at my dad's funeral that I was curious and wondered who all of these people were who had come to pay their respects. I recognized my relatives, but many were entirely new faces.

After that, I was nervous about going back to school, not sure how my classmates would react or treat me. Would they be kind? Would they not understand, and distance themselves from me? I wondered if they would think I was different or wouldn't know what to say to me, so wouldn't say anything at all. However, when I got back, the nervousness quickly passed, because my friends and teachers were all supportive. Everyone was sad for me. My classmates, although not really knowing what to do, made cards and were as supportive as they could be. One time, on the playground, I just sat down and started to cry. When my friends saw me, they tried to talk to me, and eventually got a teacher who took me inside. The teachers were very understanding. They all told me to just let them know if I needed to leave the classroom and go out into the hallway for a while. The initial support from my teachers and friends was very helpful in my recovery.

We started counseling soon after that, more individual than group, but we did do some family counseling as well. My brother and sister still see a counselor, not for the suicide specifically but for aftereffects like anxiety and depression. Depression runs in both sides of our family. I never really liked or got into the counseling thing, and I quit at least three years ago. I continued to take some medication, so was required to see a psychiatrist for monitoring, but stopped that medication the summer after my sophomore year in high school. I continued counseling for a couple more months after that until they decided that I did not need it anymore. I am very glad to be off the medication.

Both sides of my family have been a support to me and my siblings over the years. My dad's family has probably been more so, just because they are closer in proximity. They took us fishing, biking, and camping. In fact, we did a lot of camping. I am still close to my uncles, and just went to the movies with one of them the other night.

The suicide happened in elementary school, and in middle school I was with the same classmates. In high school, we combined with another city, and not everyone knew each other. So, nobody really knew whose parents were alive or divorced or anything. So, it wasn't like I was made fun of for having only one parent. However, I was not able to get as much help or support with school and other things, because people didn't know, and also because my mom had to take care of the other two children. Obviously our family helped, but you can't really replace a dad and family cannot be there 24 hours a day, 7 days a week. So, I always thought that I didn't get as much help as other kids. I had to figure out a lot of things for myself. Recently, in a scholarship essay, I actually wrote about how my dad's death positively influenced my life. It added to my independence, because I just had to figure out things on my own.

Some of my friends and I were talking about something recently. I was much more confident when I was younger, and we wondered why that would have changed. At age 7, I was very outgoing, but after my dad's death that all changed. I am a lot more shy and reserved now. I think the shyness is a result of my dad's death. My friends agree. I used to do plays and theater and sang a lot. Now, I hate singing in front of people and I cannot act unless I am in a group of people acting. I guess I didn't really have that father-son relationship where he taught me things. I do not know a lot of things that other guys do about cars or fixing stuff. We have a bunch of tools in the basement, and I don't know any of that. I feel like I kind of missed out a little bit on that stuff, and it affected my confidence. My uncles have been a support, but they can only do so much. My friends have been a great support in that they are pushing me to overcome my shyness. It is working, and I am getting more confident every day.

I will talk openly about my dad's suicide if it is brought up. If someone asks me about my dad, I will talk about it, but I never bring it up in conversation. Most of my friends definitely do not know.

My dad was bipolar. He was a family practitioner and found it difficult to accept that he had this disorder, and even more difficult to accept help from others. He thought he could handle his depression himself. He was taking lithium for a while, but knew the side effects and did not like them, so he stopped taking it. That is what led to him killing himself. He took his own life by severing the femoral artery. He did this at night in his bathroom, and my mom found him the next morning.

While this defining moment in my life was painful, it affected me positively in two ways. First, it forced me to rapidly develop my independence, and through this a strong commitment. I learned to persevere and find a way to accomplish my goals. If at first I failed at something, I developed a new method or approach to accomplish the task at hand. I believe in constantly expanding my horizons, and besides excelling in academics, I have participated in sports, theater, volunteer work, and leadership roles. It is my hope that these commitments, talents, and experiences will serve me well through college and medical school.

Choosing to follow a similar path to my father's and entering the medical community is the second positive effect from such a painful moment in life. As a young child, I was awed by the number of people who came to my dad's funeral. I later learned that many of them were colleagues and patients. A feeling of pride rushed over me upon hearing this. My dad was able to help others with their problems, and, in doing so, developed many long-lasting relationships and touched the lives of so many people. He was well respected for his service to the community, and that made me proud. It also sparked a drive in me to become someone with the ability to positively impact the lives of others and improve the quality of my community. I chose the medical field to greatly improve the value of my life by aiding others and improving theirs.

When you are a child, no matter how a parent dies, you are losing someone who should not be lost that early. If it is cancer or a car accident, it is harder to find blame. With a suicide, there is a sense of guilt. After time, you realize that you cannot blame yourself. You just have to keep going. One life has ended, but it cannot end yours. What is most important is for those around you in daily life to be supportive and understand. Family is, of course, going to be supportive, but teachers and friends are not a certainty. What I believe worked out best was that they treated me like a normal kid when I was feeling good. When I was not doing well, they were understanding and gave me the time and space to heal. This helped me realize that my dad's death did not have to define my life. It would affect it, but I had a choice. I could decide how much.

CASE STUDY

Jenna's Story

Relief

Even after I realized my mom had just learned of my dad's suicide, I was still rather confused about why she was so upset. We hadn't seen my dad in months, and even I didn't really know how to feel or react. His death angered me, but at the same time I felt relief.

My father was a truck driver, and like any other truck driver, he was on the road a lot. This meant his time spent at home was little. While he was gone, Mom was responsible for taking care of our family, which at the time included one older sister, three older brothers, four younger sisters, and one more sister on the way. My mom took pride in raising our family. Her full-time job was raising her kids and homeschooling each one of us. We spent a lot of time together, so you can imagine our relationship with our mom formed a strong bond.

Life at our house was pleasant except for those times, usually on a Friday or Saturday night, when Dad came home. He wouldn't stay for long, one or two days at the most, but every time he was home I felt like I had to walk on pins and needles. Dad was a very abusive man. I never really understood why he had such a short temper, but over time I got good at working the system to stay out of the way of his temper. The abuse happened to all of us, including my mom, but, unlike some of my siblings, I learned to avoid my father most of the time. How we acted upon his demands really determined whether we triggered his abuse. So if he asked me to do something, I did it.

As time passed, friends and neighbors and some people from our church began to notice my father's aggressive behavior. My mother was also told that he had been abusing alcohol and drugs while on the job. In the blink of an eye, my family was separated. Most of us were placed with separate families, but I was fortunate enough to be left with my mom and one of my older sisters. The only time that I could see my brothers and sisters was once a week at church on Sunday afternoon. Life was pretty unstable at this point in our lives.

One day while we were still separated, my youngest brother had to cancel his plans to hang out with my dad because he was called in to work. While he was gone, my dad had left a message on the answering machine. His message told us how much he loved us and that he sincerely apologized for the way things were going. We were the ones my father called that day. His family had moved away, his job was stressful, and he was struggling with his drug and alcohol addiction. Dad must have felt overwhelmed. Unfortunately these issues have no easy answers, and his solution was to take his own life.

I remember that day vividly. When my mom was told, I was sitting at the table playing with some rubber stamps, and I remember hearing her cry in the background. Her cry was something I was accustomed to, but this time it was unexpected, considering she had so much going on in her life at the time. To be quite honest, even after I realized she had just learned of my dad's suicide, I was still rather confused about why she was so upset. We hadn't seen my dad in months, and even I didn't really know how to feel or react. His death angered me, but at the same time, I felt relief.

After my father's death, I began to feel as though I was the person in the family that held things together. Even though I went to some counseling, it really never helped my recovery. Instead, I found strength in helping my family. There were times that I felt like I was the only person in the family who held things together. Our family needed my help. One sister was bipolar and also suffered from ADHD. My mom and another sister were dealing with depression. A brother had knocked up his girlfriend, and, on top of it all, my sisters had now suddenly forgotten who our father really was! They talked about how great a person Dad was and spoke again and again of the few but fortunate encounters they had with him. I, unfortunately, was the one who had to bring the truth back to life, and I continually reminded them that Dad was not a perfect person and did not put the time or effort into having a good relationship with his children.

I was not really going through any difficult issues like the rest of my family, so Mom was either preoccupied or she seemed to think that I was doing just fine. The truth was I felt alone and angry. I began to look for support elsewhere, and I found it through babysitting. Babysitting gave me a stable environment, and some of the families I work for had either gone through divorce or had marital issues. Knowing that they were able to recover gave me the understanding that I needed to and could recover too.

five
Posttraumatic Growth

The notion that suffering can be transformative is not new. It is thousands of years old and reflected in the ideas and writings of the ancient Hebrews, Greeks, and early Christians as well as in Hindu, Buddhist, and Islamic belief systems (Tedeschi & Calhoun, 1995; Tedeschi, Park, & Calhoun, 1998). Friedrich Nietzsche, a late-1800s philosopher and writer, famously stated "*to live is to suffer; to survive is to find some meaning in the suffering*" and "*that which does not kill us makes us stronger.*" Though mental health professionals have tended to focus on the negative consequences of stress and trauma, this way of thinking has been more recently applied in the counseling world and has significance for working with individuals impacted by parental suicide.

The term posttraumatic growth (PTG) has been used in reference to the heightened levels of personal development or positive change that can occur alongside the distress resulting from trauma or a challenging life crisis (Linley & Joseph, 2004; Tedeschi & Calhoun, 2004). PTG refers to the capacity to move beyond pretrauma levels of adaptation and functioning, instead of just being damaged by a highly stressful circumstance (Tedeschi & Calhoun, 2004). PTG can manifest in a number of ways, including an increased appreciation for life, a sense of new life possibilities, more meaningful interpersonal relationships, an increased sense of personal strength, altered priorities, and a richer existential and spiritual self (Tedeschi & Calhoun, 2004; Tedeschi et al., 1998). A model of PTG has been proposed, highlighting individual and contextual factors that are significant to its development (Tedeschi & Calhoun, 2004). They include individual characteristics, styles of managing distressing emotions, self-disclosure about emotions and how others respond to the self-disclosure, perspective on the crisis, social support, and cognitive processing.

Most research on PTG and related concepts has focused on survivors of illness, disability, combat, rape, accidents, disaster, and the Holocaust (e.g., Chodoff, Friedman, & Hamburg, 1964; Frankl, 1963; Tedeschi & Calhoun, 1995, 2004; Tedeschi et al., 1998). Studies exploring responses following a variety of traumatic events have suggested that most individuals involved report some degree of positive outcomes, including changes in self-perceptions, social relationships, and life perspective (Stewart, Sokol, Healy, & Chester, 1986; Taylor, 1983; Wallerstein, 1986; Yarom, 1983). Both during the immediate aftermath of traumas and over the course of long-term stressors, positive emotions appear to be as prevalent as negative ones (Park & Folkman, 1997; Silver, Boon, & Stones, 1983; Wortman & Silver, 1989). Across all studies that have examined perceived benefits resulting from severely stressful life events, three important and consistent domains of change have surfaced: (a) self-concept, (b) relationships with social networks, and (c) personal growth and life priorities (Taylor, 1983). Positive changes in self-concept include the belief that one is a stronger person for the experience and is better able to handle the blows that life will inevitably deal. Overall, research suggests that stressful life events can have long-term positive effects and can help people to understand more about themselves, their social network, their priorities, and their lives in general (Updegraff & Taylor, 2000).

A small body of research has highlighted bereavement as a trigger to PTG or meaning reconstruction (Coleman & Neimeyer, 2010; Keesee, Currier, & Neimeyer, 2008; Kessler, 1987; Neimeyer, 2011; Schaefer & Moos, 2001). For example, participants in a study examining positive outcomes for bereaved adults described increased maturity and independence, enhanced capacity to face other life crises, and positive changes in their social support systems (Calhoun & Tedeschi, 1990). Over two thirds of the participants described themselves as stronger and more competent people, and more than 80% felt that they were wiser, stronger, more mature, and better able to cope with other crises. The most common benefit that survivors cited was the realization that other people were available to help and rely upon. In another study focusing on positive implications for bereaved adults, 84% of participants stated that positive things had occurred as a result of the death, such as bringing family closer together, learning to appreciate life more, and feeling stronger and more capable than previously thought (Frantz, Trolley, & Farrell, 1998). Illustrating more attention to the personal growth and transformative aspects of bereavement, Schaefer and Moos (2001) provide a theoretical framework designed to understand how personal, developmental, and environmental factors may foster this potential. They discuss the possibility of increased self-understanding, maturity, coping skills, and the ability to self-regulate as potential life-enriching consequences. Frantz, Farrell, and Trolley (2001) present an overview of previous research on the positive outcomes of bereavement and share the results of their study of nearly 400 adults who had lost a loved one approximately one year before. Positive aspects detailed include social bonds, spirituality, lifestyle, and emotion.

Little has been written regarding growth related to suicide bereavement. One explanation for the lack of attention is that growth after suicide may be more difficult to acknowledge than growth after other traumas that have different social implications (Smith, Joseph, & Das Nair, 2011). One study of parents who experienced the suicide of a child suggests that personal growth represents an important part of the healing process (Feigelman, Jordan, & Gorman, 2009). Another study of suicide bereavement reveals "purposefulness," the determination to find meaning in life after a loss, as a master theme (Begley & Quayle, 2007). A third study specifically aiming to explore experiences of PTG in adults bereaved by suicide suggests positive growth can be applied to suicide bereavement in terms of life view (e.g., greater awareness of certain aspects of life, place in the world, mortality), knowledge of self (e.g., greater awareness of who they are, psychological capabilities, coping strategies), and relation to others (e.g., increased awareness of others' feelings, not upsetting others, not making assumptions about others, wanting to meaningfully contribute to others' lives) (Smith et al., 2011). This study further elucidates how social context has implications for growth experiences and seems to be a distinctive feature of bereavement by suicide (Smith et al., 2011). It suggests that factors like how people perceive being viewed by others, the ability to portray a public guise or presence to give the impression of being "functional" or "over it," the ability to find relief in the attention of others, and the ability to drop the public guise when with other survivors are significant to growth.

Though suicide bereavement may parallel bereavement from other causes in many ways, even with respect to PTG, some authors suggest thematic differences in posttraumatic growth narratives, and the significant roles of rumination and cognitive reconstruction processes in posttraumatic growth (Sands, Jordan, & Neimeyer, 2011; Taku, Cann, Calhoun, & Tedeschi, 2008). In discussing narratives, Sands et al. (2011) suggests the following. *Redemptive narratives* transform the death, validating the suffering of the deceased but not the action of suicide and separating the deceased from the trauma of death. *Narratives of containment* function to control and contain a range of fearful and toxic elements associated with the death to assist in the reconstruction of order and safety. *Narratives of forgiveness* allow the bereaved person to talk about forgiving both themselves and the deceased. *Narratives of reconnection* foster the need to reconstruct an ongoing connection with the deceased and repair connections damaged by issues of blame, guilt, and stigma within the bereaved family.

Some survivors of parental suicide are able to generate a new purpose in life, derived from pain that motivates them to make continual positive changes (Clark & Goldney, 1995). They may identify value changes as a result of the death, no longer placing importance on trivial issues and being more sensitive to the needs of others (Clark & Goldney, 1995). Many parental suicide survivors, with time and support, become aware of how precious life is and develop increased compassion, which leads to seeking meaningful work and living life to its fullest (Requarth, 2006). They carry newfound understandings into their families, work, and social life. Some are able to help others as a result of their experience, which creates meaning in itself.

Our survivors were remarkably resilient, not only describing challenges but also identifying positives that came from their difficult experiences. The impact of loss

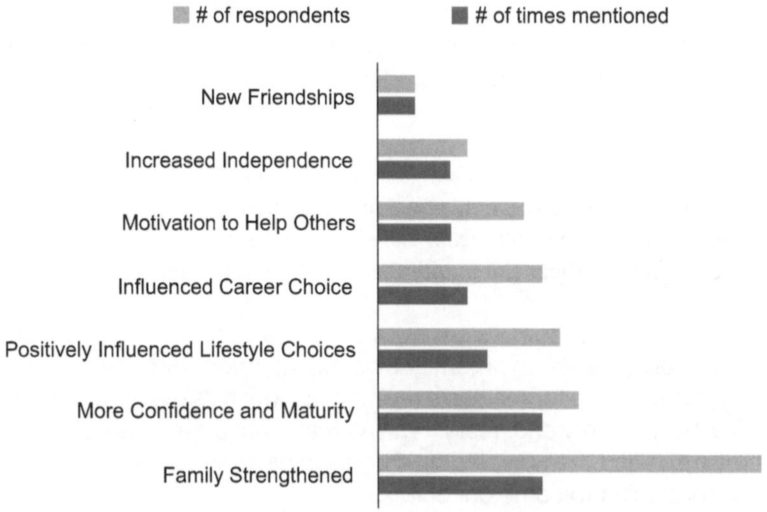

FIGURE 5.1 Posttraumatic growth: Types and frequencies.

can depend to an important extent on young people's perception of how it has changed their lives (Harrison & Harrington, 2001). As they gained insight into the death and progressed through the healing process, many of our participants began to recognize positive influences the experience had on their lives. While the intense emotions, communication difficulties, and social implications that come with losing a parent to suicide are challenging, those experiences can also create something meaningful. Survivors described the meaning from their experiences in various ways (see Figure 5.1).

Strengthened Relationships

The positive outcome told about most often was that the death actually strengthened the surviving family as a unit or improved relationships with siblings or a surviving parent. Although physical and emotional reactions among suicide bereaved children are severe and enduring, there is some evidence that families can be strengthened by suicide (Clark & Goldney, 1995; Ratnarajah et al., 2008; Requarth, 2006; Rudestam, 1977). In several cases the suicide actually allowed family members who were apart from each other to reconnect and either establish or renew their relationships. Becoming stronger as a family was a notable outcome described by Kevin, who lost his father to suicide at age 13. He indicated that "*we are all stronger than we were before emotionally it drew all of us together.*" Trevor described how he personally became "*more family-oriented.*" In other instances, survivors spoke about how their families "*banded together*" following the suicide, such as Suzanne, who reflected on what the suicide meant to her family years later:

> I strongly believe that families are made stronger by a crisis and this was certainly a crisis in my family if you band together and not blame one another and concentrate on supporting one another, then it can make families stronger.

Improved relationships among siblings and with surviving parents were one way in which families were strengthened. Dirk indicated, for example, that "*it's made me, my brother and my mom really close.*" Charlotte and Fred also described how the suicide brought them closer with their brothers and sisters.

> It's my mom, it's my mom It's just my mom I mean, I have my friends, but nobody knows me like my mom knows me, and nobody's there for me like my mom's there for me she's my best friend, she's everything to me And it's thanks to my dad, really. I wasn't really that close to her she was just my mom and then my dad died and she became my best friend it's a very good thing to come out of it.
>
> I try to do a little more be more proactive and wanting to have that friendship with my older three sisters. We talk about it and open up about it and everything the biggest thing was to open up to them granted nobody wants to lose somebody but I don't know if my relationship with my siblings would have been as good if it wasn't for him committing suicide I think it has made us stronger.

In other cases the suicide allowed previously separated family members to get back in touch with each other. In Lisa's case, she was able to reconnect with her dad and several siblings who because of divorce were not a big part of her life until her mother's suicide.

> After that my dad became a huge presence It took a huge loss to get him to become a huge presence it was phenomenal. I was finally starting to build that father-daughter relationship that you are supposed to have and it was phenomenal Then my dad died when I was going into my freshman year, and I had information about my little brother who lived in another state and I finally picked up the phone, and I dialed the number, and my palms were sweating and I'm just freaking out what is his mother going to say? Is she going to know who I am? We talked for hours and I found out my little brother was 8 She actually took my gesture and introduced me into their lives. And so, I've watched him grow up they are all on Facebook and they always send me "Hey, sister" messages, and oh, I love it.

Later in her interview, Lisa reflected on how the positive outcomes and stronger family relationships continued to be a source of strength for her later in life as she became a wife and mother.

> When people hear what I've been through, they're always like, "I'm so sorry, I'm so sorry." I'm like, I don't want your sympathy don't tell me you're sorry because to be quite honest if I hadn't experienced all the loss and the heartache that I've experienced, I wouldn't be where I am today I wouldn't have the wonderful husband that I have and the three beautiful children.

A number of participants spoke of the positive influence on friendships that resulted from the suicide. For Dirk, the suicide seemed to encourage others to initiate friendships with him out of concern. Jared quite differently worked to emulate his dad's outgoing personality, which he attributed to his ability to make friendships.

> I did have one of my friends that I actually talked to on the phone once in a while. She kind of brought me along out to lunch once in a while and I made a lot of friends that year. Kind of ironic in a sad way to make friends that way, but that's pretty much how I made all of my friends. I guess people just felt bad for me and wanted to be a friend and got to know me and become my friend.
>
> I try a lot harder to be a better person in the aspect of seeing people and being friends with people and that's the way he was he would make friends anywhere. He would just go out and be with people and just make friends. I guess I want to go out and make friends with people, and I want to be there for them.

More Maturity and Independence

Several participants told of gaining confidence, especially when expressing and sharing feelings. Guy described becoming "*more mature and more logical.*" Jeffery, Charlotte, Kevin, and Shane all agreed that it made them "*emotionally stronger.*" Shane, a young teen at the time of his dad's suicide, added that his dad's death affected him "*more so in a positive way than a negative because I've grown up so much it's made me stronger as a person,*" and Brooke added that the suicide had actually "*led to a more positive place because I don't think I would be anywhere close to where I am today if it wasn't for what happened.*" Trevor and Kevin mirrored these sentiments by stating the following:

> It made me a stronger person actually. I mean, it's hard to say just because it's such a horrible thing that you never want to think, well, oh, well, gee, if somebody dies in my family I'm going to be a better person.
>
> It just gave me a positive outlook on life and I realize how short life is and how suicide is not an option. Suicide ruins everyone else's life around you. I will never commit suicide and I will never condone it or

> be okay with people doing it for any reason. I don't see any reason why anyone should resort to that. It definitely influenced me positively in that way, and it sucks that I had to grow up like that, but it's made me a stronger person for sure.

In the following excerpts Amber and Dirk talk about gaining maturity, especially with handling and expressing feelings. This is an especially important achievement for Dirk, whose mother described him as a child who had trouble controlling his temper shortly after the suicide.

> I feel more confident and able to express to people what I think it is that they want to know, what they should know, what they need to know. I am much more available for interrogation without it seeming like interrogation. I can talk about it without getting offensive.
>
> If I'm overwhelmed or depressed I know the feeling will pass and I work myself through it. It's definitely helped me as I got older it made me more aware of how I feel and how to fix how I feel. I now understand it is just a feeling that I can overcome that it will pass.

Several participants in our study cited "independence" as one major outcome of the suicide, using phrases like "*a lot*," "*a whole lot*," and "*a whole bunch*" to try to quantify their personal growth. Zach, Kevin, and Melissa all spoke of the suicide propelling them toward more independence.

> I actually wrote about this in a scholarship essay, but I think it's added to my independence just because I had to figure things out.
>
> I gained a lot of independence Mom was there for me, but I had to learn everything on my own.
>
> Homework was something I had to do on my own rather than my father standing over my shoulder to make sure I got it done I wasn't a great student prior to this and I hate to say it but it's better that he wasn't there. He was too overbearing and too much of a helicopter parent My mom said my personality benefitted from a whole lot of independence.

Lifestyle Choices

A number of participants suggested that the suicide had a positive effect on their lifestyle choices. In one instance a suicide note left for Trevor by his father was the source of advice on lifestyle. He reflected on the impact of his father's written words.

> my dad had wrote all four of us kids and my mom also a letter that he just didn't know what to do anymore, and he was encouraging to us to pay attention to people when they were talking about alcoholism so that we didn't get wrapped up in it didn't get involved with it. He definitely

cared about us and didn't want us to get wrapped up into that lifestyle. I really took what he had written to me in that letter to heart that's why throughout high school I did not want anything to do with alcohol didn't want to have anything to do with the party scene, and just completely stayed away from it. So that was a positive.

Others spoke of the decision to stay away from drugs because of the suicide.

To this day, none of us has taken Vicodin. I broke my finger once, and my mom wouldn't let me fill a prescription for Vicodin I think it has to do with what happened with my dad, knowing how addicting that stuff is my mom wouldn't allow it in the house. It was definitely a fear of the same thing happening.

It made me stop and think about life in general. When I was 14 I was smoking pot with my brothers and I don't anymore. I stopped because of him, stopped because it wasn't the right thing to do. The suicide just made me who I am today, like I don't know where I would be if he was still alive but, I'm glad that I'm where I'm at right now in my life.

Still others described the positive influence in terms of choices regarding parenting.

And now being a parent and everything I definitely don't want to make the mistakes that he made, and I worry about it as my daughter gets older I'm very aware of that kind of stuff and a lot of stuff, seeing how my dad was and what happened with him.

It made me realize that if I ever have a family of my own I would never do that to my family I made myself a promise I would never do that.

Career Choices

Some participants in our study shared how the suicide influenced their career paths. Largely because writing was personally therapeutic for her, Amber pursued creative writing in college and eventually became a writer and poet. Guy set out to be a psychologist, motivated by how his own psychologist helped his family heal and was "*such a big part*" of his life. Likewise, because of her experience with parental suicide, Suzanne described how she was drawn to a career in suicide prevention.

I got asked very early in my career to develop a program on suicide prevention I had no intention of teaching this topic at that point in time eventually, I agreed and did this one program I wouldn't have even thought of telling them about my dad. It was all just generic about suicide and after I got finished, the ladies came up and said, "Oh, you have to teach more of these programs."

It is not uncommon for a teen to follow the career path of a parent. This holds true even after a suicide, as described by Jared, who chose a military career to be like his deceased dad so that he could "*carry on the tradition.*"

> One of the reasons I went into the military was because my dad was in the air force. I wanted to carry on the tradition. I wish he was here to show him all my accomplishments.

Motivation to Help Others

Participants in our study discussed their motivation to help others with similar experiences, and commented on the therapeutic impacts such actions had on them in their healing process. Several, like Rachel, found that one of the positive results of having experienced a suicide was a heightened ability to be more "*compassionate*" and "*sensitive towards other people*" who had gone through what she had "*gone through.*" Suzanne described her work in suicide prevention as an "*inner burning desire*" to help other people.

> So there's an inner burning desire to want to help other people and even if one family didn't have to go through it and I believe that I've impacted more than that in my life time and I'm not judgmental about it and so people just flood me come up and you know tell me their stories and talk to me that's therapy it really is good therapy.

Amber described her feelings of being driven, even "*obliged*" to help others who have experienced a loss to suicide.

> I've taken it upon myself. I feel almost obliged to help whenever I can do something about suicide.

Amber further described her work as a volunteer counselor at Camp HOPE as personally "*cathartic.*"

> In camp I would seek out the suicide kids, the people who have had to deal with suicide and be like, "I'm here for you" having been able to do what I can for and with Camp HOPE as far as counseling and being able to have that regular, kind of scheduled catharsis and knowing that I'm probably really helping somebody I feel better.

CASE STUDY

Jake's Story

A Positive Outlook on Life

The suicide gave me a positive outlook on life, the realization of how short life is and how suicide is not an option. When I've gone through difficult stuff, his death makes me think more positively, because things could always be worse.

My dad was manic depressive, and because he was off medication, he was really manic. He was put in jail for kidnapping my older brother. The kidnapping happened because my brother's mom, who is not my mom, was not fit to raise her kids, so when my dad took my brother back, she reported it as a kidnapping. Dad was in jail and was going to be sent to another state. He would have been in prison for five years if they had proven everything, which they probably would have. He committed suicide by hanging himself in jail the day before he was going to be extradited. He was 32. Although I was only 4 years old at the time, I remember the day pretty well. My mom was on the phone crying. We asked her to tell us what had happened, and she did.

At the funeral, my dad's mom was flipping out! She was mad at my mom, because my mom and dad were going through a divorce at the time. My dad was going to lose us kids, and obviously his other son. My grandma, who was very angry, yelled at her to leave! I also remember my 9-year-old brother walking me up to the casket. I saw my dad, and all of his friends, and a lot of family. I just remember going back and sitting down, but, to tell you the truth, I don't think I even cried. It's weird, because a lot of what I've learned in psychology class is that kids usually block that kind of stuff out. But not me; I remember it all very, very vividly.

At 4, forever is not really a concept to you. Sometimes my dad would go to work for a week or longer at a time, and I remember believing that he was just at work and thinking that I would see him again. I remember telling myself that that he would be back. I also remember going back to preschool and how the kids in my class knew about my dad and told me they were sorry. I just blew it off, because it didn't really mean much. I didn't really think anything of it at the time, but, looking back, my teacher was pretty nice to me too.

I think I was 6 when I realized he wasn't coming back. I knew he had died and I had gone to the funeral, but it never really hit me until then. When I finally realized he wasn't coming back, I was just distraught. I don't remember exactly why or how I realized he was never coming back, but I think it was the birth of my baby sister that kind of finalized it. I don't know how it clicked, but maybe it was just realizing how people are born and people die. I remember sitting in my room bawling, and my mom came in and explained to me how it *is* forever. That's when it pretty much sank in.

The exact dynamics of suicide didn't sink in until I was much older, though, because as far as I knew at the time, he had just killed himself. It wasn't until years later that I knew what the disease was and learned more about it. There was no guilt. When it clicked I only had sadness. I was just sad and thinking, "I don't have a dad now, and I won't."

It sounds weird, but I have a pretty photographic memory and remember everything about him, even from the age of 2. My dad would always walk around on his hands, and I would follow him around, picking up the change that would fall out of his pockets. When he was in his manic stage, which went on for a year and a half, he built this massive tree house. It was like eight stories tall and built around a tree. I remember him taking us up in that tree. We lived on a farm, and he took us on long walks through the woods. We had horses, and I remember him saying, "Hold on to the mane," as he put me on bareback and trotted me through the woods. I don't have any bad memories of him. Even though he didn't live with us, he was still in our lives every day. My mom definitely kept us close to him.

I definitely had support after Dad's death. My mom is a very strong woman, and she raised us all by herself. She also put us in counseling from the time when we needed it, and I was in and out of counseling for a long time. I guess overall the counseling did help. She also sent me to Camp HOPE, and that was also a great and a cool experience. It brought out a lot of emotions in the beginning, but it was really nice seeing other people with similar experiences. Just having other people who understood where you were coming from made a big difference. It was good being able to talk about it freely and open up. I caught a big bass, and overall it was a lot of fun. It was definitely important in my recovery and made an impact on my life.

It sucked not having a dad and growing up with only a mom. She tried everything to keep us involved in sports and stuff, but it wasn't the same as if you had a dad. I was involved in sports all of my life, but it was different for me because everyone else's dads were there versus only my mom being there. It was especially hard for wrestling because that was like a dad-son thing. I had father figures on and off, but no one who was influential.

The suicide really affected my family, and we all dealt with it differently. One brother is pissed off to this day, and the other brother is on the same path. I don't really talk to them about it, because they don't have anything good to say and are really negative. My sister is the same as me; she has accepted and dealt with it. My mom still really blames herself. Because my brother is a lot like my dad, I wonder if he'll ever commit suicide. I worry about that a lot and it sucks because if they end up like that, what will it be like to deal with that? I want to help him as much as I can, but if he doesn't want my help there is nothing I can do. Not that it's a burden on me, but it drags me down sometimes. It just makes me sad.

My dad's death seems like light-years away now. I still think about it on his birthday and the day that he killed himself, but it's nothing that I get too worked up over. It's something I've dealt with and is just a part of who I am now.

My dad's suicide is not something I share with people who aren't close to me. Even some of my friends don't know. It hasn't come up, and I don't bring it up. If someone asks me, I am okay talking about it. It's not something that I am ashamed of or anything, but it is just something that is personal. To explain the story and why it happened is a long process, so it's not really worth telling a lot of people about. Anyone I feel that should know, I'll tell. I will definitely open up and tell anyone about my experiences if they have lost someone too.

The suicide gave me a positive outlook on life, the realization of how short life is and how suicide is not an option. Suicide is not something you do, because it ruins the lives of everyone around you. I will never commit suicide, and I will never condone it or be okay with people doing it. I don't see any reason why anyone should resort to that. It sucks that I had to grow up without a dad, but it made me a stronger person for sure. When I've gone through difficult stuff, his death makes me think more positively because things could always be worse.

My advice to other kids like me is just to give it time. It will suck, but later you will look back on it differently. It's terrible at first, and for years it will be there. It's depressing, but definitely you do get over it, and it just becomes something that you went through. Just deal with it. Go to counseling and get help. It helped me to talk about my dad and keep his memory alive, and that helped me to accept that it is forever. If you don't open up and you hold it back, one day you could be my age and have to go through it then.

CASE STUDY

Trevor's Story

Taking His Letter to Heart

Talk to people. Move out of your house if you need to. Move on with your life because you have to. Don't look back at the things you missed out on, but look forward to the things that you will experience soon. There are a lot of things that I missed out on because of my father's death, but you know what, that's in the past. As of now, I am just trying to live my life as best I can. So far, I think I am doing a pretty good job at it.

When I was 8 years old, my father committed suicide. I was on my way home from school when my aunt, who lived about half a block away, called for me to come over. I visited my aunt and uncle all the time, so I was happy to go over and see her. When I got over to the house, she explained that my mother had asked her if I could stay over there for a few hours because my father hadn't been feeling well that morning. She explained that they had taken my dad into the hospital, but she never hinted that he wasn't going to be okay or that I should be worried about what was going on. I was young and didn't know any better, so I just said okay and proceeded to hang around with my aunt for a while. After a few hours, she walked me over to my house.

When I got home, my whole family was there sitting at the kitchen table and in the living room, except for my mom. I didn't see her anywhere. I was very confused and tried to find her to ask why everyone was at the house. When my siblings and I found her in her room, she explained to us what had happened to our dad. I don't remember a lot about it, and I am not sure that I truly understood the reality of the situation at that time.

I remember reading the note that my father left behind for me. He had left us each a letter, including my mother. I still have his letter, and I plan on having it for the rest of my life. It had a really big impact on who I am today, and even though I wish he wouldn't have committed suicide, I am still glad that he chose to leave me with some words of wisdom. That day was the only time that my family ever talked openly about the letters. We all sat down together in my mom's room, just her and us kids, sharing what our letters enclosed. My letter reasoned that he just didn't know what to do anymore. He encouraged me, and all of us, to pay attention when people talk about alcoholism and be aware of other things that cause people's lives to go downhill. He wanted to make sure that we didn't get wrapped up in all of it the way that he had. The letters showed that he definitely cared about the family and didn't want us to live the same lifestyle that he had. I really took to heart what he had written to me in his letter. What he said in his letter was why I didn't drink in high school, nor did I want anything to do with the party scene. It was the reason why I completely stayed away from all of that stuff. It was one very positive thing to come from his suicide.

My dad had a lot of problems with alcohol in his life. I remember him having a lot of treatments for severe alcoholism while I was growing up. He was diagnosed as an alcoholic with severe depression and was being treated for both problems. He tried many times to overcome his alcoholism, but it was so overwhelming that he just couldn't handle being without it. Eventually, it is what took his life.

A lot of the problems that my dad struggled with came from his childhood. He had a rough time growing up because his family didn't provide him with the best environment. His father was an alcoholic as well, and he would beat the kids. Both my grandpa and my uncles gave my dad a really hard time as he was growing up. When my dad was only 12 years old, his father would just throw him a beer and tell him to drink up. I think that's really where it all started. It just got worse from there. My dad was unable to suppress his feelings or deal with them at all really, so he tried to drink them away.

My father wrote in a journal for many years, and it wasn't until a couple years ago that my mom pulled out my father's journals and shared them with us kids. My mom hasn't always been the type to share a lot of things. She is a very strong person, but she never wants anyone to know when she is hurting. She is very independent and stubborn and won't let anyone help her out even when she needs it. Her personality was partially a benefit and partially a hindrance as I was growing up. She taught us to get over things on our own terms, but I struggled because I wasn't able to talk things out. She also didn't ever want us children to talk openly about the suicide. Honestly, I had no idea about what really happened with my father until a couple years ago, when she brought out the journals. My mom did a really good job of hiding everything from us kids while we were growing up. My father's suicide is a sore subject for her. She didn't want to talk about it then, and I still can't bring it up now without causing a big deal. Maybe it's because my dad's side of the family blamed her for the suicide, but I never believed that. I just would have liked to know the truth from the beginning.

On the other hand, a few of my aunts and uncles were really open to talking about the suicide with us kids. They knew my dad well, and it was really helpful for them to be there during that point in my life. In fact, a few of my uncles stepped in at times and became father figures in my life. They filled in during times in my life when I needed my father the most, like during hunter's safety, when they went through it with me. They really just helped out with a lot of father-son things. They would take all of us kids to places that my mom couldn't afford or to places that my dad would have taken us to if he would have been alive. That was really beneficial and really helped me out with the growing process as well. Now that my father is gone, they are a really important part of my life. I value my relationships with them a lot.

My brother took over doing the outside chores and took on a lot of father-like responsibilities too. Although he came down on us when we did something wrong, and I was sort of intimidated by him, he really just tried to be as much of a father figure as possible. Together, my brother, with my aunts and uncles, took us under their wings, which, looking back on it, was really nice.

That didn't mean that it wasn't a struggle though, because high school was a really rough time for me. As I said, I took the advice in my father's letter seriously, but that made it hard fitting in with people. It wasn't easy to find other kids like me who were so against drinking. I went to only one party throughout my entire high school career, and I didn't even stay for the whole thing. I had nothing to drink, took one look around at all the people who were acting stupid, and jumped at the opportunity to take home the first person who needed a ride.

I never really had any close friends I could talk to in high school. I mean, I had friends that I would screw around with, but no one I could really talk to about the suicide or what was going on in my life. As I said before, my mom really didn't want any of us kids to talk about my dad's death with anyone, and she would say things like, "Just tell them that your dad passed away." So, I became ashamed to say anything, and I think this is why I was really bad at communicating with people in high school. For a while it seemed like every day was a bad day.

As I get older, it gets easier to talk about my dad, and I'm noticing a lot more freedom to express myself now that I'm away from home. I've noticed life goes a lot better if you just talk and don't worry about who is going to find out about what. It's not a big deal. It happened, and it's over.

Don't get me wrong, it was a hard transition to make, but with time and a little bit of counseling, I was able to make progress. I have been going to counseling on and off since my father's death. I remember going to counseling with my mom for the first time right after my dad died. I really don't think that it helped much at the time. I honestly only remember sitting around and coloring, but I think it was important that I got introduced to it at that time. My school also had a counselor see me about once a week for probably a few months after my dad died. It was good because I got to say what was on my mind and what I was thinking about that week, which helped me express my feelings and round out my thoughts. Basically, it was just nice to know that someone outside my family cared.

Three years ago, when I started to see a counselor again, it didn't go as well as when I was in high school because I felt pressured to take antidepressant medication.

I hid my meds from my mom of course, because she doesn't believe in depression. I knew if she found out that I was seeing a counselor and sharing things about our family, she would flip out, and she did. Mom was angry with me for seeking help, so I just kind of gave up on the whole depression thing, and it has been really hard. I have really struggled with it.

Just weeks ago, I went to a new counselor, hoping to work on a few issues. This time around I chose a psychiatrist who diagnosed me with rapid-cycling bipolar disorder, a fairly common disorder. The first counselor treated me for depression and ADHD, which can cause a person with rapid-cycling bipolar disorder to get more agitated, instead of treating the actual problem. My new medication might take up to five weeks to kick in, so hopefully it will work a lot better. For now though, I still have my up and down days.

To be honest, counseling pushed me away in the beginning. Sometimes it just seemed like I was paying someone to listen, when I could have just been talking to a friend for free. It has been hard to put those feelings aside, but with my new counselor I feel like I might have found someone who can finally help me move forward with my life. I wish I would have gotten counseling sooner. The information about counseling was always around; the hard part was picking up the phone and calling. It's like a leaky roof—you only want to fix it when it's raining. It seems like I only wanted to see a counselor when I was feeling crappy, not on a regular basis, so I just kept putting it off. In the end, I am glad I got over that.

While my sister was going through counseling of her own, she was given a book called *Adult Children of Alcoholics,* by Janet Gringer. After reading it, she bought a copy for each of us siblings. Basically, it describes my mother to a T. In fact, it describes my whole family to a T. It was an amazing read for me because it showed me that I am not the only one out there dealing with this. It's a sad thing really, but I am still glad not to be the only one. I think a big part of overcoming a suicide is overcoming the feeling that you are the only one out there dealing with this. It is so good to hear that you're not alone.

Anyone who is dealing with the death of a parent should just keep talking about it. Find people you are comfortable talking to and don't let them go anywhere. It is fine to be picky and choosy about who you talk with, because there are some people who will have no idea what you are going through. What is important, though, is that you find at least one person who does. Don't let your emotions build up, because that only leads to worse problems. Everything can be going right in your life, and then all of a sudden one thing happens that is just a hair of a thing but it sets your life astray, and it is so good to have someone to talk to during a time like that. Don't ever feel ashamed to talk to somebody or think that you are too tough to talk to someone, because I felt that way for a really long time, and it is not true for anyone. Once you find someone who cares for and comforts you, everything gets so much easier.

Here's my advice. Talk to people. Move out of your house if you need to. Move on with your life, because you have to. Don't look back at the things you missed out on, but look forward to the things that you will experience soon. There are a lot of things I missed out on because of my father's death, but you know what, that's in the past. As of now, I am just trying to live my life as best I can. So far, I think I am doing a pretty good job at it.

CASE STUDY

Jerome's Story

Tomorrow Is a New Day

Suicide is not something you can control. The decision to commit suicide is solely the decision of the one doing it. I know that my dad had depression issues and was bipolar, and so I know it was not my fault. If I could, I would remind other children of that, and to remember that tomorrow is a new day.

Mom and I had just gone to the store. I was only 3, so I stayed right by my mom's side as we came into the house. We had bought some things at the store, and we were excited to show my dad what we bought. As we came down the stairs, my mom became very upset and screamed when she saw my dad. It scared me as she pushed me up the stairs, trying to prevent me from seeing what had happened. But I did see, and I was so confused. I wondered why he had painted his neck.

The next thing that I can remember was walking to the neighbor's house and watching the cops coming into our house from across the street. There were family members showing up and people talking to me, but I did not know what had happened. I just knew that something was really wrong and everyone was upset. My sister, who was 7 or 8 at the time, had just gotten back from a weekend at my aunt's house. She too was sent over the neighbor's house to be with me. Everyone was so upset, but I was too young to understand why.

We stayed with some of my mom's side of the family in the next few months because it was hard, mostly for my mom, to be in the house. I had lots of cousins my age around me, and we played a lot, which kept my mind off of things. My dad's parents lived close by too, but they were not around as much as my mom's family. I guess they were dealing with a lot too.

My mom and I went to a counselor together when I was young, but the counselor kind of scared me. He asked really bizarre questions like, "What would I say to my dad if I saw him now?" This made me scared because it made me think of ghosts and things. I quit going.

My dad must have liked baseball, because he had a ball glove that my mom saved, and sometimes I find myself wondering if I would have been more athletic if I had someone to play sports things with. I really didn't have a father figure to do sports with. Even when my mom remarried, my stepfather wasn't around much, because he worked a lot. My stepdad did fill a big part of my life though, and I have a lot of respect for him. As a little kid, I found myself worrying about my mom a lot. When I was at a friend's house, I would think about how my friend had a dad and wondered how my mom could take care of me and my sister by herself. So, my stepdad gave us all some relief. I find myself getting mad sometimes at my dad for leaving my mom all alone with two kids.

I didn't feel guilty, but my sister told me when we got older that she felt guilty because she said my dad had wanted to talk to her in a serious way, and she did not know what to do because she was a little kid too. She wonders if she would have talked to him when he wanted to, if things would have been different.

I never really talked about my dad's death to people, and I am sure that others just thought that my stepdad was my real dad, and in a way he was. I recently finished my technical college degree in graphic design and web development, which was not very easy for me, but I have finally figured out what I like to do.

I went to a camp with a friend whom I met in third grade, when we were about 9. We are still friends after all of these years. I don't remember much about going, and I don't think that I was in much grief or anything, but it made me think back on things, and it gave me a lot of respect for my mom, because I realized that she did a lot for us. I don't think that any of this has made a difference to me as an adult. I feel that I am doing fine and my family is too.

Suicide is not something you can control. The decision to commit suicide is solely the decision of the one doing it. I know that my dad had depression issues, and was bipolar, and so I know it was not my fault. If I could, I would remind other children of that, and to remember that tomorrow is a new day.

CASE STUDY

Suzanne's Story

It Hits You in Ways That You Don't Expect

That day, 48 years ago, is a day of intense, intense sadness, a day of reflection, a day of change, and a day of regret. It is also a day that has forced me to teach about suicide, in hopes that someone else can possibly save a life.

Today I turned 50 years old. I can't begin to explain to you how proud I am of our children and my wonderful husband, who I have been married to for almost 35 years now. I am so very thankful for every second I have with them. This day is particularly a time of immense emotion for me, which is precisely why I am writing today. Writing is a strength of mine, and I have found it to help me tell a true and accurate story about the wonderful life my dad led when he was still alive. On this day, 42 years ago, my father took his own life. It is a day that vividly sticks out in my mind and a day that I will never forget. I was 8 years old at the time.

It was a beautiful, sunny day. My mother and I were out in the garden picking strawberries on our farm. She seemed uneasy that day and kept suspiciously sending me to check on my dad as he sat crouched on an old bench seat beneath a beautiful shade tree in our yard. As we continued to pick strawberries, we heard his footsteps and noticed as he abruptly headed toward the road. I was too young to really understand what was happening, but I do remember hearing the sharp tone of my mother's voice as she yelled, "Jerry! Jerry! Stop! Jerry! I love you! Come back!" She also yelled for me to get my oldest sister, who was home from college. In the meantime, our neighbors were called, and they began searching the woods. They brought back tragic and devastating news. Dad had hung himself at the young age of 50.

My dad, although probably bipolar or manic depressive, still had many wonderful things going for him, which will always leave me with one question: Why did he commit suicide? Why did he feel the need to take his own life? I completely understand that there is not a simple answer to that complicated question, yet I will never ever stop searching for the answer. It's a mystery.

Being a farmer, Dad wanted to support the family. He worked very hard, and my mother and he had a very loving relationship. They had their faults, don't get me wrong, but for the most part he was a gentle and nurturing man whom we all dearly, dearly loved. Unfortunately, my dad had some strange paranoia, once even believing that our whole family was going to die as a result of the Cuban Missile Crisis. Thinking that Cuba was going to invade the U.S., Dad believed we were all going to die by a nuclear disaster, and he risked our lives in many ways to avoid it. You see, these are the things that played vastly into my dad's medical condition. These are the reasons that my dad attempted suicide five times prior to his death.

The research tells us that when someone attempts suicide one or more times, they are at higher risk than if they had never attempted suicide at all, and my father followed this pattern of behavior. His attempts kept getting more and more lethal. My mother was thankfully there to have saved him from each of his previous attempts, and I always wonder why something couldn't have happened so that he would have been saved on this day as well. Over the years, I've come to realize that my dad really didn't want to die—in fact he wanted to live—but didn't know how to deal with the issues that bothered him most.

The funeral was an intensely sad day for all of us. We were all in such a state of shock. I keenly remember one of the pastors at the little Catholic church we devotedly belonged to for many, many years. He obviously did not want more of his parishioners to commit suicide, and so he gave a bold sermon that will forever stick in my mind. Here we are, so very raw in the grieving process, and he stood before us preaching about how committing suicide is a sin and that anyone who commits suicide is going straight to hell.

Because my sister and I were so young at the time, my mother told us that my father had died of a heart attack, rather than suicide. I had no idea that my mother was not telling us the truth at the time, yet the kids at school would tease me about the way in which my father died. Sometime later, my sister and I confronted my mother about the suicide, and that is when she told us that by not telling us the truth, she was only trying to protect us from the pain. My father's death was painful for my mother, and she was in a state of denial for many years. In fact, I recall finding my father's old, original death certificate and noticing that my mother had obviously attempted to cross off the words that described the cause of my dad's death. It is common for families who have a loved one die by suicide to deny or cover the death up for as long as they have to, to preserve their own sanity.

My mother was a strong woman, but my father's death really took a toll on her and everyone else. There were more responsibilities for her and for us. My mother never had outside employment, although she did cook for weddings, make Christmas wreaths, and sell our farm produce, which brought in little bit of income. Because she did not want any handouts from the government, she didn't apply for social security until I was in college. I believe this is due to her independent spirit. She wanted to make it on her own. My mother also rejected the idea of ever being married again. She was afraid that there was absolutely no one who would love her children as much as my father and she had, and in multiple ways she dedicated her life to us children and didn't want to devote her time to a relationship.

It is important to understand that my mother did not make my father out to be a perfect person. Even though she loved him very much, she understood that he had his faults. It's a whole lot easier to point out the positive attributes of a person when they die, and of course there were many positive aspects in my father's life, but my mother did not deny his mental health issues and the fact that he too had his weaknesses.

Dad's death was emotionally hard on my brothers and sisters, and they all were affected in some way. Even though my brother was only 15 at the time of my dad's death, we depended on him to keep the farm up and running. He loved farm work and eventually did dairy farming for a living. He was a real asset to the farm after my dad died. He would sprain an ankle, and it was a major event for the family. He did all the milking, so when he wasn't able to do it, we were forced to learn quickly. There was little support for him after my father's death. The teachers were absolutely horrible. They said all kinds of things to my brother like, "Your father was crazy, and you're going to be crazy also." Or they would say, "You'll never amount to anything, because your father was crazy." You would have expected the teachers to be somewhat supportive, but they were almost worse than the kids in some ways.

There were people who reached out to us during this time whom we will never forget. My sister had a very close relationship with one such family. They were well known in the area, had a beautiful house, and were just wonderful, wonderful people both before and after my dad died. My sister, at the time, cleaned, cooked, and regularly took care of their children. This family was more than generous, inviting us to play games over at their house, taking us to the movies, and they would sometimes take us to one of the nicest supper clubs in town. Little things that people did for us to reach out meant the world to my family during this time.

As for myself, I was the youngest child in the family, and, although too young to comprehend a lot of the details related to the suicide, I was still very, very involved. Going back to school and facing the kids and the teachers was probably one of my toughest tasks. My school was a one-room country school where everybody knew everybody else. The kids obviously knew my situation and would say things to me like, "You're going to lose your farm." Or they would chide, "You're not going to have food to eat."

All of the children who attended this school were basically from poor farm families, but we were not any poorer than anyone else. The cows on our farm were a little run down due to my dad's illness. He was unable to replace them as quickly as he might have been if his health had not been deteriorating. The point is, however, that our farm was certainly an above-average farm, and, although at times we may have struggled without the help of my father, we were doing just fine. Food was sometimes a concern of mine, and the lunch you brought to school every day really determined your economic status, but for the most part my mother would make delicious homemade bread and homemade jams and jellies from the strawberries that we had in abundance. I never felt rich, but I never felt poor either.

I never really had any formal support, definitely no counseling. There was never really money for that, but we got strength from praying. We prayed every night for my father, and I found my strength in playing the piano. My elementary school teacher offered to give me piano lessons, and even though my mother didn't have the extra money to pay for the lessons, she made sure that I was always able to take them. She was concerned about me and wanted to make sure that I did something that I wanted to do.

The only emotion that I can remember being faced with is intense, intense sadness, especially on special holidays or other occasions such as my first communion, when his presence would have meant the most. I don't ever remember being what I would describe as clinically depressed. In fact, other than sadness, my childhood was filled with wonderful memories from before and after my dad's death. I never did feel guilt either. Guilt is not the right word; it's more regret that I felt. Even today, there are times when I reflect back to my father's death and all of his attempts and wonder if there was something that could have saved him. Yes, my mother saved him a few times as well as other members of my family, but is there something that could have saved him on that day? Is there something I could have done, or someone else could have done that would have changed his mind?

Grieving is one of those things that hits you when you least expect it, and it hits you in ways that you don't expect it. For instance, the anniversary date of his death is always hard, and when my own children were 8 years old, I couldn't help but look at them and remind myself of how very young and fragile an 8-year-old actually is. These were two exceptionally hard days for me, but that's the way grieving is. It is impossible to ignore a parent's death date, especially when you lose a loved one by suicide. His death, in my mind, will never be put to rest. Another day that brought back a flood of memories for me was the day of my mother's funeral. It was the same church as my father's ceremony, and there lay the same gravestone boldly inscribed with birth and death dates of each parent, and of course we had lost another parent. You can only imagine how emotional this day was for all of us.

I believe that families are made stronger by some sort of a crisis, and my dad's death was certainly a crisis for my family. If you concentrate on supporting one another rather than blaming, families are able to connect and become even stronger. You come out of these tragedies with a greater appreciation for one another.

It's been 48 years since my father's death, and I'm still searching for an answer. At one point in my career in community education I was asked to organize a program on suicide prevention. After repeatedly failing to find people willing to do this, I decided that I would create and present the program for this organization, but just one time. I researched the topic and eventually put on the program. My program contained generic information about suicide, and I purposefully failed to mention anything about the loss of my father. After finishing that first program, some of the ladies from the organization flooded me with praises, and what I found was that I couldn't put it down. I couldn't stop reading. I kept developing materials. I needed to do more programs on suicide prevention, which I did for many different community organizations.

I did eventually bring my father into the conversation, which in turn helped people to share their own stories. Most of the people at these programs have something to share. In some cases, they themselves have attempted suicide and want to understand their own situation and compare it with other people, and in other cases they've had a brother, a sister, or even a parent or close friend who have attempted. I've learned so much from both reading and hearing stories that other people have shared with me. It's definitely therapy for me, and it also brings the subject matter into the open, which is exactly what we need.

What many people don't understand is that you need to talk to people who are exhibiting warning signs of suicide. You can't shy away from those people and expect that they are going to get better. You don't need to have a PhD in psychology with this topic to be able to possibly save someone's life. These programs on suicide prevention, the stories that I've shared with others, as well as the research and other reading materials, have helped me understand suicide better, and what's more, it has helped me put my father's suicide into perspective.

Even all of this has not provided closure about whatever my father was thinking when he committed suicide. It will always remain a mystery to me. That day, 48 years ago, is a day of intense, intense sadness, a day of reflection, a day of change, and a day of regret. It is also a day that has forced me to teach about suicide, in hopes that someone else can possibly save a life.

six
Professional Implications and Best Practices

Research on grief counseling and other general bereavement interventions demonstrates distressingly low efficacy (Jordan & McMenamy, 2004; Jordan & Neimeyer, 2003), and research on interventions specific to children also indicates surprisingly small effect sizes (Currier et al., 2007). Though possible reasons for these results may relate to research design (e.g., timing and length of intervention, participant selection), the ultimate result is little clarity about the forms of support that actually benefit bereaved children (Akerman & Statham, 2011). Research evidence does support the importance, though, of identifying high-risk subgroups of bereaved individuals, as studies indicate more intervention effectiveness with high-risk or high-distress mourners (Akerman & Statham, 2011; Jordan & McMenamy, 2004). Individuals bereaved through violent, unexpected, or untimely deaths are more likely to experience complicated grief reactions and are more likely to benefit from a structured intervention.

Even so, little effort has been made to develop empirically based interventions for suicide survivors (Clark, 2001; Constantino, Sekula, & Rubinstein, 2001; Farberow, 2001). Numerous positive descriptions of groups or programs for suicide survivors exist, though only a few empirical studies have been conducted to examine program effectiveness (Jordan & McMenamy, 2004). Existing studies, though generally weak in methodological rigor, have demonstrated a bit more promise for interventions specific to suicide survivors than general bereavement interventions, as most demonstrate at least some effect and most see high levels of participant satisfaction (Jordan & McMenamy, 2004). The most carefully designed studies have tended to find the least success, causing the efficacy of formal interventions for suicide survivors to remain largely unknown (Jordan & McMenamy, 2004).

In considering young people impacted by the suicide of a loved one, little research and resource attention has been devoted to how to best provide support (Hung & Rabin, 2009) with an even larger gap in information regarding those bereaved by parental suicide. The biggest focus for young people has been in the area of suicide prevention, though some feel that postvention *is* prevention as children who have experienced parental suicide are at an increased risk for suicide themselves (Schneidman, 1981). Research on children impacted by parental suicide is challenging in that such children are perceived as somewhat vulnerable, and there is often secrecy surrounding suicide. Also, bereavement related to parental suicide shares some characteristics of bereavement related to other kinds of death; however, some argue that interventions specific to parental suicide are needed (Mitchell et al., 2007; Ratnarajah & Schofield, 2007), and others suggest that cause of death is not always useful in identifying whether a child will benefit from intervention (Brown et al., 2007).

Given the dearth of research evidence particular to intervention with this population, it is difficult to present "best practices" for professionals. The term "best practices" refers to current state-of-the-art approaches, interventions, and models for a particular problem and client population (Petr & Walter, 2005). The traditional approach to determining best practices involves a thorough and systematic review of the *quantitative* literature in an attempt to identify the most effective, empirically validated interventions (Petr & Walter, 2005). Few studies relevant to this population can stand up to the type of methodological scrutiny needed to qualify as an "evidence-based" intervention, though. As such, we must adopt the expanded view of "best practices" suggested by Petr and Walter (2005), including both qualitative and quantitative research evidence, the practice wisdom of professionals, and consumer/client perspectives. While the importance of empirical data should not be minimized, this broader view provides additional depth when attempting to understand the often complex dynamics and issues surrounding parental suicide. Additionally, because of the lack of research specific to parental suicide survivors, we must include in our discussion interventions related to general childhood bereavement, loss of a parent to death by any means, and general suicide survivor approaches. While a full examination of these areas is beyond the scope of this chapter, we have identified sources with clear relevance to serving those impacted by parental suicide.

General Counseling Strategies

It would be ideal for children bereaved by parental suicide to see counselors with expertise in that particular realm. In reality such services may not be readily available in the child's community or a counselor may already have an established relationship with the child prior to the suicide and be best equipped to continue counseling. As such, it is important to acknowledge the convincing evidence demonstrating that the nonspecific, relational, and contextual aspects of counseling are the most "active ingredient," rather than specific techniques or procedures

(Deegear & Lawson, 2003; Wampold, 2001). The most important factor, even in bereavement intervention, may be the encounter with a compassionate and empathically attuned professional who is able to provide a healing, understanding, and supportive context (Jordan & Neimeyer, 2003).

Working models for counseling and psychotherapy appropriate for normal and pathologic bereavement are readily available. Evidence-based grief interventions include allowing the client to repeatedly retell the story of the loss from his or her own perspective, the facilitator guiding the client through memories, and the promotion of restoration-oriented coping (Neimeyer & Currier, 2010). Also important to any grief intervention is the ability of the counselor to listen, provide accurate information, and adapt methods to the developmental level of the child (Allen-Heath et al., 2008). One common notion behind a positive grief outcome is the need for "grief work," tasks in which the bereaved needs to do such things as experience the pain, acknowledge the reality of death, experience the emotions associated with the loss of the relationship with the deceased, adjust to life without the deceased, integrate aspects of the deceased into one's own self-identity, establish a continuing bond with the deceased, convert the relationship from one with interactions to one of memory, find meaning in the death, and expend energy toward establishing new relationships (Cohen et al., 2004; Stroebe & Stroebe, 1993; Wolfelt, 1996; Worden, 1982/1991).

The literature points to a number of needs that children have after the death of a parent, which counselors might consider when determining approaches. Adams-Greenly and Moynihan (1983) identify five related suggestions: (a) provide clear, honest, and age-appropriate information; (b) actively involve them in their own grief work; (c) provide reassurance about the grief process that they are going through; (d) let them know their thoughts and feelings are normal; and (e) allow them to continue to be children by staying involved in age-appropriate activities and interests. Others point to the need to increase self-esteem and adaptive control beliefs; facilitate positive parent-child relationships; encourage parental warmth, parent-child communication, and effective discipline; reduce parental distress; increase positive family interactions; and reduce child exposure to negative life events (Akerman & Statham, 2011; Haine et al., 2006). Others speak of a broader systems approach that involves restructuring the family unit, taking into account all forces that impact a child's grieving process (e.g., loss of friends, change of school or location, economic status, family interactions), and including family members' different views of the suicide and diverse coping reactions (Heikes, 1997; Hurley, 1991; Ratnarajah & Schofield, 2007).

We learned much from our participants to inform counselors and other helping professionals. First and foremost, because suicide often breaks a bond of trust between the person who took his or her life and the surviving child, trust may be difficult for the child in future relationships. Counselors should be prepared to put additional effort into trust-building through remaining consistent, reliable, and compassionate. Support should continue to be offered, even if a child is initially refusing help (Dyregrov, 2009a). Processing and revealing emotions can take time, and when a child is ready for assistance, it should be clearly available. This may involve not always taking a first response at face value, but being patient, digging deeper, and using a variety of approaches to build trust and elicit conversation.

In terms of handling client emotions, counselors should avoid making empathetic assumptions, as there is no universal emotional response to parental suicide. Counselors should ask about feelings and then follow the client's lead. If emotions like guilt, anger, and, in some cases, relief manifest, do not downplay them, but rather attend to their source and help the client to explore them by (a) validating these feelings as natural and encouraging their expression; (b) helping the client understand the role of mental illness in suicide and encouraging forgiveness as part of the healing process; and (c) normalizing suicide death through open and honest communication about suicide, sharing age-appropriate books and stories about suicide loss, and connecting the client with other children who share similar losses. Such activities can diminish the feelings of shame that sometimes accompany parental suicide.

Counselors must also understand the reasons behind absent emotions and provide opportunities to identify feelings, without forcing expression. Children who appear stoic or do not show any emotion may be at risk for complicated grief. Lack of emotions can be misinterpreted as "doing fine," though it is more likely a sign that the child is struggling. One participant in our study shared, "*Coping with the death shouldn't be left to somebody by themselves, especially not a child. You can't let them be quiet, even if they look okay. Try to get them to talk. Find a group of people that they're comfortable with to talk to or just be there. Ask them for who they would be most comfortable to talk to.*"

Remember that children of parental suicide may have experienced adverse reactions from others. Professionals (e.g., first responders, law enforcement, medical professionals), for example, often must ask difficult questions during an emotionally intense and confusing time and interactions can come across as blaming or accusatory. Extended family and friends may place blame on the family for the suicide. Peers often do not have the skills and knowledge to respond in a helpful way. Thus, allow children to process the reactions of others, advocate for them when needed, and provide reassurance to the child that he or she did not do anything to cause the death. One participant offered the following advice: "*Don't say 'it's not your fault' say 'people still love you and it's not because of you' say it and repeat it, repeat it, repeat it, repeat.*"

Whenever a death occurs, there is a rearrangement of household duties, even more so when a primary caretaker dies. Early on, encourage families to make permanent changes such as seeking flextime at work and distributing household duties appropriately among family members. Rally extended family, faith networks, and schools in support of the family. It is helpful to try to understand the needs of the family and assist, or make referrals for practical support such as child care, transportation, financial help, and tutoring. Children who lose a parent to suicide may experience additional losses related to less available support and diminished opportunities.

Challenging life events are complicated by the history of suicide within the family. Emotions often surface if the surviving parent chooses to remarry. Relocation to a new home may occur, and with it the loss of a familiar environment, or the fear that important artifacts will be lost in the move. Mental health issues might manifest in late adolescence or early adulthood. The death of a loved one or friend later in life can cause grief to resurface, especially if factors such as the type of death, similarities in age of the deceased, or the time of year of the death mirror the original loss. It is supportive to help clients anticipate and respond to the emotional reactions that can surface when people revisit their loss in relation to life changes and events, providing opportunities to process, generate awareness, and solve problems. Happy life events (e.g., graduation, weddings) can also trigger emotions. Creating a memory ritual, looking at pictures or videos from the past, visiting a special place, or considering what the deceased person might do or say if he or she were there can provide support and reassurance, and help preserve memories.

As children understand aspects of death differently at different developmental stages, their grief may be delayed or manifest differently throughout life. For example, a 4-year-old child may grieve the loss of support that a mother would give a young child and then "regrieve" at age 6, when he first recognizes the permanence of the loss. An 8-year-old child might grieve the absence of a parent at school functions and then make adjustments to cope with that loss, yet "regrieve" as a teenager at a significant life event such as a graduation. By understanding age-appropriate grief reactions counselors can provide information and support accordingly. Remember, providing support is a "marathon," not a "sprint," as counseling may be needed initially following the suicide, throughout adolescence and young adulthood, and at critical points throughout life.

The Importance of Assessment

Most young people who experience the death of a loved one during childhood do not feel a need for professional services (Harrison & Harrington, 2001). Children are resilient, and even children bereaved by parental suicide often demonstrate low levels of distress in the face of such trauma (Ratnarajah & Schofield, 2007). While most children experience some negative impact on psychosocial well-being in the short term regarding the death of a parent to any cause, for the majority, these difficulties do not persist or require specialist intervention (Akerman & Statham, 2011). As such, psychotherapeutic treatment should be reserved for those in genuine need (Bonano & Mancini, 2002).

Professionals must determine and implement "best practices" according to the unique needs and situations of their clients. The nature of support and intervention should be based on an assessment of each child's particular needs, as there is no "one size fits all" approach for assisting children bereaved by parental suicide. In fact, a risk of harm is present if services are offered that are not appropriate to need (Akerman & Statham, 2011; Nicholson, Foote, & Grigerick, 2009). Assessment might include level of distress following the death, as those with higher levels of distress tend to benefit most from intervention (Akerman & Statham, 2011). Gender differences should also be accounted for, since males and females tend to respond differently to typical interventions (Akerman & Statham, 2011). Timing of intervention should also be a consideration, as brief interventions taking place early in bereavement may be inadequate to address the magnitude of disruption produced by suicide (Murphy, Johnson, & Lohan, 2003). Additional factors that have bearing on selection of approach include age, stage of development, personality structure, previous losses, trauma and psychiatric history, coping style, presence of protective factors in their social environment (such as family and economic support), and how the child understands and makes sense of the death (Akerman & Statham, 2011; Jordan & Neimeyer, 2003; Ratnarajah & Schofield, 2007).

Our participants also revealed the need to assess for symptoms of mental illness when counseling children bereaved by parental suicide. In many of our participants, mental health issues existed prior to the suicide and continued or were exacerbated after the fact, suggesting both genetic and social predispositions. Mental health issues will influence choice and frequency of intervention, and should be accounted for in a treatment plan. Further, child survivors of parental suicide experience a six-fold increased risk of attempting or completing suicide in their lifetimes (Brent et al., 2002; Hung & Rabin, 2009; Sorensen et al., 2009). As such, counselors should know the signs of suicide and assess for suicide risk (see Table 6.1).

Our participants also revealed the need to assess long-standing family communication patterns. Cycles of poor family communication present before the parental suicide will subsequently influence family responses and the healing process. Clients, especially young clients, often lack skill and confidence in expressing themselves or find it difficult to put feelings into words. Survivors suggested that

TABLE 6.1 Signs of Suicide

According to the American Foundation for Suicide Prevention (2011), some suicides occur without any outward warning, but most people do give warnings, including the following:

- Observable signs of serious depression including unrelenting low mood, pessimism, hopelessness, desperation, anxiety, psychic pain, inner tension, withdrawal, loss of pleasure from activities that had once been enjoyable, and sleep problems
- Increased alcohol and/or other drug use
- Recent impulsiveness and taking unnecessary risks
- Threatening suicide or expressing a strong wish to die
- Making a plan, including giving away prized possessions, sudden or impulsive purchase of a firearm, or obtaining other means such as poisons or medications
- Unexpected rage or anger

Note. For more information on what to do if you suspect someone is suicidal, visit the American Foundation for Suicide Prevention website at http://www.afsp.org/index.cfm?fuseaction=home.viewPage&page_id=1.

because avoidance and distraction are often used by children of parental suicide to protect emotions, they may not raise red flags at home or school. They may be well-behaved, good students who are suffering in silence, and they may not take the initiative to seek help. This possible response should be reflected in assessment to avoid overlooking needs that are not overtly manifest.

A Differentiated Response

Children do not recover in isolation from others, and support must include their family and community (Kaslow & Aronson, 2004), with multiple layers of support available. Based on their review of the treatment literature, Hung and Rabin (2009) cite the potential usefulness of individual therapy for those experiencing complicated grief due to suicide bereavement (Webb, 2003), family therapy (Brown et al., 2007), and a combination of individual, family, and group sessions (Sandler et al., 2003) to allow a child to express feelings in different contexts. Heikes (1997) calls for a multidimensional approach following parental suicide, asserting that the family and larger support system of the child need to be involved in recovery. Widening the safety net of support to include other caring adults can counteract the negative effects of missing parental bonds. This becomes particularly important if the surviving parent is unable to provide support due to his or her own grief.

A differentiated response to childhood bereavement is important, one that accounts for each child's needs and circumstance, including both proactive and reactive elements (Akerman & Statham, 2011). Proactive elements are strategies that strengthen all children's resilience and the preparedness to address grieving and trauma, while reactive approaches address the specific needs of bereaved children with varying supports and interventions (Akerman & Statham, 2011). The "Grief Matters for Children" campaign based in the UK promotes this multifaceted approach that is designed for schools but can be applied to other settings as well (Figure 6.1).

In discussing their experiences with parental suicide, our participants agreed, suggesting a broader, multifaceted approach. The less-than-helpful responses from clergy, school personnel, and other professionals suggest a need for additional training in childhood grief and loss. School personnel, for example, might proactively incorporate material on grief and loss or life-change into their curricula so that children are taught to better support one another through difficult times. Another aspect of a broader approach is to provide additional public education regarding the link between mental illness and suicide, not only for the purpose of suicide prevention but also to reduce stigma, uncertainty, insecurity, and misinformation.

A Focus on the Whole Family

Studies indicate a need to strengthen the protective factors within the child's life by providing support to parents of bereaved children, particularly for the surviving parent when one parent has died (Akerman & Statham, 2011). Hung and Rabin

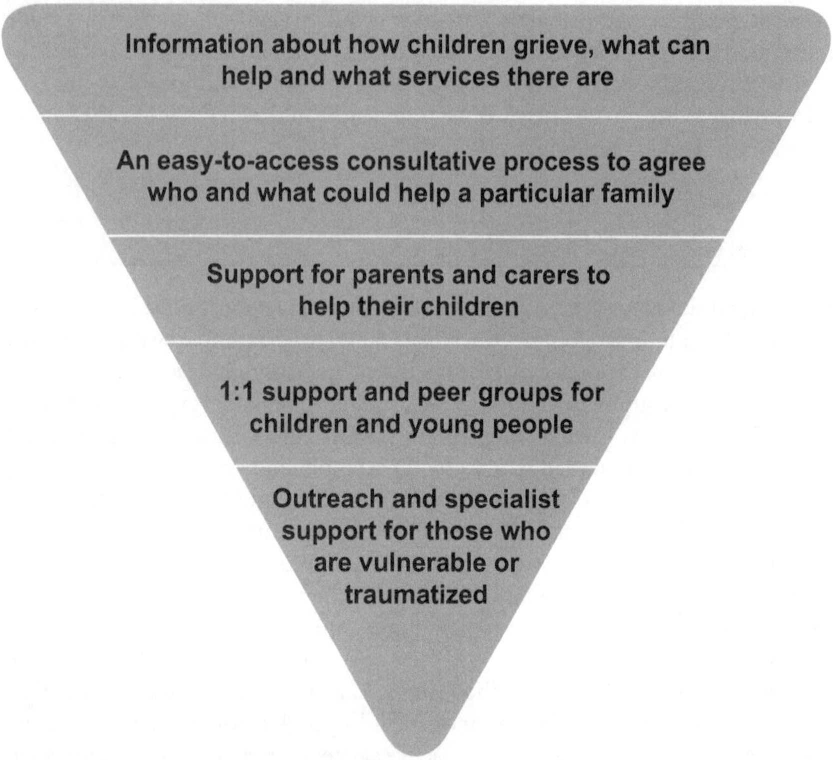

FIGURE 6.1 A multifaceted approach to supporting bereaved children.
Source: Childhood Bereavement Network: Grief Matters for Children Call to action briefing paper. Reprinted with permission.

(2009), based on their comprehensive review of the literature, assert that how the surviving parent copes with the death of a spouse has a huge impact on how well surviving children fare. Resilience is largely cultivated through strong bonds with loving adults, and unavailable surviving parents can severely disrupt those ties (Dyregrov, 2009b; Ratnarajah & Schofield, 2007; Requarth, 2006). Kaslow and Aronson (2004) contend that adults should be supported first, connecting them with resources and educating them about children's grief reactions so as to facilitate a safe environment that cultivates healing.

Clinicians and researchers alike agree on the need for family-based intervention (Dyregrov & Dyregrov, 2005). Parental suicide survivors may seek refuge in their families. As such, family relationships should be nourished, and loved ones should be prepared to facilitate this coping strategy. Higher levels of primary caregiver warmth and discipline and lower levels of mental health issues after a death have been associated with more resilience and better child outcomes (Lin et al., 2004). "Positive parenting" has been found to be a protective factor against mental health problems for children who have had a parent die (Haine et al., 2006). One framework for what parents can do to assist their children in managing challenges and to progress in their recovery utilizes the fundamental tasks of parenting (e.g., safety and sustenance, socio-emotional support, stimulation, surveillance, structure, and social connectedness) to discuss the challenges, responsibilities, and roles parents play in their child's recovery from such a developmentally challenging circumstance (Bradley, 2007). Family-oriented approaches for suicide survivors have received increasing recognition in the literature (e.g., Kaslow & Aronson, 2004).

One specific family intervention, the Family Bereavement Program, has been evaluated rigorously and found to be effective for children and young people experiencing problematic grief (Sandler et al., 1992). The program is designed to prevent potential mental health complications that may result from a parent's death by targeting mediating factors such as parental demoralization, negative life events, parental warmth, and stable positive events in the family. It targets the entire family, educating members about the grief process, creating a support network for families by connecting them with others who have experienced similar events, and using a trained family advisor who has also experienced significant bereavement (Akerman & Statham, 2011).

Haine and colleagues (2006) identify mediating factors that the literature suggests could be incorporated into interventions for parentally bereaved children. Those relevant to a family focus include increasing self-esteem and adaptive control beliefs; improving coping skills; supporting children to express emotion in adaptive ways; facilitating positive parent-child relationships; enhancing parental warmth; improving parent-child communication; fostering effective discipline; reducing parental distress; increasing positive family interactions; and reducing children's exposure to negative life events.

Warmbrod (1986) identifies three stages of grief counseling when working with bereaved children and parents. She advocates treatment of the parent and child together in an effort to break through the barriers of pain, confusion, and isolation experienced by all family members. Counselors model, for the parent, appropriate responses to children's questions and reactions. The first stage of counseling used is "The Beginning: The Death and Funeral," which encourages the family to talk about what happened and share their reactions. The second stage, "The Middle: The Past Memories," encourages survivors to talk about and share memories of the deceased. And finally, "The End: The Present and Future," invites the family to focus on future plans and hopes.

Our participants' stories mirrored the need for a family-focused approach, providing depth to the argument that the family context is an important element of the healing process. We learned the importance of counseling not only for the child but also for the surviving parent, as he or she plays a key role in modeling healthy grieving. Surviving parents should be urged to seek out support for themselves and to encourage their children to make best use of available services. Surviving parents should not attempt to handle their child's recovery in isolation. Survivors of parental suicide need the support of their parents to best engage in community services, as children may resist formal and informal support. Parents should be encouraged to openly discuss the loss experience with new teachers and discuss special needs that their children may have in school. Surviving parents and other family members should attend to the child's mental health needs, even in the face of such resistance. One participant in our study shared that "*the rest of the family has such a big impact on the child. The family needs to get help and be an example and try and help the kid get through it.*"

If the surviving parent is not functioning well due to their own grief, increased responsibilities, or mental health issues, the counselor might identify additional community and family supports. Otherwise, children tend to inappropriately assume more responsibility, and they then lack the support, structure, and direction they need to thrive. Counselors should watch for the tendency to take on adult responsibility, become overly compliant, or maintain few peer friendships. Some children feel responsible for the care of the entire family, at the expense of their own needs as children. In some instances, adults make misguided comments that foster this perceived sense of responsibility—for example, suggesting that they are the "man of the house now."

Another role for counselors is to work with the family to utilize developmentally appropriate terms and communication methods to reveal the truth about the death. Children should be told the death was a suicide soon after the event, in a developmentally appropriate, accurate, careful, and loving fashion (Cain, 2002). This approach is critical in helping to construct meaning out of the experience (Hung & Rabin, 2009; Ratnarajah & Schofield, 2007). Language that is neither euphemistic nor metaphoric should be used; the use of the word suicide with even a young child may provide the basis for future discussions and serve to destigmatize the experience (Mitchell et al., 2006). Open and honest communication is essential, and children should be encouraged to ask questions and work through what occurred (Davies, 1998). Others who have understanding of the realities of suicide and the deceased parent are an important source of support. The telling must not be an event, but a process, with experiences being retold at different points in the child's life; as children mature, they will need new information about the death (Cain, 2002; Mitchell et al., 2006). Further, although the end of the deceased person's life may have been filled with difficulty, also reminiscing about happier times can aid in coping and preserving important family history.

Parental suicide survivors benefit from truthful information about the suicide, contributing mental health issues, and the struggles of the deceased person. Healthy family communication has been found to serve a protective role, creating resiliency in children affected by the experience of parental suicide (Grossman et al., 1995). Closed communication in which children are "protected" by hiding the cause of death or not talking about it creates a dishonest communication cycle that delays grieving, leads to anger, and results in feelings of betrayal later in life. When children are not told the true cause of death from the beginning, they lose trust in others when the facts finally do come out (Clark & Goldney, 1995). One participant in our study shared the following: "*open communication is needed . . . my mother tried to cover up the suicide, and she did it for the most loving of reasons, I know that . . . I confronted her and said 'Mom, why did you try and tell us that Dad didn't die by suicide?' and she said, 'You kids were too young, I didn't want you to have to go through that pain.' That was her reason, she wanted to save us from the pain, but it really didn't help because . . . you're always wondering.*"

Support for the child is essential and the family provides the most natural context for such support. Because divorce, separation, and remarriage are common in American society, some surviving children may not have a strong connection with the surviving parent. Counselors should be prepared to address this and encourage strengthened relationships when in the best interest of the child. Role models such as stepparents, older siblings, and extended family members can offset the struggles with identity from growing up without both parents that can accompany parental suicide. Siblings are also important sources of support immediately following the death and throughout life, and relationships should be nurtured and supported. Because of the nature of the death and often complex family dynamics, surviving children may experience resistance or rejection from certain family members. They should be assisted with these feelings of rejection and family conflict, and other adults can also play a positive role with the child (e.g., teachers, adult family friends).

True for child bereavement associated with any type of loss, creating normalcy and routine within the family is important, and the whole family can be engaged in this process. Carrying on with significant family events and rituals can be helpful, and family members might go out of their way to make such times special, even in the absence of the deceased parent. Surviving parents should be encouraged to allow their child to be a "kid," and to have fun, play, and engage in activities with other kids. Feelings of abandonment are common for those bereaved by parental suicide, and surviving parents and other family members should be encouraged to express their continued commitment to the child. Further, counselors might assist surviving parents in understanding how their own parenting approach may change due to their grief and the absence of the other parent and how a sense of stability for the child might be fostered alongside such changes. Surviving parents who are struggling with their own emotions can still provide an important supportive presence by simply spending time with the child.

Trauma-Informed Practice

Trauma symptoms after the loss of a parent may be present in children who have experienced a sudden death (Cohen, Goodman, Brown, & Mannarino, 2004; McClatchey, Vonk, & Palardy, 2009), and may be heightened for death involving suicide. The importance of addressing trauma symptoms when they coexist with grief systems has been established (Cohen et al., 2004). As such, the use of trauma-focused treatment for children who experience a traumatic loss such as suicide has been suggested in the literature (Cohen et al., 2004). In using this approach, children are helped to make meaning of the traumatic loss and integrate their experience into a larger vision of themselves and the world around them, recognize their fear and pain, and identify how they have grown and strengthened through the experience (Cohen et al., 2004). Specific trauma interventions like exposure, stress inoculation techniques, and cognitive restructuring have been shown to help decrease trauma symptoms (Cohen et al., 2004; Cohen, Mannarino, & Deblinger,

TABLE 6.2 Resources for Trauma-Informed Practice

EMDR Institute, Inc.: http://www.emdr.com/
International Society for Traumatic Stress Studies: http://www.istss.org/Home.htm
National Center for Trauma-Informed Care: http://www.samhsa.gov/nctic/
Trauma-Informed Practices and Expressive Arts Therapy Institute and Learning Center: http://trauma-informedpractice.org/

2006; Goenjian et al., 1997; Layne et al., 2001; McClatchey et al., 2009). Eye movement desensitization and reprocessing (EMDR), an information processing therapy that attends to past experiences that have set the groundwork for pathology, the current situations that trigger dysfunctional emotions, beliefs, and sensations, and the positive experience needed to enhance future adaptive behaviors and mental health, has been used for a wide range of trauma-related pathologies (Shapiro, 2001, 2002). Cohen et al. (2006) developed and tested a cognitive-behavioral treatment for children with traumatic grief responses related to death of a parent from traumatic causes (e.g., car accident, suicide, homicide), finding that specifically defining the nature and mechanisms of disturbed grief reactions could be more helpful in designing interventions than focusing on specific causes of death.

A number of our participants reflected the need for trauma-informed care, revealing the impact of discovering the body and the aftermath of the suicide. They discussed symptoms of posttraumatic stress disorder and experiences in therapy with EMDR and systematic desensitization. While avoidance of people and places associated with the suicide may help people cope in the short term, at some point survivors may want to directly address their fears and emotions. They should not be pushed to do so, but rather offered support as they face such encounters. A full discussion of trauma-related therapies and their efficacy for serving children of parental suicide is beyond the scope of this chapter, though the reader may seek out further information through the resources listed in Table 6.2.

Meaning-Making and Growth

A growing body of literature suggests that finding meaning is an important issue for most people coping with loss and trauma (e.g., Bulman & Wortman, 1977; Chodoff et al., 1964; Davis, Nolen-Hoeksema, & Larson, 1998; Kast, 1998; Kushner, 1981; Neimeyer, 2009; Silver et al., 1983; Taylor, 1983; Thompson & Pitts, 1993). Research demonstrates that bereaved people struggling to make sense of their loss could benefit from interventions that foster this process (Neimeyer et al., 2010), using approaches appropriate to developmental level. When the loss is more objectively traumatic, data suggest that a search for sense or significance in the loss is more common (Davis, Wortman, Lehaman, & Silver, 2000). Because not all parental suicide survivors view themselves as being on a quest for meaning derived from their experience, though, caution should be used in incorporating such strategies. Many find meaning and consolation in systems of secular and spiritual beliefs and practices that have served them well in the past (Attig, 2000) and may not need additional efforts in this regard.

Finding meaning in the face of suicide loss satisfies the need to make sense of the loss, restores sense of self-worth, reframes assumptions about how the world works, and finds benefit in the experience of loss (Begley & Quayle, 2007; Davis & Nolen-Hoeksema, 2001). Sands et al. (2011) propose the tripartite model of suicide bereavement (TMSB), which focuses on key themes that those who are bereaved struggle with as they restory their loss. The themes focus on meaning making "within the context of the bereaved person's relationship with self, the deceased, and significant others" (p. 261). The model focuses on "psychological, relational, and existential tasks faced by survivors as they attempt to grasp, step into, and ultimately differentiate from the mindset that led their loved one toward a tragic relinquishment of life" (p. 278).

Research suggests the importance of normalizing the concept of "growth" among people who are grieving, viewing it for some as a natural extension of the grieving process, perhaps beyond the end point of "acceptance" discussed by Kubler-Ross (Smith et al., 2011). Under a constructivist framework, people are motivated to develop and maintain a meaningful self-narrative, which contains deeply ingrained beliefs and assumptions that they are deserving of positive outcomes, that they have significant control over their lives, and that the world is generally compassionate and fair (Janoff-Bulman, 1992; Neimeyer et al., 2010). The death of a loved one challenges the validity of such core beliefs and damages the soundness of the self-narrative, with violent, sudden, or seemingly meaningless deaths causing the world to appear dangerous, unpredictable, or unjust (Janoff-Bulman, 1992; Neimeyer, 2011; Park & Folkman, 1997).

Therapists may draw on constructivist ideas to help people assimilate the loss experience into their pre-loss beliefs and self-narratives, or accommodate the loss by reorganizing, deepening, or expanding their beliefs and self-narratives to embrace the reality of the loss (Janoff-Bulman, 1992; Park & Folkman, 1997). Strategies that may assist children in reestablishing a coherent self-narrative that integrates the loss while also allowing life to move forward along new lines include retelling the narrative of the loss, therapeutic writing, attention to language and metaphor, the use of evocative visualization, and encountering the prosymptom position (Neimeyer et al., 2010). Neimeyer (2011) discusses strategies to advance the goal of meaning reconstruction, beginning with fostering a sense of presence to the needs of the client, progressing to a delicate attention to the process of therapy, and finding ultimate expression in a great variety of specific therapeutic procedures. Bereavement work should focus not only on understanding and managing the emotional and physical challenges of grief but also on constructing a meaningful narrative of a world that integrates the loss into the survivor's life narrative and reestablishes those ideals that we take for granted—security, predictability, trust, and optimism (Neimeyer, 2002). Indeed, helping children make meaning of a loss creates the conditions for personal growth and a positive grief outcome.

Our participants also shared important information regarding meaning making. Through them, we learned the importance of encouraging reevaluation of the event and its meaning over time, as maturity and developmental stage can be factors in how the death is processed and integrated. Participants also alluded to the difficulty surrounding unanswered questions and the nature of the death. One participant recounted repeatedly asking "*why*" in a lengthy letter written to his deceased father. "*I think I asked 'why' probably a hundred times. 'I love you, I miss you, but why, why would you do that?'*" Counselors should provide calm, nonjudgmental, repeated reassurance in the face of repeated questions such as, "Why would a parent commit suicide?" or "What would my life have been like?" A child who asks, "Why didn't my dad tell me he was thinking about suicide?" may be feeling guilt and abandonment, and may feel reassured by the response: "When people aren't thinking clearly there is no one who they would confide in. Your father loved you very much. I am sure that he would have told you if he could have." Grieving children who ask the same questions repeatedly may not be seeking concrete answers; they may be seeking reassurance and meaning. It is important to understand the need behind any question a child asks.

Expressive Techniques

The use of various expressive therapies has gained increasing attention in the research and professional literature. Such approaches allow children to express and process their feelings, and can be particularly helpful to those who have difficulty verbalizing. Expressive therapies can reduce the impact of the loss, increase self-esteem, open up social opportunities, and provide nonverbal ways to express feelings. They may be used in individual, family, or group sessions, providing opportunities for the participant to communicate his or her bereavement experience in symbolic form (Bowman, 1994; Rubin, 2005; Webb, 2003). Expressive methods have been used in grief groups, retreats, and workshops (Cates, 1986; Masterman & Reams, 1988; Zambelli & DeRosa, 1992).

Particular methods should be selected and perhaps combined based on child needs, circumstances of the death, and the family/community narrative about it (Webb, 2003). Bibliotherapy (Doka, 1990; Rudman, Kabakow, Gagne, & Bernstein, 1993), art therapy (Brountas, 1988; Zambelli, Clark, Barile, & DeJong, 1988), play therapy (Kronick, 1985), creative writing, journal writing, and music are among the most popular techniques. Writing memories of the deceased person, for example, can be important to children who may be afraid that their loved one will be forgotten (Noonan, 2000). Writing interventions have also demonstrated promise particular to suicide bereavement, particularly for males who are less likely to disclose traumatic experiences to others (Kovac & Range, 2000; Pennebaker, Zech, & Rime, 2001; Smyth, 1998). Memory books, photos, and letters further provide opportunities to share memories and also connect concrete objects to the deceased. Additionally, traditional play activities can serve as an outlet for emotions, and may facilitate comfort in sharing the bereavement story (Deblinger,

TABLE 6.3 Journaling

Fire in My Heart, Ice in My Veins is a journal for teenagers who have experienced loss. The journal can be ordered at http://fireinmyheartjournal.com/, which also provides an online environment to share stories and illustrations.

McLeer, & Henry, 1990). Because children may not be able to tolerate strong or painful feelings for an extended period of time (Deblinger et al., 1990; Samide & Stockton, 2002), expressive therapies may be ideal brief therapeutic strategies to use when facilitating relaxation and connection with others.

Our participants provided testament to the value of expressive activities. We learned that writing and art can be powerful vehicles for saying good-bye to the deceased parent or for symbolically expressing thoughts and feelings to them. Such activities allow more private ways of expressing thoughts and emotions needed by some children. Writing and art can also be utilized to process dreams and might be recommended as a comforting or therapeutic approach. Professionals can introduce and encourage personal ways of dealing with grief that are age-appropriate. Young children, for example, may not be able to journal, but they can certainly draw or talk about dreams (see Table 6.3). Professionals might help children to write their own stories.

Rituals and ceremonies are additional expressions that can be important in progressing through grief, transitioning roles, and keeping a continuing bond with the deceased (Cameron, 1991; Klass, Silverman, & Nickman, 1996; Rando, 1992; Wolfelt, 1996; Worden, 1996). Ceremonies such as a balloon lift, candle lighting, or cemetery visit are all widely viewed as effective in allowing children and adolescents the opportunity to share, express emotions, and bring a sense of finality to the death.

Support Groups

Most authors argue in support of the effectiveness and adequacy of social support interventions, though only a handful of empirical studies on the effectiveness of self-help groups overall have been conducted (Lieberman, 1986). The majority of participants in a study examining the needs of suicide survivors indicated they had sought support from suicide grief groups, and 94% found them helpful (McMenamy et al., 2008). Talking one-on-one with another survivor was seen as helpful by 100% of participants who had received that type of support. Though there is much literature on support groups for those bereaved by suicide, it consists mainly of clinical descriptions and models of existing programs for survivors, with little empirical investigation (Cerel, Padgett, Conwell, & Reed, 2009; Jordan, 2011). There is, however, considerable anecdotal and some empirical support for the conclusion that bereavement support groups overall are an important and valuable form of postvention for many suicide survivors (Jordan, 2011).

Suicide support groups have been described and recommended for many years in the literature, with Jordan and McIntosh (2011) providing a recent overview with general guidelines for facilitators. Most studies report positive outcomes for adult participants (Farberow, 1992; Mitchell et al., 2003; Murphy et al., 1998; Rogers, Sheldon, Barwick, Letofsky, & Lancee, 1982; Renaud, 1995). While our focus in this book is on children, such results may have implications for others in the child's family who are impacted by the loss, as well as the child who may require support later in life. Many bereaved children experience social isolation and lack friends who understand their experience (Worden, 1996), with children bereaved by suicide more significantly impacted due to stigma. Peer acceptance is a great concern for all children and adolescents, and those who have experienced the death of a loved one are not exempt (Fleming & Balmer, 1996). Support groups are an intuitively appealing approach given the potential for reducing the isolation and embarrassment that often accompanies the social stigma of suicide (Hung & Rabin, 2009). Internet support groups have gained popularity for those living in rural areas, as well as for others who have difficulty accessing or are uncomfortable with face-to-face support groups (Feigelman, Gorman, Beal, & Jordan, 2008).

In general, the past six decades have produced an evolution in general children's bereavement groups in terms of scope and content. An art therapy group for bereaved children with a coinciding parent support group has demonstrated positive reactions by parents, who reported more expression of feelings from their children and improved family communication (Zambelli et al., 1988). Similar results were found in another group intervention for bereaved children, who appeared less constricted and angry over time, and were better able to understand and cope with the emotional reactions associated with their grief (Masterman & Reams, 1988). Parents of the children reported a decrease in behavior problems at home and school, and increased communication with their children about bereavement issues. Masterman and Reams (1988) advocate an eight-session program with school-age children, as well as preschoolers ages 3 to 6, where bereavement issues are dealt with intermittently with activities and play time. Kandt (1994) suggests using a 12-session format for bereaved adolescents, incorporating activities like journal writing, creating a family tree and memory book, and a balloon lift to give a sense of finality to the grieving process. Gray (1988) also found promising results with a support group intervention with bereaved adolescents, who reported high levels of satisfaction, experience of positive difference in their lives as a result, and the ability to express their grief upon meeting others who were going through similar difficulties.

In terms of helping children process the loss of a parent, the effectiveness of traditional bereavement groups is low (Currier et al., 2007), and support groups designed on the basis of grief theory have demonstrated mixed results (Graham, 1999; Huss & Ritchie, 1999; Samide & Stockton, 2002; Sandler et al., 1992; Sandler et al., 2003; Schilling, Koh, Abramovistz, & Gilbert, 1992). Grief groups based on both grief theory and trauma theory, however, have shown promising results, with findings indicating that trauma symptoms need to be addressed first in order for children to process their grief (Goenjian et al., 1997; Layne et al., 2001; Saltzman,

Pynoos, Layne, Steinberg, & Aisenberg, 2001). Mitchell et al. (2007) present a case for a support group designed specifically for child survivors of parental suicide, providing a theoretical framework for support group interventions and a structure for an eight-week group.

One controlled study has evaluated the effectiveness of a bereavement support group specific to children who have experienced parental or sibling suicide (Pfeffer et al., 2002). The manual-based intervention, which also included a psychoeducational intervention for parents, focused on reactions to death and suicide and strengthening coping skills. Results showed significant decreases for children in the treatment group in depression and anxiety symptoms, although not in trauma or social adjustment. There were no significant changes in parents' depression scores, which makes sense, given that the intervention was designed to educate parents about bereavement in children rather than directly affect their own grief responses. Although the study by Pfeffer et al. (2002) on a suicide-specific group experience did show promising results, other researchers generally agree that suicide-bereaved children do not need a specially designed group intervention (Brown et al., 2007; Requarth, 2006). Group facilitators are trained to work with each child's unique experience of grief, and differences for those who are suicide-bereaved are outweighed by similarities of those bereaved by other causes. The same recommendation, however, does not hold true for adults seeking support. It is difficult for adult survivors of suicide to integrate with more general bereavement groups due to the stigma and unique grieving needs surrounding this type of death (McMenamy et al., 2008; Requarth, 2006). Perhaps children are more forgiving and less tainted than adults, allowing acceptance of loss as a more universal experience.

Participants in our study also reflected the benefits of using support groups. They discussed the need to connect with others who have experienced parental suicide, the death of a parent, or another significant life trauma in that they felt they had no one to talk to who understood. They noted the healing that can come from not only being supported by others who understand but also using their experiences to assist others. One participant offered this advice: "*I would set up a circle of people who volunteer to be there, some teachers, some friends, and even clergy, and get together and talk.*" See Tables 6.4 and 6.5 for resources to help start a suicide bereavement support group or to locate an existing support group.

School-Based Support

As schools are often part of the bereaved child's life in the aftermath of parental suicide, it is essential that they are prepared to provide adequate support and a context conducive to healing. In addition to a school's focus on suicide prevention and intervention for youth at risk of suicide themselves, a comprehensive, school-based suicide program also contains postvention services for those who have experienced the suicide of a loved one (Ward, 1995). While much has been written about the school's role in suicide prevention and response to a youth suicide,

TABLE 6.4 Resources for Starting a Support Group

Online Resources

Children's Grief Education Association: http://www.childgrief.org/supportgroups.htm

HEARTBEAT: Grief Support Following Suicide: http://heartbeatsurvivorsaftersuicide.org/index.shtml

Suicide Prevention Action Network. The Basics: Facilitating a Suicide Survivors Support Group: http://www.spanusa.org/files/General_Documents/The_Basics_Facilitator_Guide.pdf

World Health Organization. Preventing Suicide: How to Start a Survivors' Group: http://www.who.int/mental_health/prevention/suicide/resource_survivors.pdf

Books

Jordan, J. (2011). Group work with suicide survivors. In J.J. Jordan & J.J. McIntosh (Eds.), *Grief after suicide: Understanding the consequences and caring for the survivors* (pp. 283–300). New York: Taylor & Francis.

Jordan, J., & Harpel, J. (2007). *Facilitating suicide bereavement support groups: A self-study manual*. New York: American Foundation for Suicide Prevention.

TABLE 6.5 Locating Existing Support Groups

American Association of Suicidology: http://www.suicidology.org/web/guest/home

American Foundation for Suicide Prevention: https://www.afsp.org/preventing-suicide/our-education-and-prevention-programs

Association for Death Education and Counseling: www.adec.org/

Camp HOPE: www.camphopeforkids.org

Dougy Center: National Center for Grieving Children & Families: http://www.dougy.org/

GriefNet: http://www.griefnet.org/support/sg2.html

Suicide Grief Support Forum, Friends and Families of Suicides: http://www.pos-ffos.com/

Survivors of Suicide: http://www.survivorsofsuicide.com/

little work has provided guidance on postvention services for children and youth who have experienced suicide within their own families. Some services focus on support and further prevention following the suicide of a peer, and those who experience the suicide of a parent may not fit into existing frameworks.

Schools can play an important role in ensuring that the needs of a bereaved child are recognized and approached in an appropriate fashion, including raising awareness among school personnel and students about how to respond, providing school-based counseling and groups, and providing appropriate referral for other community resources. Various sources outline strategies that schools can use to assist bereaved students, though the approaches are not necessarily grounded in research evidence. Recommendations for school psychologists regarding childhood bereavement have been cited (e.g., Ayyash-Abado, 2001), as have group interventions such as SHIFT (Safe, Hopeful, Inclusive Environment for Feelings and Thoughts), play therapy, family intervention, and various ways of making memorials that a school can undertake (O'Connor & Templeton, 2002). Holland (2004) describes "good practice" for school personnel in the immediate aftermath of the death, such as preparing classmates for the child's return, providing access to a "quiet room," and allocating a "special person" for the child to talk to. In the Project Iceberg Study (Holland, 2004), adults recalling their experiences of losing a parent during childhood reported feeling isolated, ignored, embarrassed, or different upon return to school and suggested that a simple acknowledgment of their loss and a kind word may have been adequate, with no need for more intense intervention.

Few examples of empirically evaluated school-based interventions for bereaved children exist in the literature. An Australian-based study evaluated an eight-week education program for youth ages 12–18 who experienced the loss of a parent or significant other through separation, divorce, or death (Frydenberg, Muller, & Ivens, 2006). Results indicate that it helped female students to cope with loss, but had a less pronounced impact on male students. Music therapy and trauma/grief-focused school-based brief psychotherapy were found to be promising treatment models in a meta-analysis of 27 studies (Rosnera, Kruse, & Hagl, 2010). The incorporation of art therapy into school-based groups is also used frequently, though with little empirical evidence as to its effects (Finn, 2003).

A study of 32 young suicide survivors (20% of whom had lost a parent) provides insight about the difficulties faced and overall experiences with support from school (Dyregrov, 2009b). Survivors had problems with intrusive thoughts and concentration, but they also desired a "psychological time out" from the sad atmosphere at home. As such, school served as an important reprieve. Survivors also expressed feeling pressure to perform at school at the same level as before the death and wanted schools to be aware that it was not helpful to their healing. They further encouraged teachers to use caution when approaching them, suggesting that they demonstrate understanding of their situation, "without falling all over them in front of everybody else" (Dyregrov, 2009b, p. 155). Dalke (1994), in a case study of two girls who lost a father to suicide, described one young girl's anger at a teacher who waited six months to offer a hug and an invitation to talk. The girl felt abandoned because the teacher knew what had happened, but waited so long to reach out. The teacher's gesture also caused the girl to relive the event and rekindled the girl's anger with her deceased father.

Participants in our study also helped us to gain insight about how schools can support children impacted by parental suicide. Though it is somewhat common for school personnel to receive training on working with bereaved children, specific training regarding suicide bereavement may be warranted. Schools may want to develop crisis plans that involve attention to the special needs of children following the loss of a parent to suicide. School counselors, psychologists, and social workers have a significant role in responding to students' emotional, psychological, social, and family needs. They should receive training, pursue continuing education, consult with other professionals, and proactively develop strategies for working with bereaved students. Beyond existing bullying prevention programs within the school, school staff should help children understand and develop empathy. Children may make comments about the death to one another, the bereaved child, or school staff. School staff should be prepared to respond to such comments, clarify misinformation, and advocate for students who are being teased.

School personnel can also play a role in fostering connections for the child impacted by parental suicide. Because of the stigma and trust issues associated with suicide, long-term, selective friendships can be significant sources of support. Such friendships should be nurtured and strengthened. School personnel can assist friends in sending flowers, making cards, or calling their friend following the death. Kind gestures from friends can mean a lot, though often children do not know what to say or do. New friendships might also be fostered, particularly with other children who have experienced traumatic life events. School staff should refer students to existing support groups that are available and consider developing their own support group if none exist.

School personnel themselves may also be a source of support. Caring gestures like sending cards or flowers, making supportive phone calls, or attending the funeral can go a long way with this type of loss. One participant in our study suggested to school personnel, "*sometimes you say nothing and you just sit with them. I mean just chill out, you just go whewwwww, like that, that was intense be available.*" Children who experience the death of a parent to suicide have genuine emotional needs that manifest in the school environment. School personnel should proactively express empathy and support, encourage the processing of emotions (through such means as talking, writing, and drawing), respond to emotions that arise, and allow reasonable accommodations in school work. They might consider reaching out to the family outside of the school environment. Further, the impacts of parental suicide do not diffuse quickly, and ongoing support may be needed. Designating a specific staff member, perhaps the school counselor, social worker, or a special teacher, to regularly check in with the student may be helpful. See Table 6.6 for resources to help support school professionals.

TABLE 6.6 Resources for School Professionals

American School Counselor Association: http://schoolcounselor.org/
Children's Grief Education Association: http://www.childgrief.org/childgrief.htm
School Social Work Association of America: http://sswaa.org/
Suicide Prevention Resource Center: http://www.sprc.org/featured_resources/customized/teachers.asp

Grief Camps

Innovative at the time, Moyer (1988) describes a novel 3-day camping program specifically for children who had experienced the death of a family member or close friend. The program was created by a hospice due to the increasing need and corresponding lack of services available for children experiencing death and loss. The goals of the weekend were to have children be with others who had also experienced a death and have fun, allow expression of feelings of grief and loss, and provide opportunities to ask questions about their experiences. Grief camps are now found throughout the world (McClatchey & Wimmer, 2012), with a list provided by the Association of Death Education and Counseling containing 108 camps located in 39 different states, and 3 camps that operate in multiple locations throughout the U.S. (a state-by-state list of grief camps can be found at www.camphopeforkids.org).

Little has been done to determine the efficacy of camps for bereaved children, which follow a variety of formats and generally target children bereaved by a variety of causes. Studies that have been conducted demonstrate somewhat mixed results. One study reported positive experiences of a weekend camp in which children participated in grief theory-based activities such as painting feeling masks, creating and playing a board game, participating in memorial services, letter writing, and working on grief coping skills (Nabors et al., 2004). However, the results suggest no change in anxiety and sadness levels as measured by rating scales. Another study evaluated a camp with a psychodynamic and cognitive-behavioral therapy–oriented curriculum that aimed to help campers cope while working through their grieving process and to reduce psychological distress linked to cognitions of the loss (Farber & Sabatino, 2007). Children who attended one camp session demonstrated heightened difficulties in psychosocial functioning, while children attending a second camp session showed a decrease in such difficulties. This study included only reports from parents, adult volunteers, and camp clinicians. In another study relying on semistructured interviews and archival data, campers who had lost a family member gave mostly positive comments (Barrett, 2004). One study examining a grief theory–based camp for siblings of deceased cancer patients demonstrated perceived feelings of being better equipped to deal with grief and express feelings among attendees, and parent reports of heightened acceptance of grief feelings and increased family communication (Creed, Ruffin, & Ward, 2001).

No studies have specifically examined the efficacy of a camp intervention for children bereaved by parental suicide. One very small study of a residential bereavement group for children, young people, and families bereaved through suicide in general reported that children felt happier and parents felt better able to cope (Braiden, McCann, Barry, & Lindsay, 2009). Also, one line of research has more rigorously investigated a camp approach specific to loss of a parent from any cause. Camp MAGIK (Mainly About Grief in Kids) focuses on a child's grief issues, but also the trauma symptoms that may surround the loss of a parent, and it includes a parallel retreat for parents and guardians of the campers. A controlled outcome study of Camp MAGIK demonstrated that it reduced both posttraumatic stress disorder and childhood traumatic grief symptoms in participating campers (McClatchey et al., 2009). A program evaluation of the camp before trauma interventions were incorporated demonstrated that trauma symptoms did not decrease and in some cases increased (Searles, 2006). Though results were promising and lend credit to the trauma-focused approach, the study did not identify the components of the camp sessions that were most responsible for a reduction in symptoms. As such, the researchers further qualitatively examined the camp intervention to determine which elements were perceived to be most helpful by campers and their guardians. Therapeutic interventions deemed important included counseling sessions, memorial service, balloon release, and journaling. Traditional camp activities viewed as most healing were connecting with other campers, canoeing, and the talent show.

CASE STUDY

Camp HOPE

I sobbed when I left Camp HOPE because I didn't want to leave. Those same people, who dropped me off kicking and screaming because I didn't want to go to the camp, now were there to pick me up, and I didn't want to leave. They were like, HELLOOO! You were crying yesterday because you didn't want me to leave you here, and now you don't want to go home?! (Lisa)

Camp HOPE, attended by many of the survivors featured in this book, is one example of a camp intervention aimed at meeting the needs of grieving children, many of whom have experienced parental suicide. This overview provides basic program components and gives a sense of the usefulness of this type intervention, perhaps compelling the reader to develop a similar program, adopt program components in their own work, or refer children to programs in their areas.

Camp HOPE Overview

Camp HOPE is a nonprofit organization located in central Wisconsin, providing resources and services for grieving children and their families. Since its inception in 1989, Camp HOPE has served over 4,000 children and their families, including approximately 500 who have experienced the death of a parent to suicide. The primary program is a weekend camp offered to children and teenagers who have experienced the death of a family member or close friend. The camp is held at a private campsite in May, October, and February of each year. All services are offered free of charge to the participants and their families.

The main objective of the camp is to allow participants the opportunity to work through the grieving process in a supportive environment. Programming is designed to guide the children through the complex emotions of grief, to help normalize their grief, and to provide social support. Among the primary goals of the camp is to incorporate as much age-appropriate fun as possible. Through play, the children are able to express themselves in an emotionally safe social context, created with their developmental abilities in mind. Additionally, the children learn that it is okay to laugh and play as well as discovering that to do so is not disrespectful to the memory of the person who has died. Playing, sharing, and being with peers who have also experienced a loss through death encourages acceptance of their emotions as normal elements of grieving. Participants have the opportunity to enjoy many recreational and outdoor activities associated with camping. Many of these activities, such as storytelling, folk singing, reading, and art, provide opportunities for participants to reflect and share their stories. Similarly, a memory collage, a question-and-answer session with a physician, and a candlelight ceremony are featured activities designed to guide the children through their grief in a social milieu where they are most comfortable.

Results of a study done on Camp HOPE have indicated several aspects of the camp as beneficial (Loy, 1999). Among those were counselor competence; the fun nature of the camp; and the opportunity to share thoughts and emotions. Additionally, participants reported changes in their thoughts about being normal, their knowledge and understanding of death and loss, and the intensity of and ability to share their feelings. Both participants and guardians reported positive changes following camp, such as opening up, becoming more willing to talk about the deceased, and becoming more able to share feelings. Furthermore, they reported changes in attitude and self-esteem, better behavior at home and in school, and better understanding of others. Additionally, surveys of all participants and their parents reveal an overwhelmingly positive view of the camp and its effectiveness. Teens and preteens attending the camp expressed that it helped to normalize their feelings, increased their self-esteem and knowledge about death, and improved their behavior (Loy, 1999).

Staffing the Camp

A volunteer counseling staff is recruited and intentionally modified prior to each session; new and veteran counselors are assigned to work together to assure consistency between camps while simultaneously encouraging novice excitement. Because professional credentials are not prerequisite to serving as a counselor, the main purpose of staff training is to ensure a knowledgeable, cohesive camp.

On-site staff training is conducted during the evening prior to the children's arrival. It begins with team building activities designed to introduce staff to the campsite, the programming, and each other. Name games and beginning trust activities are typical during this session. Early on during staff training, each counselor is asked to share aspects of his or her own grief history. As counselors share, they realize that even though their grief experiences appear different on the surface, they are in fact very similar; they each experienced the pain and loss of bereavement. The importance of reflecting on one's own grief experience, and the ability to appropriately express this experience prior to working with grieving children, must be underscored. Sharing encourages cohesiveness among the counselors. The awareness and sharing of similar experiences contribute to group dynamics and bring a group together in a relatively short period of time (Worden, 1982/1991). Prior to working with grieving children, counselors must feel comfortable witnessing the pain of others and must not allow their own losses, feared losses, or anxieties interfere with their helpfulness or understanding (Worden, 1982/1991). Through sharing, counselors examine their own grief and how it might affect their work with children. After sharing grief experiences with each other, counselors are encouraged to relate their experiences to those of the children. This discussion enables the counselors to consider the grief experience of the child and to begin to formulate a plan for helping.

Each counselor receives a copy of the application form submitted on behalf of each child who enrolls in the camp. This form includes a biography, a brief grief history, grief-related difficulties and behavior problems, and a counseling history. It also includes medical information and the child's hobbies and nickname. Each piece of information allows the counselor to build a camper profile and facilitates preparation for the children's arrival.

A camp schedule is provided for each counselor. The schedule is a detailed time line for the weekend and provides the structure essential for a smoothly running camp. The activities are ordered in a progression that (a) allows the campers time to become acclimated to the surroundings and develop trust in their camp mates and counselors, (b) alternates activities that are more emotional with those designed for fun, and (c) allows a better utilization of camp facilities and staff.

The importance of an emotionally and physically safe camp, set in a fun atmosphere, is stressed. Staff training reinforces the expectation that all counselors exhibit an inviting disposition when campers arrive, participate fully in all activities during the camp, and keep the children's best interests in mind. This part of the training session highlights each phase of the camp experience and each activity. Following this session, neophyte counselors are asked to couple with veteran counselors to discuss each activity and take a tour of the campsite. Part of creating an inviting atmosphere involves cabin decor. Counselors are asked to decorate their cabins in an appealing manner, appropriate for the ages of their campers.

Components

Camp HOPE relies on six components developed through research of similar bereavement programs, trial and error, and a thorough investigation of grief literature. The six components forming the framework are (a) sharing opportunities, (b) normalizing grief, (c) developmentally appropriate activities, (d) family support, (e) trained, knowledgeable staff, and (f) an environment that is fun. The following activities support these components.

The Board of Losses

A sign displays the names of each child, counselor, and support person involved in the camp weekend, the person(s) who have died in their lives, and causes of death. It also displays colored-balloon stickers representing the relationship to the bereaved person. A blue balloon sticker may signify the death of a father, red the death of a mother, and so on.

Zambelli and DeRosa (1992) describe grief normalization as the process of seeing others with similar grief experiences. The Camp HOPE loss board is a visual representation of each loss individually, and a reminder that each person at camp has suffered the loss of a similar significant person in his or her life.

Balloon Badge

The balloon badge, a plastic name tag made in the shape of a balloon, is also designed to help normalize grief. In addition to the name of the wearer, it displays the same colored balloon sticker as on the camp board of losses. Therefore, as campers and counselors interact, they have immediate knowledge of who they are interacting with and the relationship they had with the deceased. As an example, a child can easily see and identify with other children and counselors who are also mourning the death of a father.

Camper Check-In

Children are often apprehensive about attending a grief camp; therefore initial impressions are designed to be as inviting as possible. The registration area is decorated with bright colors, balloons, and banners, and a table with cookies, juice, and coffee is available. Staff members and therapy dogs are positioned in the parking lot and at registration, and are instructed to be helpful and reassuring to parents as they begin to establish rapport with the arrivals. Staff at a check-in table record emergency telephone numbers, give cabin assignments, and introduce the children to their adult counselors.

Opening Ceremony

The camp opens with the director telling a story illustrating the importance of feeling safe and being able to share feelings. It is suggested that those in attendance be understanding and empathetic listeners, because each is experiencing a significant loss. Introductions are made, and a few important rules are covered. This session is ended on a lighthearted note, usually through the use of a satire of the camp rules.

Free Time

The first activity for all campers is free time. This is a time to establish the fun tone of the camp and allow the children and counselors an opportunity to interact and build relationships. Each counselor has been informed of a large variety of free-time activities, including canoeing and boating, fishing, hiking, and arts and crafts. The children and counselors choose an activity and begin their camp experience.

One characteristic that distinguishes children's grief from that of adults is that children need to work through their grief intermittently (Baker, Sedney, & Gross, 1992). Therefore, periods of emotional sharing are followed by fun and play. Abundant free time and varied activities are available over the course of the weekend, interspersed with grief work activities. Furthermore, games and play help to develop solid peer relationships with others in like circumstances, further normalizing grief and encouraging the adoption of healthy social meanings, norms, and behavior (Zambelli & DeRosa, 1992).

Parent Session

Families and family grief processes are inextricably linked to individual grief recovery (Moos, 1995; Costa & Holliday, 1994; Saler & Skolnick, 1992). Therefore, a parent session is an important component of Camp HOPE, designed to provide support for the entire family. The 30-minute parent session begins with a description of camp activities and suggestions of how the principles of each activity might be supported within the family when the child returns home. For example, the camp weekend supports open communication and the sharing of feelings. However, for some, that may not be the case back at home. Parents are reminded of its importance and given suggestions on how to create a sharing environment in their homes. Likewise, some children may not want to tell a parent what happened at camp upon their return home. Therefore it is important that parents know not to pressure the child, and not to feel rejected by this common reproach.

The second aspect of the parent session is the opportunity for parents to ask questions about their own grief and that of their children. A child-and-family counselor is on hand to answer questions and offer suggestions in a nonthreatening format. This session provides the opportunity for parents to learn from experts as well as each other. In many cases, they begin a healing conversation with an understanding peer, which is often carried on at their hotel that evening, and in some cases much longer. The parent session ends with a tour of the camp facilities and lunch.

Meals and Hot Chocolate Chip Cookies

Meals provide an informal time for cabin mates to share nourishment and conversation. In some cases, the conversation is quite casual; however, in others this can be a time when the campers share stories and listen to the stories of others. The menu is designed to appeal to the likes of children, featuring typical camp foods such as hot dogs, tacos, and macaroni and cheese. Early on during the first afternoon of camp, a tray of warm chocolate chip cookies and cold milk is served as a reward for attending camp and to signify fun as a top priority.

Camper Team Building

Another early activity at Camp HOPE is team building; staff members trained in teaching team building and challenge activities lead this session. Activities are designed initially to allow campers and counselors to get to know and interact with each other and later to build group unity, develop trust, and build self-esteem. Designed with the ages of the campers in mind, team building activities are conducted in age-similar groups.

Stories

In *Therapeutic Metaphors for Children and the Child Within*, Mills and Crowley (1986) explain that stories can ease isolation and normalize the experiences of children. Stories allow children to identify with the characters or elements of a story and relate them to their own situation. At Camp HOPE, a professional storyteller conducts age-appropriate story time throughout the weekend. Some of her stories are simply planned for fun; others provide a healing metaphor with the needs of bereaved children in mind. The staff storyteller is also assigned the duty of telling calming stories to the younger children at bedtime.

Visualization and Journal Writing

Journal writing helps bereaved adolescents focus thoughts and feelings (Kandt, 1994). It provides campers an age-appropriate avenue for the expression of their grief and also a visual guide to record their progress. The quote from Isak Dinesen that "All sorrows can be borne, if you put them in a story" captures the essence of the visualization and journal writing session at Camp HOPE. The adolescent equivalent of story time, this session introduces teenagers to journal writing as a vehicle of expression to use to help cope with their loss. Each teen is given a journal book to use during the activity and keep as a gift.

This session begins as the camp storyteller plays her guitar, leads a visualization designed to bring about a relaxed state, and encourages the campers to consider their loss. A story format asks campers to recall memories and emotions, consider their loss, and reflect on ways they can cope. It gently concludes by giving the participants control over their images and encouraging their future use. At the conclusion of the visualization, campers are asked to complete their first journal entry by recording their visualization experience.

Games

To begin group discussion and initiate sharing informally among groups, camp counselors use board games. The Un-Game and To Tell the Truth are designed for adolescent and adults; players respond to a series of life situation questions by sharing personal beliefs and feelings. Our Home, which has a similar purpose, is designed for younger children. Playing games such as these enables children to practice new ways of coping and relating (Zambelli & DeRosa, 1992). In addition to the therapeutic board games, the camp offers a wide selection of games and activities. An abundance of games such as Monopoly and Yahtzee, as well as the availability of footballs, basketballs, and Hula-Hoops, allows children opportunities to engage in enjoyable activities.

Nature Activities

A 45-acre lake surrounded by a 400-acre wildlife refuge provides each camper the opportunity to enjoy nature. Summer activities may include hiking or a hay ride on the many trails, weaving their way through the woodland; swimming, fishing, or boating on the lake; or simply enjoying the sunset behind a campfire. During the winter, camp activities include cross-country skiing or snow shoeing, sledding, ice-skating, and ice fishing. In addition, a wildlife expert leads several activities designed to teach about the outdoors and stimulate an appreciation of nature.

Bibliotherapy

Reading books (a) offers an opportunity to identify with others, (b) helps children realize they are not alone, (c) helps children express feelings that aid the catharsis process, (d) can facilitate the sharing of problems, and (e) leads to insights and expanded horizons (Rudman, Gagne, & Bernstein, 1993). Like stories, books allow children to identify with the characters or elements of a story and relate them to their own situation. Furthermore, written words are less intrusive and demanding than spoken words; as with play and art, children approach books with a minimum of defensive posturing (Wolfelt, 1996).

Camp HOPE's library features an extensive array of books appropriate for all ages. In addition, one camp session is devoted to bibliotherapy, where counselors read excerpts or entire books to their campers and discuss possible meanings. The youngest campers read *Saying Goodbye*, by Jim and Joan Boulden (1992). Children 8 through 12 years of age read *A Child Remembers*, by Enid Samuel Traisman (1994), and the adolescents read selected pages from *Fire in My Heart, Ice in My Veins*, also written by Traisman (1992).

Memory Collage

Art allows for the expression of conscious and unconscious thoughts and feelings. An effective medium for children of all ages, it is especially beneficial for young children who have difficulty finding the right words to say and for older children who may find it easier to express feelings through art. Camp HOPE's art room, staffed by arts-and-crafts volunteers, is stocked with a large variety of art supplies. Among other things, children can tie-dye hats or T-shirts, make wristbands or necklaces, create pottery, or practice wood burning.

The memory collage activity encourages children to share memories of the person in his or her life who has died. First, the children create collages featuring images and pictures reminiscent of the deceased one that are drawn or taken from magazines. The children are then asked to share their collage and memories with their group. As children compare and discuss their creations, new social meanings for the loss are found. The collage also becomes a symbolic portrayal of the child's memories, feelings, perceptions, and reactions to the death that can be taken home and shared with family.

Candlelight Ceremony

Perhaps the most emotional activity conducted at camp is the candle-lighting ceremony. This ritual is conducted in the evening at the end of the first day of camp, after a day full of fun, beginning relationships, and feelings of comfort and security have set in. It is a simple yet powerful activity allowing children to express some of the deep sadness that, for some, may rarely surface. In this activity, counselors and children sit in a circle by the campfire where they are given candles with glass holders. They are asked to light their candles one by one and to share a special memory of the person who has died. It is explained that memories are a special way to keep a loved one in your life, this is a safe place to share memories, and that it is okay to cry.

Most participants share stories, some remember funny events, and some sad times. In all cases, children share only what they are comfortable with and can take as much time as they want. Counselors are asked to sit among the children to provide safety and support; they also serve as role models who are able to share and not afraid to cry. When all candles are lit and stories shared, several moments are given to reflect.

The children are encouraged to keep their candles and to light them on special occasions. Children have reported lighting their candles on birthdays, death anniversaries, and special holidays. This emotionally draining event usually marks a transition point in the camp, where the children realize that camp is a safe place, everyone has suffered similar experiences, and it is healthy to share memories and express emotions. After the candlelight ceremony is concluded and bedtime arrives, the atmosphere at camp is intentionally lightened. In a short period of time, the children are able to let go of some of their sadness and get on with the rest of the evening's activities.

Physician Session

Children often have misconceptions and maladaptive fantasies about death (Zambelli & DeRosa, 1992). They also often harbor important questions that remain unanswered. In the absence of reliable information, children often formulate their own incorrect conclusions that, if left unresolved, can complicate the grieving process (Stokes & Crossley, 1995). One attempt to provide children with reliable information is through the physician session. During this session the children are encouraged to ask any questions that they may have about illness, accidents, or emotional states involved in the deaths that they are grieving. In order to stimulate appropriate questioning, counselors are encouraged to formulate questions they suspect some of their campers would have. For example, one counselor whose teenage camper lost a father to suicide asked the question, "Do people who commit suicide always tell others before they do it?" Another, whose 9-year-old camper lost a sister to cancer, asked why people lose their hair from chemotherapy. Both questions were asked in an attempt to anticipate likely questions and underlying concerns of the children in their group. The children are divided into two groups to better accommodate age-appropriate questions and responses: one of younger children, and a second with adolescents.

There are generally five areas of questions that are asked at the physician session. They include questions concerning (a) factual medical information such as treatment, medication, hereditary conditions, and pain, (b) emotional issues where children wonder if it is normal to have certain emotions and fears, (c) spiritual issues that question cultural and family beliefs, (d) searching questions a child uses to try to make sense out of an unexplainable circumstance such as, "Why do people die?," and (e) suicide issues that attempt to understand the confounding issues involved in this type of death. Great care is taken to answer questions in an honest, unbiased manner, with the best interest of the children in mind. The physicians leading the question-and-answer session are pediatricians, chosen because they have demonstrated concern for children and can speak to their level. They are also comfortable speaking about issues surrounding death, and are willing to share their own personal experiences with death.

Clean Cabins and Pack

Time is reserved near the end of camp to clean cabins and pack for a return home. Packing ahead of time facilitates a smooth departure, allowing time at the end to talk to parents and say goodbye, rather than a rush of last-minute packing. This also signifies to the children the beginning of the end of camp and allows them to emotionally prepare for their departure. Counselors have been prepared to help smooth the transition by discussing what has been learned at camp and memories of the weekend, and by providing reassurance that they will be okay when back at home.

Closing Ceremony

The closing of camp is a festive occasion where children are praised for their accomplishments and parents are reunited with their children. Parents are welcomed, cookies are served, and a folk-singer leads the entire group, singing and gesturing to uplifting songs. The final song, "Love Grows," acknowledges the friendships formed during camp and the personal growth that has occurred.

The final ritual of the camp is the balloon send-off, where each group of children releases a balloon to signify their letting go of some of their pain. Significant in its representation of finality to the painful part of the grieving process, this metaphor also promotes a new beginning, when the family can take on a new view of their experience.

Camp HOPE Adult Component

While children attend Camp HOPE, their parents, grandparents, guardians, or adult caretakers are invited to attend a Camp HOPE for Adults session. This session, held at a nearby location, separate from the children, is designed to serve as a retreat and support group weekend that mirrors the experience of the children. The primary goals of Camp HOPE for Adults are to provide opportunities for adult caretakers of the children attending Camp HOPE with opportunities to share their experiences with others who are grieving a similar loss, to learn how to better support their children following their camp experience, and to relax knowing that their children are well cared for at Camp HOPE. Camp HOPE for Adults provides a common experience that all family members can use to grow, or as a starting point for healing.

Transition to Adult Component

Adult Campers attend the child camp opening ceremony, where they meet the camp staff and hear the philosophy of Camp HOPE. Following the opening ceremony, while their children are enjoying team-building and free-time activities, adults are invited to attend a parent session that ends with a tour of the camp facilities and lunch. Following lunch, adults depart for Camp HOPE for Adults.

Adult Opening Ceremony

The adult camp opens with a drumming session, which is led by a professional musician. During this session adult campers sit in a circle and one by one introduce themselves; then they build group unity by drumming common beats and learn how to express their emotions through music. The session ends with each camper sharing why he or she came to camp and what they want to accomplish during the weekend.

Free-Time Activities

Free-time activities for adults consist of recreational activities such as fishing or hiking; more contemplative activities such as craft making, wood carving, and journal writing; and relaxation activities such as yoga and massage therapy. Several massage therapists provide ample opportunities for every camper to receive at least one massage during the camp weekend. The massage session is an especially important (and well-received) aspect of the camp, because it provides a physical release of emotional stress, and for many it is the first touch that they have received in some time.

Support Groups

Two groups are facilitated by professional counselors at the adult camp: one for those campers who have experienced child loss and one for campers who have experienced spouse loss. In each case, campers share experiences, receive guidance on how they can adjust to new challenges brought on by their loss, and gain support from each other.

Candlelight Ceremony

At the same time their children are sharing memories around a campfire a few miles away, so are the adults. Adults are reminded of this fact as they sit in their circle, light a candle in memory of their deceased loved one, and share a chosen memory. This emotional session can carry on well into the night as adult campers continue to tell stories and share poignant memories. At the end of the evening, the adults are encouraged to take their candles home, exchange memories that were shared with their children, and together continue to light their candles on special occasions.

Confidence Building

The final activities before the closing are the low-ropes course and the climbing-wall activities, which are led by staff members trained in facilitating challenging activities. These two activities are designed to provide a variety of challenge levels to ensure that all campers can be successful. The facilitator uses the activities to acknowledge their accomplishments over the course of the weekend and to build their confidence and self-esteem.

Closing Ceremony

Adults and children attend the closing of the camp together.

Epilogue

Completing this work has been a long but significant journey for us, one that has left us both more in tune with the needs of survivors of parental suicide and inspired by their resilience. We feel fortunate to have had the opportunity to interact with the individuals whose stories formed the basis of this book, and it has been a privilege to allow their voices to be heard. At the onset, we were concerned that asking people to share their stories might be an emotional burden for them. For reassurance, we reviewed the literature on the impacts of participating in emotionally demanding research, finding evidence that the research process can actually be therapeutic to participants in some way. Since the interviews, we have also been reassured by the participants whom we have been in contact with, many of whom expressed gratitude for the opportunity to share their experiences to benefit others. One noted that *"completing this study has definitely impacted me. Being able to sit down and recount all of my memories from so long ago has helped me to reconnect with who I am inside. It has made me realize that the things that I went through as a child will always be with me, but do not have to shape who I am. I live my days for me and my family. I don't try to please others. I just make sure my family is taken care of."* We truly hope that reading this book has been as helpful to you as doing this research has been meaningful to us. It seems that when a person helps others, they also help themselves. We have had this experience, as have our participants. We invite you to share in it as well as you carry these new insights forward in your professional practice.

References

Adams-Greenly, M., & Moynihan, R.T. (1983). Helping the children of fatally ill parents. *American Journal of Orthopsychiatry, 53*(2), 219–299.

Akerman, R., & Statham, J. (2011). *Childhood bereavement: A rapid literature review.* London: Childhood Wellbeing Research Centre.

Allen-Heath, M., Leavy, D., Hansen, K., Ryan, K., Lawrence, L., & Gerritson, A. (2008). Coping with grief: Guidelines and resources for assisting children. *Intervention in School and Clinic, 43,* 259–269.

American Association of Suicidology. (2005). Suicide prevention is everyone's business. Retrieved from http://www.suicidology.org

American Foundation for Suicide Prevention. (2011). Warning signs of suicide. Retrieved from http://www.afsp.org

Andress, V.R., & Corey, D.M. (1978). Survivor-victims: Who discovers or witnesses suicide? *Psychological Reports, 42,* 759–764.

Angell, G.B., Dennis, B.G., & Dumain, L.E. (1998). Spirituality, resilience, and narrative: Coping with parental death. *Families in Society, 79*(6), 615–630.

Antonovsky, A. (1979). *Health, stress and coping.* San Francisco: Jossey-Bass.

Armour, M. (2006). Violent death: Understanding the context of traumatic and stigmatized grief. *Journal of Human Behavior in the Social Environment, 14*(4), 53–90.

Attig, T. (2000). *The heart of grief: Death and the search for lasting love.* New York: Oxford University Press.

Auman, M.J. (2007). Bereavement support for children. *Journal of School Nursing, 23*(1), 34–39.

Avrami, S. (2005). "I wish he had died in the war": Suicide survivors—The Israeli case. *Omega: Journal of Death and Dying, 51*(1), 65–75.

Ayyash-Abado, H. (2001). Childhood bereavement: What school psychologists need to know. *School Psychology International, 22*(4), 417–433.

Baker, J.E., Sedney, M.A., & Gross, E. (1992). Psychological tasks for bereaved children. *American Journal of Orthopsychiatry, 62*(1), 105–116.

Barbato, A., & Irwin, H.J. (1992). Major therapeutic systems and the bereaved client. *Australian Psychologist, 27,* 22–27.

Barrett, C. (2004). Bereavement camp: A qualitative analysis of a therapeutic program for grieving youth. *Dissertation Abstracts International Section A: Humanities and Social Sciences, 64*(7-A), 2391.

Beavers, W.R., & Hampson, R.B. (1990). *Successful families: Assessment and intervention.* New York: W.W. Norton.

Begley, M., & Quayle, E. (2007). The lived experience of adults bereaved by suicide: A phenomenological study. *Crisis: The Journal of Crisis Intervention and Suicide Prevention, 28*(1), 26–34.

Belle, D. (1988). Gender differences in the social moderators of stress. In R.C. Barnett, L. Beiner, & G.K. Baruch (Eds.), *Gender and stress* (pp. 257–277). New York: Free Press.

Bonano, A. D., & Mancini, G.A. (2002). Resilience in the face of potential trauma: Clinical practices and illustrations. *Journal of Clinical Psychology, 62*(8), 971–985.

Boulden, J., & Boulden, J. (1992). *Saying goodbye.* Weaverville, CA: Boulden.

Bowlby, J. (1979). *The making and breaking of affectional bonds.* London: Tavistock.

Bowlby, J. (1980). *Attachment and loss: Vol. 3. Loss: Sadness and depression.* London: Harper Collins.

Bowman, D.O. (1994). The application of poetry therapy in grief counseling with adolescents and young adults. *Journal of Poetry Therapy, 8*(2), 63–73.

Bradley, R.H. (2007). Parenting in the breach: How parents help children cope with developmentally challenging circumstances. *Parenting: Science & Practice, 7*(2), 99–148.

Braiden, H. J., McCann, M., Barry, H., & Lindsay, C. (2009). Piloting a therapeutic residential for children, young people and families bereaved through suicide in Northern Ireland. *Child Care in Practice, 15*(2), 81–93.

Brent, D.A., & Mann, J.J. (2005). Family genetics studies, suicide, and suicidal behavior. *American Journal of Medical Genetics, 133C*(1), 13–24.

Brent, D.A., Oquendo, M., Birmaher, B., Greenhill, L., Kolko, D., Stanley, B., . . . Mann, J. (2002). Familial pathways to early-onset suicide attempt: Risk for suicidal behavior in offspring of mood-disordered suicide attempters. *Archives of General Psychiatry, 59*(9), 801–807.

Brountas, M. (1988). Adam: A love story. *Teaching K–8,* 73–78.

Brown, A.C., Sandler, I.N., Tein, J.Y., Liu, X., & Haine, R.A. (2007). Implications of parental suicide and violent death for promotion of resilience of parentally-bereaved children. *Death Studies, 31*(4), 301–335.

Bulman, R.J., & Wortman, C.B. (1977). Attributions of blame and coping in the "real world": Severe accident victims react to their lot. *Journal of Personality and Social Psychology, 35,* 351–363.

Cain, A.C. (2002). Children of suicide: The telling and the knowing. *Psychiatry, 65*(2), 124–136.

Cain, A.C. (2006). Parent suicide: Pathways of effects into the third generation. *Psychiatry, 69*(3), 204–227.

Cain, A.C., & Fast, I. (1972). Children's disturbed reactions to parent suicide: Distortion of guilt, communication, and identification. In A. Cain (Ed.), *Survivors of suicide* (pp. 93–111). Springfield, IL: Charles C. Thomas.

Calhoun, L. G., Selby, J. W., & Selby, L. E. (1982). The psychological aftermath of suicide: An analysis of current evidence. *Clinical Psychology Review, 2,* 409–420.

Calhoun, L.G., & Tedeschi, R.G. (1990). Positive aspects of critical life problems: Recollections of grief. *Omega: Journal of Death and Dying, 20*(4), 265–272.

Callahan, J. (2000). Predictors and correlates of bereavement in suicide support group participants. *Suicide and Life-Threatening Behavior, 30,* 104–124.

Cameron, E.C. (1991). Creative ritual: Bridge between mastery and meaning. *Pastoral Psychology, 40*(1), 3–13.

Campbell, F., Cataldie, L., McIntosh, J., & Millet, K. (2004). An active postvention program. *Crisis: The Journal of Crisis Intervention and Suicide Prevention, 25*(1), 30–32.

Campbell, F.R. (1997). Changing the legacy of suicide. *Suicide and Life-Threatening Behavior, 27,* 329–338.

Cates, J. (1986). Grief therapy in residential treatment. *Child Care Quarterly, 15*(3), 147–158.

Cerel, J., Fristad, M.A., Weller, E.B., & Weller, R.A. (1999). Suicide-bereaved children and adolescents: A controlled longitudinal examination. *Journal of the American Academy of Child & Adolescent Psychiatry, 38*(6), 672–679.

Cerel, J., Fristad, M.A., Weller, E.B., & Weller, R.A. (2000). Suicide-bereaved children and adolescents: II. Parental and family functioning. *Journal of the American Academy of Child & Adolescent Psychiatry, 39*(4), 437–444.

Cerel, J., Jordan, J.R., & Duberstein, P.R. (2008). The impact of suicide on the family. *Crisis: The Journal of Intervention and Suicide Prevention, 29*(1), 38–44.

Cerel, J., Padgett, J., Conwell, Y., & Reed, G.A. (2009). A call for research: The need to better understand the impact of support groups for suicide survivors. *Suicide and Life-Threatening Behavior, 39*(3), 269–281.

Cerel, J., & Roberts, T.A. (2005). Suicidal behavior in the family and adolescent risk behavior. *Journal of Adolescent Health, 36*(4), 352-e8.

Childers, P., & Wimmer, M. (1971). The concept of death in early childhood. *Child Development, 42,* 1299–1301.

Chodoff, P., Friedman, S.B., & Hamburg, D.A. (1964). Stress, defenses and coping behavior: Observations in parents in parents of children with malignant diseases. *American Journal of Psychiatry,* 120, 743–749.

Clark, S. (2001). Bereavement after suicide: How far have we come and where do we need to go? *Crisis: The Journal of Intervention and Suicide, 22,* 102–108.

Clark, S.E., & Goldney, R.D. (1995). Grief reactions and recovery in a support group for people bereaved by suicide. *Crisis: The Journal of Intervention and Suicide Prevention, 16*(1), 27–33.

Clark, S.E., & Goldney, R.D. (2000). The impact of suicide on relatives and friends. In K. Hawton & K. van Heeringen (Eds.), *The international handbook of suicide and attempted suicide* (pp. 467–484). New York: Wiley & Sons.

Cohen, J., Goodman, R. F., Brown, E. J., & Mannarino, A. (2004). Treatment of childhood traumatic grief: Contributing to a newly emerging condition in the wake of community trauma. *Harvard Review of Psychiatry, 12*(4), 213–216.

Cohen, J.A., Mannarino, A.P., & Deblinger, D. (2006). *Treating trauma and traumatic grief in children and adolescents.* New York: Guilford Press.

Cohen, J.A., Mannarino, A.P., & Knudsen, K. (2004). Treatment of childhood traumatic grief: A pilot study. *Journal of Clinical Child & Adolescent Psychology, 33*(4), 819–831.

Coleman, R.A., & Neimeyer, R.A. (2010). Measuring meaning: Searching for and making sense of spousal loss in later life. *Death Studies, 34,* 804–834.

Constantino, S.E., Sekula, L.K., & Rubinstein, E.N. (2001). Group intervention for widowed survivors of suicide. *Suicide and Life-Threatening Behavior, 31,* 428–441.

Costa, L., & Holliday, D. (1994). Helping children cope with the death of a parent. *Elementary School Guidance and Counseling, 28,* 206–213.

Cotton, C., & Range, L. (1990). Children's death concepts: Relationships to cognitive functioning, age, experience with death, fear of death and hopelessness. *Journal of Clinical Child Psychology, 19,* 123–127.

Creed, J., Ruffin, J.E., & Ward, M. (2001). A weekend camp for bereaved siblings. *Cancer Practice, 9*(4), 176–182.

Creswell, J.W. (1998). *Qualitative inquiry and research design: Choosing among five traditions.* Thousand Oaks, CA: SAGE.

Crosby, A., & Sacks, J. (2002). Exposure to suicide: Incidence and association with suicidal ideation and behavior, US 1994. *Suicide and Life-Threatening Behavior, 32,* 321–328.

Currier, J.M., Holland, J.M., Coleman, R.A., & Neimeyer, R.A. (2008). Bereavement following violent death: An assault on life and meaning. In R. Stevenson & G. Cox (Eds.), *Perspectives on violence and violent death* (pp. 175–200). Amityville, NY: Baywood.

Currier, J.M., Holland, J.M., & Neimeyer, R.A. (2006). Sense-making, grief and the experience of violent loss: Toward a mediational model. *Death Studies, 30,* 403–428.

Currier, J.M., Holland, J.M., & Neimeyer, R.A. (2007). The effectiveness of bereavement interventions with children: A meta-analytic review of controlled outcome research. *Journal of Clinical Child & Adolescent Psychology, 36*(2), 253–259.

Dalke, D. (1994). Therapy-assisted growth after parental suicide: From a personal and professional perspective. *Omega: Journal of Death and Dying, 29*(2), 113–151.

Dane, B.O. (1991). Counselling bereaved middle aged children: Parental suicide survivors. *Clinical Social Work Journal, 19*(1), 35–48.

Davies, B. (1998). *Shadows in the sun: The experiences of sibling bereavement in childhood.* Washington, DC: Taylor & Francis.

Davies, R. (2004). New understandings of parental grief: Literature review. *Journal of Advanced Nursing, 46*(5), 506–513.

Davis, C., & Hinger, B. (2005). Assessing the needs of survivors of suicide: A needs assessment in the Calgary Health Region (Region 3), Alberta. Report for the Calgary Health Region, Alberta. Retrieved from http://www.albertahealthservices.ca/InjuryPrevention/hi-ip-pipt-chc-pro-assessing-needs-of-survivors-report-lit.pdf

Davis, C.G., & Nolen-Hoeksema, S. (2001). Loss and meaning: How do people make sense of loss? *American Behavioral Scientist, 44*(5), 726–741.

Davis, C. G., Nolen-Hoeksema, S., & Larson, J. (1998). Making sense of loss and benefiting from the experience: Two construals of meaning. *Journal of Personality and Social Psychology, 75*(2), 561–574.

Davis, C., Wortman, C.B., Lehaman, D.R., & Silver, R.C. (2000). Searching for meaning in loss: Are clinical assumptions correct? *Death Studies, 24,* 497–540.

Deblinger, E., McLeer, S.V., & Henry, D. (1990). Cognitive behavioral treatment for sexually abused children suffering post-traumatic stress: Preliminary findings. *Journal of the American Academy of Child and Adolescent Psychiatry, 29,* 747–752.

Deegear, J., & Lawson D.M. (2003). The utility of empirical supported treatments. *Professional Psychology: Research and Practice, 54,* 271–277.

Demi, A.S., & Howell, C. (1991). Hiding and healing: Resolving the suicide of a parent or sibling. *Archives of Psychiatric Nursing, 5*(6), 350–356.

Doka, K. (1990). The therapeutic bookshelf. *Omega, 21*(4), 321–328.

Dowdney, L. (2000). Annotation: Childhood bereavement following parental death. *Journal of Child Psychology and Psychiatry, 41*(7), 819–830.

Dunn, R.G., & Morrish-Vidners, D. (1987). The psychological and social experience of suicide survivors. *Omega: Journal of Death and Dying, 18*(3), 175–215.

Dyregrov, A. (2004). Educational consequences of loss and trauma. *Educational and Child Psychology, 21*(3), 77–84.

Dyregrov, K. (2009a). How do the young suicide survivors wish to be met by psychologists? A user study. *Omega: Journal of Death and Dying, 59*(3), 221–238.

Dyregrov, K. (2009b). The important role of the school following suicide in Norway. What support do young people wish that school could provide? *Omega: Journal of Death and Dying, 59*(2), 147–161.

Dyregrov, K., & Dyregrov, A. (2005). Siblings after suicide—"The forgotten bereaved." *Suicide and Life-Threatening Behavior, 35*(6), 714–724.

Elder, S.L. (1995). Helping bereaved children and adolescents cope with the aftermath of suicide. In D. W. Adams & E. J. Deveau (Eds.), *Helping children and adolescents cope with death and bereavement* (pp. 137–151). Amityville, NY: Baywood.

Farber, M., & Sabatino, C. (2007). A therapeutic summer camp for grieving children: Results from community based research. *Child & Adolescent Social Work Journal, 24*(4), 385–402.

Farberow, N. (2001). Helping suicide survivors. In D. Lester (Ed.), *Suicide prevention: Resources for the millennium* (pp. 189–212). Philadelphia, PA: Brunner-Routledge.
Farberow, N.L. (1992). The Los Angeles survivors after suicide program: An evaluation. *Crisis: The Journal of Crisis Intervention and Suicide Prevention, 13,* 23–24.
Feigelman, W., Gorman, B.S., Beal, K.C., & Jordan, J.R. (2008). Internet support groups for suicide survivors: A new mode for gaining bereavement assistance. *Omega: Journal of Death and Dying, 57*(3), 217–243.
Feigelman, W., Jordan, J.R., & Gorman, B.S. (2009). How they died, time since loss, and bereavement outcomes. *Omega: Journal of Death and Dying, 58*(4), 251–273.
Fine, C. (1999). *No time to say goodbye: Surviving the suicide of a loved one.* New York: Doubleday.
Finn, C. (2003). Helping students cope with loss: Incorporating art into group counseling. *Journal for Specialists in Group Work, 28*(2), 155–165.
Flarity, K.L. (1993). The clergy and the suicide-bereaved: A phenomenological analysis of twenty case interviews. *Dissertation Abstracts International, 54,* 2198B. (UMI No. DA9318367).
Fleming, S., & Balmer, L. (1996). Bereavement in adolescence. In C.A. Corr & D.E. Balk (Eds.), *Handbook of Adolescent Death and Bereavement* (pp. 139–154). New York: Springer.
Frankl, V.E. (1963). *Man's search for meaning: An introduction to logotherapy.* New York: Pocket Books.
Frantz, T.T., Farrell, M.M., & Trolley, B. C. (2001). Positive outcomes of losing a loved one. In R.A. Neimeyer (Ed.), *Meaning reconstruction & the experience of loss* (pp. 191–209). Washington, DC: American Psychological Association.
Frantz, T.T., Trolley, B. C., & Farrell, M.M. (1998). Positive aspects of grief. *Pastoral Psychology, 47*(1), 3–17.
Frantz, T. T., Trolley, B. C., & Johll, M. P. (1996). Religious aspects of bereavement. *Pastoral Psychology, 44*(3), 151–162.
Freud, S. (1917). *The standard edition of the complete psychological works of Sigmund Freud: Vol. 14. Mourning and melancholia (1914–1916).* London: Hogarth Press.
Frydenberg, E., Muller, D., & Ivens, C. (2006). The experience of loss: Coping and the seasons for growth program. *Australian Educational and Developmental Psychologist, 23*(1), 45–68.
Fulmer, R. (1983). A structural approach to unresolved mourning in single parent family systems. *Journal of Marital and Family Therapy, 9*(3), 259–270.
Furman, E. (1974). *A child's parent dies: Studies in childhood bereavement.* New Haven, CT: Yale University Press.
Garmezy, N. (1987). Stress, competence, and development: Continuities in the study of schizophrenic adults, children vulnerable to psychopathology, and the search for stress-resistant children. *American Journal of Orthopsychology, 57,* 159–185.
Giovanola, J. (2005). Sibling involvement at the end of life. *Journal of Pediatric Oncology Nursing, 22*(4), 222–226.
Glass Jr., J.C. (1991). Death, loss, and grief: Real concerns to young adolescents. *Middle School Journal, 22*(5), 15–17.
Goenjian, A.K., Karayan, I., Pynoos, R.S., Misessian, D., Najarian, L.M., . . . Steinberg, A. M. (1997). Outcome of psychotherapy among early adolescents after trauma. *American Journal of Psychiatry, 154*(4), 536–542.
Graham, H.M. (1999). Help or hindrance? An examination of the effectiveness of children's grief support groups. *Dissertation Abstracts International, 60*(6), 2227A.
Gray, M.J., Prigerson, H.G., & Litz, B.T. (2004). Conceptual and definitional issues in complicated grief. In B.T. Litz (Ed.), *Early intervention for trauma and traumatic loss* (pp. 65–86). New York: Guilford Press.
Gray, R.E. (1988). The role of school counselors with bereaved teenagers: With and without peer support groups. *School Counselor, 35*(3), 185–193.

Greeff, A. P., & Human, B. (2004). Resilience in families in which a parent has died. *American Journal of Family Therapy, 32*(1), 27–42.

Green, B., Krupnick, J., Stockton, P., Goodman, L., Corcoran, C., & Petty, R. (2001). Psychological outcomes associated with traumatic loss in a sample of young women. *American Behavioral Scientist, 44*, 817–837.

Grollman, E. (1977). Explaining death to children. *Journal of School Health, 47*(6), 336–339.

Grossman, J. A., Clark, D. C., Gross, D., Halstead, L., & Pennington, J. (1995). Child bereavement after paternal suicide. *Journal of Child & Adolescent Psychiatric Nursing, 8*(2), 5–17.

Haine, R. A., Wolchik, S. A., Sandler, I. N., Millsap, R. E., & Ayers, T. S. (2006). Positive parenting as a protective resource for parentally bereaved children. *Death Studies, 30*(1), 1–28.

Harrison, L., & Harrington, R. (2001). Adolescents' bereavement experiences: Prevalence, association with depressive symptoms, and use of services. *Journal of Adolescence, 24*(2), 159–169.

Harwood, D., Hawton K., Hope J., & Jacoby R. (2002). The grief experiences and needs of bereaved relatives and friends of older people dying through suicide: A descriptive and case-control study. *Journal of Affective Disorders, 72*, 185–194.

Heikes, K. (1997). Parental suicide: A systems perspective. *Bulletin of the Menninger Clinic, 61*(3), 354–367.

Heron, M. (2012). Deaths: Leading causes for 2009. *National Vital Statistics Reports, 61*(7). Hyattsville, MD: National Center for Health Statistics.

Himebauch, A., Arnold, R., & May, C. (2008). Grief in children and developmental concepts of death #138. *Journal of Palliative Medicine, 11*, 242–244.

Holland, J. (2004). "Lost for words" in hull. *Pastoral Care in Education, 22*(4), 22–26.

Holland, J. M., Currier, J. M., & Neimeyer, R. A. (2006). Meaning reconstruction in the first two years of bereavement: The role of sense-making and benefit-finding. *Journal of Death and Dying, 53*, 175–191.

Horacek, B. (1991). Toward a more visible model of grieving and consequences for older persons. *Death Studies, 15*(5), 459–472.

Houck, J. A. (2004). *Comparing grief reactions and religious/spiritual coping methods among cancer, AIDS-related, and suicide bereavement* (Doctoral dissertation). Retrieved from Dissertation Abstracts International.

Howarth, R. A. (2011). Concepts and controversies in grief and loss. *Journal of Mental Health Counseling, 33*(1), 4–10.

Hung, N. C., & Rabin, L. A. (2009). Comprehending childhood bereavement by parental suicide: A critical review of research on outcomes, grief processes, and interventions. *Death Studies, 33*(9), 781–814.

Hurley, D. J. (1991). The crisis of paternal suicide: Case of Cathy, age 4 1/2. In N. B. Webb (Ed.), *Play therapy with children in crisis: Individual, group, and family treatment* (pp. 237–253). New York: Guilford Press.

Huss, S., & Ritchie, M. (1999). Effectiveness of a group for parentally bereaved children. *Journal for Specialists in Groupwork, 24*(2), 186–196.

Janoff-Bulman, R. (1992). Happystance. A review of subjective well-being: An interdisciplinary perspective. *Contemporary Psychology, 37*, 162–163.

Johnson, P. (2002). After a child's parent died. *Child Psychiatry and Human Development, 12*(3), 160–170.

Jordan, J. R. (2001). Is suicide bereavement different? A reassessment of the literature. *Suicide & Life-Threatening Behavior, 31*(1), 91–102.

Jordan, J. (2011). Group work with suicide survivors. In J. J. Jordan & J. J. McIntosh (Eds.), *Grief after suicide: Understanding the consequences and caring for the survivors* (pp. 283–300). New York: Taylor & Francis.

Jordan, J., & Harpel, J. (2007). *Facilitating suicide bereavement support groups: A self-study manual.* New York: American Foundation for Suicide Prevention.

Jordan, J.R. & McIntosh, J.L. (2011). *Grief after suicide: Understanding the consequences and caring for the survivors.* New York: Routledge.

Jordan, J.R., & McMenamy, J. (2004). Interventions for suicide survivors: A review of the literature. *Suicide and Life-Threatening Behavior, 34*(4), 337–449.

Jordan, J.R., & Neimeyer, R.A. (2003). Does grief counseling work? *Death Studies, 27*, 765–786.

Kalish, R.A. (1985). *Death, grief, and caring relationships* (2nd ed.). Monterey, CA: Brooks/Cole.

Kandt, V.E. (1994). Adolescent bereavement: Turning a fragile time into acceptance and peace. *School Counselor, 41*(3), 203–211.

Kane, B. (1979). Children's concepts of death. *Journal of Genetic Psychology, 134*, 141–153.

Kaslow, N.J., & Aronson, S.G. (2004). Recommendations for family interventions following a suicide. *Professional Psychology: Research & Practice, 35*(3), 240–247.

Kast, V. (1998). *A time to mourn: Growing through the grief process.* (D. Dachler & F. Cairns, Trans.). Einsiedeln, Switzerland: Daimon Verlag.

Keesee, N.J., Currier, J.M., & Neimeyer, R.A. (2008). Predictors of grief following the death of one's child: The contribution of finding meaning. *Journal of Clinical Psychology, 64*, 1145–1163.

Kendler, K.S., Neale, M.D., Kessler, R.C., Heath, A.C., & Eaves, L.J. (1992). Childhood parental loss and adult psychopathology in women: A twin study perspective. *Archives of General Psychiatry, 49*(2), 109–116.

Kessler, B.G. (1987). Bereavement and personal growth. *Journal of Humanistic Psychology, 27*(2), 228–247.

Klass, D., Silverman, P.R., & Nickman, S. L. (Eds.). (1996). *Continuing bonds: New understandings of grief.* Briston, PA: Taylor and Francis.

Kovac, S.H., & Range, L.M. (2000). Writing projects: Lessening undergraduates' unique suicidal bereavement. *Suicide and Life-Threatening Behavior, 30*, 50–60.

Kronick, D. (1985). Children's books and games dealing with death. *Academic Therapy, 20*, 5.

Kubler-Ross, E. (1969). *On death and dying.* New York: Springer.

Kuramoto, S.J., Brent, D.A., & Wilcox, H.C. (2009). The impact of parental suicide on child and adolescent offspring. *Suicide and Life-Threatening Behavior, 39*(2), 137–151.

Kushner, H.S. (1981). *When bad things happen to good people.* New York: Shocken Books.

Layne, C.M., Pynoos, R.S., Slatzman, W.R., Arslanagic, B., Savjak, N., . . .Popovic, T. (2001). Trauma/grief-focused group psychotherapy: School-based postwar intervention with traumatized Bosnian adolescents. *Group Dynamics: Theory, Research, and Practice, 5*, 277–290.

Lieberman, M.A. (1986). Self-help groups and psychiatry. *American Psychiatric Association Annual Review, 5*, 744–760.

Lin, K. K., Sandler, I. N., Ayers, T. S., Wolchik, S. A., & Luecken, L. J. (2004). Resilience in parentally bereaved children and adolescents seeking preventive services. *Journal of Clinical Child and Adolescent Psychology, 33*(4), 673–683.

Lincoln, Y., & Guba, E. (1985). *Naturalistic inquiry.* Beverly Hills, CA: SAGE.

Lindemann, E. (1944). Symptomatology and management of acute grief. *American Journal of Psychiatry, 101*, 141–148.

Linley, P.A., & Joseph, S. (2004). *Positive psychology in practice.* Hoboken, NJ: Wiley & Sons.

Lohan, J.A., & Murphy, S.A. (2002). Family functioning and family typology after an adolescent or young adult's sudden violent death. *Journal of Family Nursing, 8*(1), 32–49.

Loy, M.J. (1999). *A study of the effectiveness of a camp intervention for bereaved adolescents* (Unpublished doctoral dissertation). University of Wisconsin-Madison, Madison, WI.

Luecken, L.J. (2008). Long-term consequences of parental death in childhood: Psychological and physiological manifestations. In M.S. Stroebe, R.O. Hansson, H. Schut,

& W. Stroebe (Eds.), *Handbook of bereavement research and practice: Advances in theory and intervention* (pp. 397–416). Washington, DC: American Psychological Association.

Malikow, M. (1991). *The preparedness of evangelical pastors for the provision of suicide postvention* (Unpublished doctoral dissertation). Boston University: Boston, MA.

Mandelco, B. L., & Peery, J. C. (2002). An organisational framework for conceptualising resilience in children. *Journal of Child and Adolescent Psychiatric Nursing, 13*(3), 99–113.

Maple, M. (2005). Parental bereavement and youth suicide: An assessment of the literature. *Australian Social Worker, 58*(2), 179–187.

Masterman, S.H., & Reams, R. (1988). Support groups for bereaved preschool and school-age children. *American Journal of Orthopsychiatry, 58*(4), 562–570.

Matter, D.E., & Matter, R.M. (1982). Developmental sequences in children's understanding of death with implications for counselors. *Elementary School Guidance and Counseling, 17*(2), 112–118.

McClatchey, I.S., Vonk, E.M., & Palardy, G. (2009). Efficacy of a camp-based intervention for childhood traumatic grief. *Research on Social Work Practice, 19*(19), 19–30.

McClatchey, I.S., & Wimmer, J.S. (2012). Healing components of a bereavement camp: Children and adolescents give voice to their experiences. *Omega: Journal of Death and Dying, 65*(1), 11–32.

McCown, D.E., & Davies, B. (1995). Patterns of grief in young children following the death of a sibling. *Death Studies, 19*, 41–53.

McIntosh, J.L. (1993). Control group studies of suicide survivors: A review and critique. *Suicide and Life-Threatening Behavior, 23*, 146–161.

McIntosh, J.L., & Wrobleski, A. (1988). Grief reactions among suicide survivors: An exploratory comparison of relationships. *Death Studies, 12*(1), 21–39.

McMenamy, J.M., Jordan, J.R., & Mitchell, A. M. (2008). What do suicide survivors tell us they need? Results of a pilot study. *Suicide & Life-Threatening Behavior, 38*(4), 375–389.

Melhem, N.M., Day, N., Shear, M.K., Day, R., Reynolds, C.F., & Brent D. (2004). Traumatic grief among adolescents exposed to a peer's suicide. *American Journal of Psychiatry, 161*, 1411–1416.

Melhem, N.M., Moritz, G., Walker, M., Shear, M.K., & Brent, D. (2007). Phenomenology and correlates of complicated grief in children and adolescents. *Journal of the American Academy of Child & Adolescent Psychiatry, 46*(4), 493–499.

Melvin, D., & Lukeman, D. (2000). Bereavement: A framework for those working with children. *Clinical Child Psychology & Psychiatry, 5*(4), 521–539.

Middleton, W., Raphael, B., Martinek, N., & Misso, V. (1993). Pathological grief reactions. In M. S. Stroebe, W. Stroebe, & R. O. Hansson (Eds.), *Handbook of bereavement: Theory, research and intervention* (pp. 44–61). New York: Cambridge University Press.

Mills, J.C., & Crowley, R. (1986). *Therapeutic metaphors for children and the child within.* New York: Brunner/Mazel.

Mitchell, A. M., Gale, D.D., Garand, L., & Wesner, S. (2003). The use of narrative data to inform the psychotherapeutic group process with suicide survivors. *Issues in Mental Health Nursing, 24*(1), 91–106.

Mitchell, A. M., Wesner, S., Brownson, L., Dysart-Gale, D. D., Garand, L., & Havill, A. (2006). Effective communication with bereaved child survivors of suicide. *Journal of Child and Adolescent Psychiatric Nursing, 19*(3), 130–136.

Mitchell, A. M., Wesner, S., Garand, L., Gale, D.D., Havill, A., & Brownson, L. (2007). A support group intervention for children bereaved by parental suicide. *Journal of Child and Adolescent Psychiatric Nursing, 20*(1), 3–13.

Moore, J., & Herlihy, B. (1993). Grief groups for students who have had a parent die. *School Counselor, 41*, 54–59.

Moos, N.L. (1995). An integrative model of grief. *Death Studies, 19*(4), 337–364.

Moyer, J.A. (1988). Bannock bereavement retreat: A camping experience for surviving children. *American Journal of Hospice Care, 5*(2), 26–30.

Munholland, K. (1997). *Attachment and parental loss.* Unpublished manuscript, University of Wisconsin-Madison.

Murphy, F.C., Sahakian, B.J., Rubinsztein, J.S., Michael, A., Rogers, R.D., Robbins, T.W., & Paykel, E.S. (1999). Emotional bias and inhibitory control processes in mania and depression. *Psychological Medicine, 29*(6), 1307–1321.

Murphy, S.A., Johnson, C., Cain, K.D., Das Gupta, A., Dimond, M., & Lohan, J. (1998). Broad-spectrum group treatment for parents bereaved by the violent deaths of their 12- to 28-year-old children: A randomized controlled trial. *Death Studies, 22,* 209–235.

Murphy, S.A., Johnson, L.C., & Lohan, J. (2003). Finding meaning in a child's violent death. *Death Studies, 27,* 381–404.

Nabors, L., Ohms, M., Buchanan, N., Kirsch, K.L., Nash, T., Passik, S.D., . . . Brown, G. (2004). A pilot study of the impact of a grief camp for children. *Palliative Supportive Care, 2,* 403–408.

Nagy, M. (1948). The child's view of death. *Journal of Genetic Psychology, 73,* 3–27.

Neimeyer, R.A. (2002). Traumatic loss and the reconstruction of meaning. *Journal of Palliative Medicine, 5*(6), 935–942.

Neimeyer, R.A. (2005). From death anxiety to meaning making at the end of life: Recommendations for psychological assessment. *Clinical Psychology: Science and Practice, 12*(3), 354–357.

Neimeyer, R.A. (2009). *Constructivist psychotherapy.* New York: Routledge.

Neimeyer, R.A. (2011). Reconstructing meaning in bereavement. In M. Watson & D. Kissane (Eds.), *Handbook of psychotherapy in cancer care* (pp. 247–258). Hoboken, NJ: Blackwell.

Neimeyer, R.A., Burke, L.A., Mackay, M.M., & van Dyke Stringer, J.G. (2010). Grief therapy and the reconstruction of meaning: From principles to practice. *Journal of Contemporary Psychotherapy, 40*(2), 73–83.

Neimeyer, R.A., & Currier, J.M. (2010). Grief therapy: Evidence of efficacy and emerging directions. *Current Directions in Psychological Science, 18,* 352–356.

Neimeyer, R.A., Fortner, B., & Melby, D. (2001). Personal and professional factors and suicide intervention skills. *Suicide and Life-Threatening Behavior, 31*(1), 71–82.

Neimeyer, R.A., Prigerson, H.G., & Davies, B. (2002). Mourning and meaning. *American Behavioral Scientist, 46*(2), 235–251.

Neimeyer, R.A., & Sands, D. C. (2011). Meaning reconstruction in bereavement: From principles to practice. *Journal of Contemporary Psychotherapy, 40,* 73–83.

Nelson, B.J., & Frantz, T.T. (1996). Family interactions of suicide survivors and survivors of non-suicidal death. *Omega: Journal of Death and Dying, 33*(2), 131–146.

Ness, D.E., & Pfeffer, C.R. (1990). Sequelae of bereavement resulting from suicide. *American Journal of Psychiatry, 147,* 279–285.

Nicholson, H., Foote, C., & Grigerick, S. (2009). Deleterious effects of psychotherapy and counseling in the schools. *Psychology in the Schools, 46*(3), 232–237.

Nikulainen-Levine, H.T. (1997). The impact of paternal suicide in childhood on women's adult love. *Dissertation Abstracts International, 57*(7-B), 4748.

Noonan, K. (2000). Coping with suicide in childhood. *Youth Suicide Bulletin, Australian Institute of Family Studies, 4,* 11–15.

Oaks, J., & Bibeau, D.L. (1987). Death education: Educating children for living. *Journal of Death Education, 60*(9), 420–422.

O'Connor, C., & Templeton, E. (2002). Grief and loss: Perspectives for school personnel. *Australian Journal of Guidance and Counselling, 12*(1), 97–106.

Oltjenbruns, K.A. (2001). Developmental context of childhood: Grief and re-grief phenomenal. In M. S. Stroebe, R. O. Hansson, W. Stroebe, & H. Schut (Eds.), *Handbook of bereavement research: Consequences, coping and care* (pp. 169–197). Washington, DC: American Psychological Association.

Padgett, D.K. (1998). *Qualitative methods in social work research: Challenges and rewards.* Thousand Oaks, CA: SAGE.

Palombo, J. (1981). Parent loss and childhood bereavement: Some theoretical considerations. *Clinical Social Work Journal, 9*(1), 3–33.

Park, C.L., & Cohen, L.H. (1993). Religious and nonreligious coping with the death of a friend. *Cognitive Therapy and Research, 17,* 561–577.

Park, C.L., & Folkman, S. (1997). Meaning in the context of stress and coping. *General Review of Psychology, 1,* 115–144.

Parkes, C.M. (1980). Bereavement counselling: Does it work? *British Medical Journal, 281,* 3–6.

Parkes, C.M. (1985). Bereavement and mental illness. *British Journal of Medical Psychology, 38,* 388–397.

Parkes, C.M. (1993). Bereavement as a psychosocial transition: Processes of adaptation to change. In D. Dickenson, M. Donna, & M. Johnson (Eds.), *Death, dying, and bereavement* (pp. 325–331). London: Open U Press, SAGE.

Parkes, C. M. (1998). *Bereavement: Studies of grief in the adult life* (3rd ed.). London: Penguin.

Pennebaker, J.W., Zech, E., & Rime, B. (2001). Disclosing and sharing emotion: Psychological, social, and health consequences. In M.S. Stroebe, W. Stroebe, R.O. Hansson, & H. Schut (Eds.), *Handbook of bereavement research: Consequences, coping and care* (pp. 517–539). Washington, DC: American Psychological Association.

Petr, C.G., & Walter, U.M. (2005). Best practices inquiry: A multi-dimensional, value-critical framework. *Journal of Social Work Education, 41,* 251–267.

Pfeffer, C.R., Jiang, H., Kakuma, T., Hwang, J., & Metsch, M. (2002). Group intervention for children bereaved by the suicide of a relative. *Journal of the American Academy of Child & Adolescent Psychiatry, 41*(5), 505–513.

Pfeffer, C.R., Karus, D., Siegel, K., & Jiang, H. (2000). Child survivors of parental death from cancer or suicide: Depressive and behavioral outcomes. *Psycho-Oncology, 9*(1), 1–10.

Pfeffer, C.R., Martins, P., Mann, J., Sunkenberg, M., Ice, A., Damore, J.P., . . . Jiang, H. (1997). Child survivors of suicide: Psycho-social characteristics. *Journal of the American Academy of Child & Adolescent Psychiatry, 36*(1), 65–74.

Pfeffer, C.R., Normandin, L., & Kakuma, T. (1998). Suicidal children grow up: Relations between family psychopathology and adolescents' lifetime suicidal behavior. *Journal of Nervous and Mental Disease, 186*(5), 269–275.

Piaget, J. (1966). *The child's conception of physical causality.* London: Routledge.

Piaget, J. (1973). *Memory and intelligence.* New York: Basic Books.

Pietila, M. (2002). Support groups: A psychological or social device for suicide bereavement? *British Journal of Guidance & Counselling, 30*(4), 401–414.

Pompili, M., Innamorati, M., Raja, M., Falcone, I., Ducci, G., Angeletti, G., Lester, D., Girardi, P., Tatarelli, R., De Pisa, E. (2008). Suicide risk in depression and bipolar disorder: Do impulsiveness-aggressiveness and pharmacotherapy predict suicidal intent? *Journal of Neuropsychiatry Disease and Treatment, 4*(1), 247–255.

Prigerson, H. G., Horowitz, M.J., Jacobs, S.C., Parkes, C.M., Aslan, M., Goodkin, K., . . . Madejewski, P.K. (2009). Prolonged grief disorder: Psychometric validation of criteria proposed for DSM-V and ICD-11. *Public Library of Science Medicine, 6*(8), 1–12.

Provini, C., Everett, J.R., & Pfeffer, C.R. (2000). Adults mourning suicide: Self-reported concerns about bereavement, needs for assistance, and help-seeking behavior. *Death Studies, 24*(1), 1–19.

Rando, T.A. (1988). *Grieving: How to go on living when someone you love dies.* Lexington, MA: Lexington Books.

Rando, T.A. (1992). The increasing prevalence of complicated mourning: The onslaught is just beginning. *Omega: Journal of Death and Dying, 26,* 43–59.

Range, L.M., & Calhoun, L.G. (1990). Responses following suicide and other types of death: The perspective of the bereaved. *Omega: Journal of Death and Dying, 21*(4), 311–320.

Range, T.A. (1998). *Treatment of complicated mourning.* Champaign, IL: Research Press.

Ratnarajah, D., Mcouns, M., & Schofield, M. J. (2008). Survivors' narratives of the impact of parental suicide. *Suicide & Life-Threatening Behavior, 38*(5), 618–630.

Ratnarajah, D., & Schofield, M. J. (2007). Parental suicide and its aftermath: A review. *Journal of Family Studies, 13*(1), 78–93.

Raveis, V., Siegel, K., & Karus, D. (1999). Children's psychological distress following the death of a parent. *Journal of Youth and Adolescence, 28*(2), 165–178.

Reilly, P., Hasazi, J. E., & Bond, L. A. (1983). Children's conceptions of death and personal mortality. *Journal of Pediatric Psychology, 8*, 21–31.

Renaud, C. (1995). Bereavement after a suicide: A model for support groups. In B. Mishara (Ed.), *The impact of suicide* (pp. 52–63). New York: Springer.

Requarth, M. (2006). *After a parent's suicide: Helping children heal.* Sebastopol, CA: Healing Hearts Press.

Resnick, R. J., & Rozensky, R. H. (1996). *Health psychology through the life span: Practice and research opportunities.* Washington, DC: American Psychological Association.

Rogers, J., Sheldon, A., Barwick, C., Letofsky, K., & Lancee, W. (1982). Help for families of suicide: Survivors support program. *Canadian Journal of Psychiatry, 27*, 444–449.

Rosen, H. (1991). Child and adolescent bereavement. *Child and Adolescent Social Work Journal, 8*, 5–16.

Rosenblatt, P. C. (1996). Grief and mourning. In D. Levinson & M. Ember (Eds.), *Encyclopedia of cultural anthropology* (pp. 548–549). Lakeville, CT: American Reference.

Rosnera, R., Kruse, J., & Hagl, M. (2010). A meta-analysis of interventions for bereaved children and adolescents. *Death Studies, 34*(2), 99–136.

Rubey, C. T., & McIntosh, J. L. (1996). Suicide survivors groups: Results of a survey. *Suicide and Life-Threatening Behavior, 26*, 351–358.

Rubin, J. A. (2005). *Child art therapy.* Hoboken, NJ: Wiley & Sons.

Rudestam, K. E. (1977). Physical and psychological responses to suicide in the family. *Journal of Consulting and Clinical Psychology, 45*(2), 162–170.

Rudman, M., Gagne, K. D., & Bernstein, J. E. (1993). *Books to help children cope with separation and loss: An annotated bibliography.* New Providence, NJ: R.R. Bowker.

Rudman, M., Kabakow, G., Gagne, K., & Berstein, J. (1993). *Books to help children cope with separation and loss: An annotated bibliography.* New Providence, NJ: Bowker.

Rynearson, E. K. (2006). *Violent death.* New York: Routledge.

Saler, L., & Skolnick, N. J. (1992). Childhood parental death and depression in adulthood: Roles of surviving parent and family environment. *American Journal of Orthopsychiatry, 62*(4), 504–516.

Saltzman, W., Pynoos, R., Layne, C., Steinberg, A., & Aisenberg, E. (2001). Trauma/grief-focused intervention for adolescents exposed to community violence: Results of a school-based screening and group treatment protocol. *Group Dynamics: Theory, Research, and Practice, 5*, 291–303.

Samide, L., & Stockton, R. (2002). Letting go of grief: Bereavement groups for children in the school setting. *Journal for Specialists in Group Work, 27*, 192–204.

Sanders, C. M. (1993). Risk factors in bereavement outcome. In M. S. Stroebe, W. Stroebe, & R. O. Hansson (Eds.), *Handbook of bereavement: Theory, research and intervention* (pp. 255–267). New York: Cambridge University Press.

Sandler, I. N., Ayers, T., Wolchik, S., Tein, J. Y., Kwok, O. M., Haine, R. A., . . . Griffin, W. A. (2003). The family bereavement program: Efficacy evaluation of a theory-based prevention program for parentally bereaved children and adolescents. *Journal of Consulting and Clinical Psychology, 73*(2), 221–228.

Sandler, I. N., West, S. G., Baca, L., Pillow, D. R., Gersten, J. C., Rogosch, F., . . . Kallgren, C. (1992). Linking empirically based theory and evaluation: The family bereavement program. *American Journal of Community Psychology, 20*(4), 491–521.

Sands, D. C., Jordan, J. R., & Neimeyer, R. A. (2011). The meanings of suicide: A narrative approach to healing. In J. R. Jordan & J. L. McIntosh (Eds.), *Grief after suicide:*

Understanding the consequences and caring for the survivors (pp. 249–282). New York: Routledge.

Schaefer, J.A., & Moos, R.H. (2001). Bereavement experiences and personal growth. In M.S. Stroebe, R.O. Hansson, W. Stroebe, & H. Schut (Eds.), *Handbook of bereavement research: Consequences, coping, and care* (pp. 145–167). Washington, DC: American Psychological Association.

Schilling, R., Koh, N., Abramovitz, R., & Gilbert, L. (1992). Bereavement groups for inner-city children. *Research on Social Work Practice, 2,* 405–419.

Schneidman, E.S. (1981). The psychological autopsy. *Suicide and Life-Threatening Behavior, 11,* 325–340.

Searles, I.E. (2006). *Effects of trauma-focused grief interventions among parentally bereaved children.* (Unpublished doctoral dissertation). University of Georgia

Seguin, M., Lesage, A., & Kiely, M.C. (1995). Parental bereavement after suicide and accident: A comparative study. *Suicide & Life-Threatening Behavior, 25*(4), 489–492.

Shapiro, F. (2001). *Eye movement desensitization and reprocessing: Basic principles, protocols and procedures* (2nd ed.). New York: Guilford Press.

Shapiro, F. (2002). *EMDR as an integrative psychotherapy approach: Experts of diverse orientations explore the paradigm prism.* Washington, DC: American Psychological Association.

Shepherd, D.M., & Barraclough, B.M. (1976). The aftermath of parental suicide for children. *British Journal of Psychiatry, 129,* 267–276.

Sherkat, D.E., & Reed, M.D. (1992). The effects of religion and social support on self-esteem and depression among the suddenly bereaved. *Social Indicators Research, 26,* 259–275.

Shneidman, E.S. (1996). *The suicidal mind.* New York: Oxford University Press.

Shuchter, S.R., & Zisook, S. (1993). The course of normal grief. In M.S. Stroebe, W. Stroebe, & R.O. Hansson (Eds.), *Handbook of bereavement: Theory, research and intervention* (pp. 23–43). Cambridge: Cambridge University Press.

Silver, R.L., Boon, C., & Stones, M. (1983). Grief and the search for meaning: Exploring the assumptive worlds of bereaved college students. *Journal of Social Issues, 39,* 81–102.

Silverman, P.R., Nickman, S., & Worden, J.W. (1992). Detachment revisited. *American Journal of Orthopsychiatry, 62*(4), 494–593.

Silverman, P.R., & Worden, J.W. (1992). Children's reactions in the early months after the death of a parent. *American Journal of Orthopsychiatry, 62*(1), 93–104.

Silverman, P.R., & Worden, J.W. (1993). Children's reactions to the death of a parent. In M.S. Stroebe, W. Strobe, & R.O. Hansson (Eds.), *Handbook of bereavement: Theory, research, and intervention* (pp. 300–316). New York: Cambridge University Press.

Simone, C. (2008). Parental suicide: The long-term impact on children and young people. *Bereavement Care, 27*(3), 43–46.

Smith, A., Joseph, S., & Das Nair, R. (2011). An interpretative phenomenological analysis of posttraumatic growth in adults bereaved by suicide. *Journal of Loss & Trauma: International Perspectives on Stress & Coping, 16,* 413–430.

Smyth, J.M. (1998). Written emotional expression. Effect sizes, outcome types, and moderating variables. *Journal of Consulting and Clinical Psychology, 66,* 174–184.

Sorensen, H.J., Mortensen, E.L., Wang, A.G., Juel, K., Silverton, L., & Mednick, S.A. (2009). Suicide and mental illness in parents and risk of suicide in offspring: A birth cohort study. *Social Psychiatry and Psychiatric Epidemiology, 44*(9), 748–751.

Speece, M.W., & Brent, S.B. (1992). The acquisition of a mature understanding of three components of the concept of death. *Death Studies, 16,* 211–229.

Stewart, A.J., Sokol, M., Healy, J.M., & Chester, N.L. (1986). Longitudinal studies of psychological consequences of life changes in children and adults. *Journal of Personality and Social Psychology, 50*(1), 143–151.

Stillion, J. M. (1996). Survivors of suicide. In K. J. Doka (Ed.), *Living with grief after sudden loss: Suicide, homicide, accident, heart attack, stroke* (pp. 41–51). Washington, DC: Hospice Foundation of America.

Stimming, M., & Stimming, M. (1999). *Before their time: Adult children's experiences of parental suicide*. Philadelphia, PA: Temple University Press.

Stokes, J., & Crossley, D. (1995). Camp Winston: A residential weekend for bereaved children. In S. Smith & M. Pennells (Eds.), *Interventions with bereaved children* (pp. 172–192). London: Jessica Kingsley.

Stroebe, M., & Schut, H. (1999). The dual process model of coping with bereavement: Rationale and description. *Death Studies, 23,* 197–224.

Stroebe, W., & Stroebe, M. (1987). *Bereavement and health*. New York: Cambridge University Press.

Stroebe, W., & Stroebe, M. S. (1993). Determinants of adjustment to bereavement in younger widow and widowers. In M. S. Stroebe, W. Stroebe, & R.O. Hansson (Eds.), *Handbook of bereavement: Theory, research, and intervention* (pp. 208–210). New York: Cambridge University Press.

Stroebe, W., Stroebe, M. S., & Domittner, G. (1988). Individual and situational differences in recovery from bereavement: A risk group identified. *Journal of Social Issues, 44,* 143–158.

Stylianos, S.K., & Vachon, M.L.S. (1993). The role of social support in bereavement. In M.S. Strobe, W. Stroebe, & R. O. Hansson (Eds.), *Handbook of bereavement: Theory, research, and intervention* (pp. 397–410). New York: Cambridge University Press.

Sveen, C.A., & Walby, F.A. (2008). Suicide survivors' mental health and grief reactions: A systematic review of controlled studies. *Suicide and Life-Threatening Behavior, 38*(1), 13–29.

Taku, K., Cann, A., Calhoun, L. G., & Tedeschi, R. G. (2008). The factor structure of the Posttraumatic Growth Inventory: A comparison of five models using confirmatory factor analysis. *Journal of Traumatic Stress, 21,* 158–164.

Taylor, S.E. (1983). Adjustment to threatening events: A theory of cognitive adaptation. *American Psychologist, 4,* 1161–1173.

Tedeschi, R.G., & Calhoun, L.G. (1995). *Trauma and transformation: Growing in the aftermath of suffering*. Thousand Oaks, CA: SAGE.

Tedeschi, R.G., & Calhoun, L.G. (2004). Posttraumatic growth: Conceptual foundations and empirical evidence. *Psychological Inquiry, 15*(1), 1–18.

Tedeschi, R.G., Park, C.L., & Calhoun, L. G. (1998). *Posttraumatic growth: Positive changes in the aftermath of crisis*. Mahwah, NJ: Lawrence Erlbaum Associates.

Thompson, K.E., & Range, L.M. (1991). Recent bereavement from suicide and other deaths: Can people imagine it as it really is? *Omega: Journal of Death and Dying, 22,* 249–259.

Thompson, S.C., & Pitts, J. (1993). Factors that are related to a person's ability to find meaning following a diagnosis of cancer. *Journal of Psychology, 11,* 1–21.

Traisman, E.S. (1992). *Fire in my heart, ice in my veins*. Canada: Centering Corporation.

Traisman, E.S. (1994). *A child remembers*. Canada: Centering Corporation.

Updegraff, J.A., & Taylor, S.E. (2000). From vulnerability to growth: Positive and negative effects of stressful life events. In J. Harvey & E. Miller (Eds.), *Loss and trauma: General and close relationship perspectives* (pp. 3–28). Philadelphia, PA: Brunner-Routledge.

Vachon, M.L., & Stylianos, K.L. (1988). The role of social support in bereavement. *Journal of Social Issues, 44,* 175–190.

Vandecreek, L., & Mottram, K. (2009). The religious life during suicide bereavement: A description. *Death Studies, 33,* 741–761.

Wallerstein, R. (1986). *Forty-two lives in treatment: A study of psychoanalysis and psychotherapy*. New York: Guilford Press.

Walter, C.A., & McCoyd, J.L.M. (2009). *Grief and loss across the lifespan*. New York: Springer.

Wampold, B.E. (2001). *The great psychotherapy debate: Models, methods, and findings*. Mahwah, NJ: Erlbaum.

Ward, B. (1995). *Good grief 2. Teacher's pack. Talking and learning about loss and death*. London: Jessica Kingsley.

Warmbrod, M.E. (1986). Counseling bereaved children: Stages in the process. *Social Casework, 67*(6), 351–358.

Warren, C.A.B. (2002). Qualitative interviewing. In J.F. Gubruim & J.A. Holstein (Eds.), *Handbook of interview research-context & method* (pp. 129–142). Thousand Oaks, CA: SAGE.

Webb, N.B. (1991). *Play therapy with children in crisis: A casebook for practitioners.* New York: Guilford Press.

Webb, N.B. (2003). Play and expressive therapies to help bereaved children: Individual, family, and group treatment. *Smith College Studies in Social Work, 73*(3), 405–422.

Weller, R.A., Weller, E.B., Fristad, M.A., & Bowes, B.M. (1991). Depression in recently bereaved prepubertal children. *American Journal of Psychiatry, 148*, 1536–1540.

Wertheimer, A. (2001). *A special scar: The experiences of people bereaved by suicide* (2nd ed.). Philadelphia, PA: Brunner-Routledge.

Willis, C.A. (2002). The grieving process in children: Strategies for understanding, educating, and reconciling children's perceptions of death. *Early Childhood Education Journal, 29*, 221–226.

Wolfelt, A. D. (1996). *Healing the bereaved child: Grief gardening, growth through grief, and other touchstones for caregivers.* Fort Collins, CO: Companion Press.

Worden, J.W. (1982/1991). *Grief counseling and grief therapy.* New York: Springer.

Worden, J.W. (1996). *Children and grief: When a parent dies.* New York: Guilford.

Worden, J.W., & Silverman, P.R. (1996). Parental death and the adjustment of school-age children. *Omega: Journal of Death and Dying, 33*, 91–102.

Wortman, C.B., & Silver, R.C. (1989). The myths of coping with loss. *Journal of Consulting and Clinical Psychology, 57*(3), 349–357.

Wright, B., & Partridge, I. (1999). Speaking ill of the dead: Parental suicide as child abuse. *Clinical Child Psychology and Psychiatry, 4*(2), 225–231.

Wyman, P. A., Brown, C. H., LoMurray, M., Schmeelk-Cone, K., Petrova, M., Yu, Q., Walsh, E., . . . Wang, W. (2010). Youth suicide prevention program delivered by adolescent peer opinion leaders: Two phases of randomized trials. *American Journal of Public Health, 100*(9), 1653–1661.

Wyss, J. (2003). Perceived open communication following parental suicide. *Dissertation Abstracts International, 64* (2-B), 977.

Yarom, N. (1983). Facing death in war: An existential crises. In S. Breznitz (Ed.), *Stress in Israel* (pp. 3–38). New York: Van Nostrand Reinhold.

Young, I.T., Iglewicz, A., Glorioso, D., Lanouette, N., Seay, K., Ilapakurti, M., & Zisook, S. (2012). Suicide bereavement and complicated grief. *Dialogues in Clinical Neuroscience, 14*(2), 177–186.

Zambelli, G.C., Clark, E.J., Barile, L., & DeJong, A.F. (1988). An interdisciplinary approach to clinical intervention for childhood bereavement. *Death Studies, 12*(1), 41–50.

Zambelli, G.C., & DeRosa, A.P. (1992). Bereavement support groups for school-age children: Theory, intervention, and case example. *American Journal of Orthopsychiatric, 62*(4), 484–493.

Zisook, S. (1985). *Biopsychosocial aspects of bereavement.* Washington, DC: American Psychiatric Press.

Zisook, S., & Shear, K. (2009). Grief and bereavement: What psychiatrists need to know. *World Psychiatry, 8*(2), 67–74.

Index

Page numbers in *italics* indicate figures and tables.

abandonment issues 163, 166, 171
abuse: family history of 107–8, 121, 122; by parents 23, 95, 109, 114, 128–9, 143; *see also* addiction/substance abuse; alcohol abuse; sexual abuse
ADD *see* attention deficit disorder
addiction/substance abuse 34–6, 38–9, 57, 59, 63, 86–7, 95–96, 103, 105, 129, 137; *see also* alcohol abuse
ADHD *see* attention deficit hyperactivity disorder
"Adjustment Disorder Related to Bereavement" (DSM-5) *15*
adolescents, reactions to death *12*, 13–14
Adult Children of Alcoholics (Gringer) 107, 145
adult components, at Camp HOPE 178, 182–4
adult-like responsibilities: by children 22, *22*, 35–8; *see also* man-of-the-house response
afterlife 115
age-appropriate grieving 10, *11–12*, 157, 164, 166–7; adolescent reactions to death 13–14; child reactions to death 12–13
alcohol abuse 35–6, 57, 59–60, 95, 109, 113, 129, 136–7, 143–5; *Adult Children of Alcoholics* (Gringer) 107; suicide attempt by alcohol 97; *see also* addiction/substance abuse
American Foundation for Suicide Prevention, warning signs of suicide *158*
American School Counselor Association *172*
anger 19, 21–4, 26, 41, 52, 60, 64, 103
antidepressant medication 144–5
anxiety 19, 21, 38; treating 79, 98
art therapy 62, 101, 102, 166–7, 168, 171, 180
assessment 157–9, *158*
Association of Death Education and Counseling 173
at-risk behavior 19
attachment theories 7–8

attention deficit disorder (ADD) 38
attention deficit hyperactivity disorder (ADHD) 38–9, 58, 78, 129, 145
aunts/uncles 70, 71, 88, 142–4, 146
avoidance 103–4; *see also* emotion-protecting measures

babysitting 82, 84, 129
balloon badges, Camp HOPE 178
balloon lifts 167, 168, 174
Before Their Time: Adult Children's Experiences of Parental Suicide (Stimming & Stimming) 18–19
behavioral treatment 79
bereavement: by age and development level 10, *11–12*, 12–14; suicide bereavement vs. bereavement from other forms of death 16–17, *18*
Bereavement and Health, (Stroebe & Stroebe) *8*
bereavement theory: contemporary viewpoints 8–10, *9*
bereavement theory: traditional theories: Bowlby, J. 7–8; Freud, S. 6–7; Kubler-Ross, E. 7; Lindemann, E. 7; Parkes, C.M. 7; summary of writings *8*
best practices *see* professional implications and best practices
betrayal 162
Bible camp 74
bibliotherapy 166, 180
Big Brother Big Sister program 92
bipolar disorder 19, 38–9, 126, 129, 145, 146, 147, 149
blame 21–2, 32, 50, 60, 105, 127, 141, 143, 156
board games 179
Board of Losses, Camp HOPE 176–7
books resources, for starting support groups *170*
Boulden, Jim and Joan, *Saying Goodbye* 180
Bowlby, J. 7–8; *Attachment and Loss: Vol. 3. Loss: Sadness and Depression 8*
bullying 29–30, 76, 150
bullying prevention programs 172
call for help 97
Camp HOPE 50–2, 88–9, 140, 174–84; adult components 182–4; balloon badges 177; bibliotherapy 180; Board of Losses 176–7; camper check-in 177; camper team building 178–9; candlelight ceremonies 181, 184; cleaning cabins and packing 182; closing ceremonies 182, 184; confidence building 184; do-nothing support at 81–2; empathizing and 84–5; free time activities 177–8, 183; games 179; goals and objectives 174–5; journaling at 101; location 174; meals, hot chocolate, and cookies 178; memory collages 180; nature activities 180; opening ceremonies 177, 183; overview 174–5; parent session 178; physician session 181–2; preserving memories at 110–11; staffing 175–6; stories 179; support groups for adults 183; survivors serving as counselors at 111–12; visualization and journal writing 179; volunteering at 138
Camp MAGIK 173–4
candlelight ceremonies 52, 167, 181, 184
canoeing 174
career choices, posttraumatic growth and 137–8
caretakers, children as 37–8, 58; *see also* adult-like responsibilities; man-of-the house response
case studies: challenges 47–64; coping mechanisms 116–29; posttraumatic growth 139–52; support systems 86–99
cemetery visits 167
ceremonies 167; candlelight 52, 167, 181, 184; closing at Camp HOPE 182, 184; opening at Camp HOPE 177, 183; *see also* rituals
challenges: case studies 47–64; checked-out parent 35–7; children notifying others 44–5; to communication and expression 25–7; delayed grief 45–6; emotional 21–5; household change 33–5;

increased sense of responsibility 36–8; ineffective support 31–3; lack of father/mother figure 27–9; mental health issues 38–40; others' reactions 29–31; revisiting the loss 40–3; types and frequencies (summary) *22*
child care 156
childhood traumatic grief 14; *see also* complicated grief
Child Posttraumatic Stress Reactions Index Scale 19
Child Remembers, A (Traisman) 180
children: overview of suicide-bereaved children 17–20; reactions to death *11–12*, 12–13
Children's Grief Education Association *172*
Child's Conception of Physical Causality, The (Piaget) *8*
child support 34
closed communication 162
closing ceremonies, at Camp HOPE 182, 184
cognitive restructuring 163
communication: challenges to suicide-bereaved children *22*, 25–7; open and closed 162; truthfulness in 162
community, educating through experiences with 112–13
community support 71–5
complicated grief (CG) 14–15, *15*, 17, 19–20, 153
confidence building: at Camp HOPE 184; posttraumatic growth and 135–6
constructivism 165
containment narratives 132
continuum, of bereavement 8–10
coping mechanisms 100–129; acknowledging the relief 113–14, 128–9; case studies 116–29; exercise as 89; gaining insight 105–8; helping others 111–13; journaling/writing/art 62, 92, 100–102; preserving and sharing memories 108–11; protecting emotions 103–4; spirituality 114–15; types and frequencies summary *101*
core beliefs 165
coroners, talking to about suicide 105
counseling *see* professional implications and best practices; professional support/counseling
creative writing 166; *see also* journaling/writing
crying 88–9, 92, 94, 106, 110, 125, 140; inability to cry 96, 140
cutting 51

death, developmental concepts of *11–12*
delayed grief 7
delinquency 19
denial 25, 103
depression 14, 17, 19, 38–9, 41, 57, 83–4, 90, 92, 146–7; exercise and 89; treating 98; viewing as illness 106–7, 117–18
destigmitization 162
developmental perspective, of bereavement 10, *11–12*, 45–6, 157
developmental regression 19
Diagnostic and Statistical Manual of Mental Disorders (DSM) 14–15; criteria for Prolonged Grief Disorder for DSM-5 and ICD-11 *15*
differentiated response 159, *160*
distraction, as coping strategy 104
divorce 84, 120, 134, 139, 171
doctors, talking to about suicide 105
"do-nothing" support 81–2
dreams *see* nightmares
"Dual Process Model of Coping with Bereavement: Rationale and Description, The" (Stroebe & Schut) 9–10, *9*

EMDR *see* eye movement desensitization and reprocessing
EMDR Institute, Inc. *164*
emotional challenges, to suicide-bereaved children 21–5, *22*
emotionlessness 25, 96, 97, 156
emotion-protecting measures, as coping mechanism 103–4
empathy 83–5
exercise, as coping mechanism 89
experiences, sharing with others 112–13

exposure therapy 163
expression, challenges to suicide-bereaved children 25–7
expressive techniques 166–7, *167*
extended families, support and 69–71, 82, 156
eye movement desensitization and reprocessing (EMDR) 78–9; EMDR Institute, Inc. *164*

faith/spirituality: as coping mechanism 114–15; support and 72, 74; *see also* religious issues
family-based interventions 159–63, *160*
family friend support 73–4, 92
family history, understanding suicide and 105, 107–8, 121, 122, 143, 158
family support 55, 59, 65–71, *133;* case studies 90–4, 99, 125–6, 146–7; posttraumatic growth and 133–5
family trees 168
Father's Day rituals 111
father/mother figures 144; lack of *22*, 27–9
fault 50, 52
fighting: children's 26; parental 56–7
financial issues 34, 58, 75, 156
Fine, C., *No Time to Say Goodbye* 40
Fire in My Heart, Ice in My Veins (Traisman) 180
first responders 29, 156
forgiveness narratives 132
free-time activities, Camp HOPE 177–8, 183
Freud, S. 6–7; *Standard Edition of the Complete Psychological Works of Sigmund Freud: Vol.14. Mourning and Melancholia 8*
friends: posttraumatic growth and 135; as support 58, 72–4, 82, 83, 91–2, 94, 98, 125, 172
funeral directors, photographs for future requests 105
funerals 36, 52, 87, 90, 96, 111, 125, 139–40, 149, 172

gaining insight 105–8
games, at Camp HOPE 179
gender differences 157–8, 166
good times, preserving memories of 109
gossip/rumors 30, 91, 121
grandparents 32, 34, 68, 69, 70–1, 80, 86–7, 90, 110, 112, 117, 139, 143, 147
Grief After Suicide: Understanding the Consequences and Caring for the Survivors (Jordan & McIntosh) 16
grief behaviors 6–10, *8*, *9;* by age and development level 10, *11–12*, 12–14; delayed *22*, 45–6; fluctuating/revisiting loss 40–3, 105; normal reactions to death 14–15; unexpected 151
grief camps 173–4; *see also* Camp HOPE, Camp MAGIK
grief counseling, three stages of 161; *see also* professional implications and best practices; professional support/counseling
grief normalization 177, 178
grief publication, children's 102
grief theory 168, 173; *see also* grief behaviors
grief work 6–10, 155; *see also* professional implications and best practices; professional support/counseling
Gringer, Janet, *Adult Children of Alcoholics* 107, 145
grounded-theory approach 103
guilt 22–5, 50, 57–60, 150, 166; about feeling relief after suicide 113–14; overcoming 105–6

halfway houses 97
Harvard Child Bereavement Study (Silverman & Worden) 13
helicopter parents 136
helping others: as coping mechanism 111–13; posttraumatic growth and 138
"hiding the pain" 103–4
higher power 114
homeless shelters 113
homeschooling 54, 128
honoring the deceased 111
hopelessness 36, 97
household change, due to a parent's suicide *22*, 33–5

independence, posttraumatic growth and 135–6
indirect support 81–2
information seeking 105, 122
in-laws 80
insecurity 89
insight, gaining 105–8
integrated grief 14
International Society for Traumatic Stress Studies *164*
Internet support groups 168
interventions: family-based 159–63; timing of 158; *see also* professional implications and best practices; professional support/counseling
isolation 17, 26–7, 31, 35, 64, 71, 83, 103, 168, 171

job losses 90, 91, 95, 120
Jordan, J.R. & McIntosh, J.L., *Grief After Suicide: Understanding the Consequences and Caring for the Survivors* 16
journaling/writing 76–7, 92, 94, 100–102, 165, 166–7, *167*, 168, 174, 179
a father's 143; professional writing 102, 148

Kane, B. 10
kidnapping 139
Kubler-Ross, E. 7, 165; *On Death and Dying 8*

language use 162, 165
later life events 79–80
law enforcement, talking to about suicide 105
law enforcement response 29, 31, 56, 61, 124, 146, 156
learning disabilities 78
legacy, preserving of deceased 110
life-defining moment case study 124–7
life events/milestones, after parental suicide 28–9, 59, 71, 79–80, 118–19, 156–7
lifestyle choices, posttraumatic growth and 136–7
Lindemann, E. 7; *Symptomatology and Management of Acute Grief 8*
little-man, little-woman response 37; *see also* adult-like responsibilities; man-of-the-house response
long-term grief issues 13
loss, revisiting *22*, 40–3
loss-orientation *9*
lying 25, 27; to professionals 103–4

mania 140
manic depression 139
man-of-the-house response 37–8; case studies of 53–60; *see also* adult-like responsibilities
marijuana 137
maturity, posttraumatic growth and 135
McCoyd, J.L.M 8
meaning-making/reconstruction 131, 164–6
medications 98
melancholia, defined by Freud 6
memorial services 174
memories: blocking/burying 103–4; preserving/sharing 108–11, 117–19, 141, 157, 166; recovering 120
memory books 166, 168
memory collages 180
mental health issues: of child survivors of parent suicide *22*, 38–40; *see also* professional implications and best practices
mental illness 22; understanding for coping 106–7
milestones *see* life events/milestones
morbid grief 7
mother/father figures: lack of *22*, 27–9; therapist as 87
mothers' support 67–8, 83–4
mourning, defined by Freud 6
mourning trajectory 32
multidimensional approach to supporting bereaved children 159–63, *160*
music therapy 171

Nagy, M. 10
narratives 132, 165
National Center for Trauma-Informed Care *164*

nature activities, at Camp HOPE 180
Neimeyer, R.A. 10
Nickman, S. 9
Nietzsche, Friedrich 130
nightmares 38–40, 50–1, 96, 98; treating with EMDR 78–9; writing about 102
nonverbal techniques 166–7
notification, by children of parent suicide *22*, 44–5
No Time to Say Goodbye (Fine) 40
numbness 25, 61–2; *see also* emotionlessness

On Death and Dying (Kubler-Ross) *8*
online resources, for starting support groups *170*
open communication 162
opening ceremonies, at Camp HOPE 177, 183
ordinary activities, as support/healing 81–2, 92, 98, 163, 174
others' reactions, to surviving children of parental suicide *22*, 29–31
"others who understand" support 83–5

panic attacks 23, 122
parents: checked-out parent *22*, 35–7; positive parenting 160–1
Parkes, C.M. 7
Parkinson's disease 93
paying it forward 111–12
peer alienation 29, 30
peer support 14, 71–5, 168
physician sessions, at Camp HOPE 181–2
Piaget, J. 10, 40; *Child's Conception of Physical Causality, The 8*
play therapy 166; *see also* Camp HOPE
poetry 102
positive outlook case study 139–41
positive parenting 160–1
postpartum depression 79–80
posttraumatic growth (PTG) 130–52; background 130–3; career choices and 137–8; case studies 139–52; characteristics of survivors 132–3; domains of change 131; lifestyle choices 136–7; manifestations of 130; maturity and independence 135–6; model of 130; motivation to help others 138; narratives of 132; outcomes 131; research/studies of 131–2; strengthened relationships 133–5; types and frequencies summary *133*
posttraumatic stress disorder (PTSD) 17, 19, 39–40, 173–4
prayer 151
preserving memories 108–11, 117–19, 157
prison 139; as therapy/benefit 63, 80, 112
professional implications and best practices 153–84; assessments 157–9, *158*; best practices defined 154; Camp HOPE 174–84; counseling stages 161; evidence-based interventions 155; expressive techniques 166–7, *167*; family focus 159–63; general counseling strategies 154–7; grief camps 173–4; journaling 166–7, *167*; meaning-making and growth 164–6; mediating factors 161; multidimensional approach 159, *160*; needs of children after death of a parent 155; reevaluation of event 166; resources for school professionals *172*; rituals/ceremonies 167; school-based support 169–72, *172*; self-narrative strategies 165; signs of suicide *158*; support groups 167–9, *170*; trauma-informed practice 163–4, *164*; tripartite model of suicide bereavement (TMSB) 165; trust issues 155–6; *see also* Camp HOPE; professional support/counseling
professional support/counseling 77–81, 91–2, 122, 125, 144–5; ineffectiveness of 32–3, 58; preserving memories and 117–18; *see also* Camp HOPE; professional implications and best practices

professional writing, as coping strategy 102
prolonged grief disorder (PGD) 14–15, *15*, 17; *see also* complicated grief
prosymptom position 165
psychiatric disorders 37
psychoanalytic theories 6–7
psychological time out 171
PTG *see* posttraumatic growth
PTSD *see* posttraumatic stress disorder

QPR *see* Question, Persuade, Refer
qualitative research evidence 154, 174
quantitative research evidence 154
Question, Persuade, Refer (QPR) 3
questions, unanswered 41–2

reactive approaches 159
reconnection narratives 132
redemptive narratives 132
reevaluation process 106, 166; case study 116–19
regret 24
regrieving 40–3, 157
relationships, strengthened 133–5
relief: acknowledging 113–14; case study 128–9
religious issues 24, 30–1, 41–2, 53; *see also* faith/spirituality
relocation 156–7
remarriage 33–4, 41, 52, 147, 156–7; *see also* stepparents
research/studies: on grief camps 173–4; on grief counseling 153–4; on posttraumatic growth 131–2; researching suicide 107
resilience 132, 160
resources 31–3; for school professionals *172*; for starting support groups *170*
restoration-orientation *9*
revisiting loss 40–3
risk factors, for suicide-bereaved children 18–20
rituals 109, 111, 157, 167, 181; *see also* ceremonies
routine 163; *see also* ordinary activities
rumors *see* gossip/rumors

sadness 60
Saying Goodbye (Boulden & Boulden) 181
schizophrenia 95
school adjustment problems 75
school-based support 75–8, 169–72, *172*
school-based support groups 77
school guidance counselors 77–8
School Social Work Association of America *172*
secondary losses 33
secrecy 25–7, 154; detriments of 108, 110; relief from not having 119
self-awareness 59
self-disclosure 130
self-discovery, case study 120–3
self-forgiveness 52, 105
self-help groups 167
self-mutilation 38, 51
self-narratives 165
self-protective responses 9, 103–4
self-stigmatization 29
sexual abuse 67, 103, 112; case study 61–4
shame 75
sharing memories 108–11
SHIFT (Safe, Hopeful, Inclusive Environment for Feelings and Thoughts) 171
short-term grief issues 13, 157
siblings 53–4, 59, 111, 163; posttraumatic growth and 134
Silverman, P.R. 9, 13
smoking 35
social networks 65; *see also* support systems
social security 34
social support *see* support systems
special occasions, commemorating 181; *see also* life events/milestones
spirituality *see* faith/spirituality; religious issues
staffing, Camp HOPE 175–6
stages of grief counseling: 1. Beginning: The Death and Funeral 161; 2. Middle: The Past Memories 161; 3. End: The Present and Future 161

Standard Edition of the Complete Psychological Works of Sigmund Freud: Vol.14. Mourning and Melancholia (Freud) *8*
stepparents 34, 41, 52, 68–9, 87–8, 147; *see also* remarriage
stigmatization: neutralizing 83, 100; of suicide 17, 26, 29, 35, 71, 75, 168, 172
Stimming, M. & Stimming, M., *Before Their Time: Adult Children's Experiences of Parental Suicide* 18–19
stress inoculation techniques 163
stressors, pre-suicide 113
Stroebe, M. & Schut, H., "The Dual Process Model of Coping with Bereavement: Rationale and Description" *9*
Stroebe, W. & Stroebe, M., *Bereavement and Health 8*
substance abuse *see* addiction/substance abuse
suicide: attempts by adults 149; attempts by children 38, 97–8; case study of both parents dying by 86–9; discovering the body 53, 114, 120; positive effects of 126–7; preventing 71, 152; researching 107; of suicide-bereaved children 18, 107; teaching about 148; understanding realities of 105; warning signs 152, *158*
suicide bereavement: characteristics of 16, *18*; overview of child survivors of 17–20; risk factors for suicide-bereaved children 18–20; vs. bereavement for other types of death 16–17, *18*, 21
suicide grief groups 167–9, *170*
suicide ideation: by parental suicide survivors 19, 67, 108, 113; by surviving parent 36–7
suicide notes 88, 136–7, 143
suicide of a parent in childhood study: overview 1–4; participant profiles 4–6
suicide prevention 152; career in 137–8
Suicide Prevention Resource Center *172*
suicide statistics 1
support groups 167–9; at Camp HOPE 183; locating existing *170*; resources for starting *170*
support systems 14, 65–99; barriers to 32; case studies 86–99; "do-nothing" support (indirect support) 81–2; extended families 69–71; familial 55, 59, 65–71, 90–2, 99; friends, faith, and community 71–5; importance of 64; ineffective *22*, 31–3; lack of early support 95–9; lack of father/mother figure 27–9; mother's support 67–8; practical support issues 156; professional counseling 78–81; school-based 75–8; stepparents and 68–9; support from "others who understand" 83–5; types and frequencies summary *66; see also* professional implications and best practices; professional support/counseling
Symptomatology and Management of Acute Grief (Lindemann) *8*

talent shows 174
teachers: nonsupportive 150; as support 76–7, 125
team building, at Camp HOPE 178–9
therapy dogs 177
TMSB *see* tripartite model of suicide bereavement
Traisman, Enid Samuel: *A Child Remembers* 181; *Fire in My Heart, Ice in My Veins* 167, 181
transformative nature of suffering 130; *see also* posttraumatic growth (PTG)
trauma-informed practice 163–4, *164*
Trauma-Informed Practices and Expressive Arts Therapy Institute and Learning Center *164*
traumatic bereavement 14; *see also* complicated grief
tripartite model of suicide bereavement (TMSB) 165
truancy 62–3, 97

trust issues 63–4, 155–6, 172
truthfulness, in communication 162
tutoring 156

uncles/aunts 70, 71, 88, 125, 142–4, 146
unresolved grief 14; *see also* complicated grief

Vicodin 137
visualization 165, 179

Walter, C.A. 8
warning signs, of suicide 152, *158*
"watching over" 115
Worden, J.W. 9, 13
workaholics 103
writing *see* journaling/writing